The Complete International SOUP Cookbook

Kay Shaw Nelson

The Complete International SOUP Cookbook

Kay Shaw Nelson

STEIN AND DAY/*Publishers*/New York

To

the

Memory

of

Mary Harris Frederickson

a dear friend

First published in 1980
Copyright © 1980 by Kay Shaw Nelson
All rights reserved
Designed by Louis A. Ditizio
Printed in the United States of America
Stein and Day/*Publishers*/Scarborough House
Briarcliff Manor, N.Y. 10510

Library of Congress Cataloging in Publication Data

Nelson, Kay Shaw.
    The complete international soup cookbook.

    Includes index.
    1. Soups.   2.   Cookery, International.   I.   Title.
TX757.N43   641.8′13   80-5409
ISBN 0-8128-2719-8

Contents

Introduction

My experience cooking and dining in many countries has provided me with a veritable treasure trove of creative soups. The text and recipes pay tribute to the fascination and versatility of these culinary creations which have nourished and delighted individuals and families since the beginning of cookery.

Consequently, this book is about all kinds of soups from around the world. It offers what I hope you'll find to be an interesting and informative story of soups—their history, amusing anecdotes and trivia, as well as valuable basic soup data on preparation and cooking, and a glossary.

These soups represent a wealth of national tastes and styles of cookery. There are superb creations for every occasion. You'll enjoy the delicate appetizer clear and cream soups and bisques. There are hearty old-fashioned chowders, great gumbos, and wholesome main-dish soups. Chilled and jellied soups are marvelous for summer meals. You can have quick and easy soup any time and an exotic soup for a special event. Garnishes enhance both flavor and appearance.

The universal appeal of soups has been celebrated in lore, fable, literature, and verse. Sentiments about soup have long been emphatic. "Of soup and love, the first is best," wrote Thomas Fuller. And, according to P. Morton Shand, "A woman who cannot make soup should not be allowed to marry."

I learned to prepare homemade soups from my mother. As a child in New Hampshire our family enjoyed nutritious chowders and soups for daily meals and in between as snacks. Thereafter, I expanded my collection of soups to include those of infinite variety and flavor, and soups have always been reliable standbys in my home wherever I lived.

While compiling the material for and writing this book, I discovered that there is no end to the repertoire of delectable international soups and that I could not possibly include them all in one volume. Unfortunately, I have not given recipes for some soups which I enjoyed in foreign homes and restaurants since they required ingredients not readily available in America or other Western countries. Such soups, prepared for feast-days or holidays involving complex procedures and native flavorings, do not taste as appealing when made in Western kitchens.

While I have included some recipes for classic stocks and tried to be faithful to old traditions for national dishes, the emphasis is on soups that can be made easily, or comparatively easily, without investing a great deal of time and effort. I have given particular attention to the element of cost, availability of ingredients and contemporary preferences in taste. The soups are designed for both beginners and kitchen veterans.

In my opinion soup has no superior among dishes in the world of gastronomy. I hope this book will lead you to the successful preparation and enjoyment of all the international soups which have given me so much pleasure.

The Complete International SOUP Cookbook

Kay Shaw Nelson

A Brief Story
of Soups

A wealth of imaginative soups has emerged from the kitchens of the world, diverse soups that you can enjoy on any occasion. Over the centuries cooks have utilized the bounty of land and sea to create a marvelous repertoire of national favorites, each prepared and flavored according to local taste.

Whether a bisque, *brodo*, bouillon, consommé, *corba*, *potage*, *shchi*, *soep*, *sopa*, *tong*, or *zuppa*, each is rewarding to make, to serve, and to eat. Indeed, there is nothing more beautiful at mealtime, or in between, than a savory soup, an important mainstay of the everyday diet in many homes.

Soup-making has long been an essential accomplishment and laudable art. In fact, soups were among man's earliest culinary creations. The saga of soup dates back to the beginning of cookery, when our ancestors hit upon the idea of filling an empty animal-skin bag with meat, bones, and liquid, along with hot stones to cook the mixture. Later, as clay containers were created, the ingredients became more varied and were cooked

1

slowly over direct heat: those cooks had devised the first *pot-au-feu* (pot on the fire).

In the eastern Mediterranean lands, where many of our soups originated, the earliest varieties were made simply with meats, greens, vegetables, and especially legumes, wisely flavored with garlic, onions, herbs, spices, yogurt, olive oil, lemon juice, or vinegar to enhance the appeal of the bland beans, peas, chickpeas, and lentils.

Although the word "soup" is not found in the Bible, the earliest literary reference to the dish is in Genesis, where we read that Esau sold his birthright to his brother Jacob for "a pottage of lentils."

In ancient China soups were made with rice, soy bean curd (*tofu*), seaweed, lotus seeds, wild game, meat innards, flower roots and blossoms, and two popular exotic ingredients, sharks' fins and birds' nests. These dishes are still enjoyed today.

The early Greeks were fond of many soups, particularly those made with lamb innards, beans, onions, and other vegetables, lettuce, and seafood. A broth prepared in great quantity and eaten as a communal dish was made with a variety of fatty meats and spiced with vinegar.

Wealthy Romans enjoyed a wide variety of intricate soups at their lengthy banquets, while lesser folk subsisted on more basic and hearty creations. From the cookbook by Apicius, believed to have been written in the first century A.D.,we learn that Roman cooks had an excellent array of earthenware and bronze pots and kettles for preparing soup. Modern-day visitors to the ruins of Pompeii can view a fascinating collection of these items, as well as other kitchen equipment recovered from the excavations.

As have other peoples, the Romans made their broths and potages with a variety of staples such as barley, dried vegetables, bulbous roots, peas, lentils, ground meat, brains, seafood, poultry, pastry, and milk, but they distinguished their soups by the addition of incredible combinations of strong flavorings. In fact, they actually disguised rather than enhanced the natural appeal of the foods by using coriander, pepper, lovage, dill, fennel, wine, honey, oil, and vinegar, among other seasonings. They also added sweet-and-sour mixtures or condiments to thick soups, a taste preference that spread to other European cuisines. A unique Roman custom was the addition of precious stones to soups served in gold dishes.

During the Dark Ages, after the fall of the Roman Empire, there were no resources for fancy experimentation with soups or any other fare. It was a time when many foraged for anything simply to keep alive, and soups became the staple of the daily diet. Basic creations filled with grains and other accessible foods provided warmth and nourishment. The first soup kitchens, which would be revived over and over again in times of need, were established in the monasteries. Countless numbers of hungry unfortunates were thus able to survive by eating hearty soups.

During the 1300s, according to written accounts, Europeans were very fond of soups, and it was customary to serve three or four different kinds at one meal. At the lively banquets of the time it was not unusual for a dinner to include six, ten, or even a dozen soups.

The first treatise dealing with soups is found in the oldest French cookbook in existence, *Le Viandier,* written about 1375 by a chef known as Taillevent, once the head cook to King Charles V. The soup recipes in his book are curious combinations. Some were based on a thick meat juice or veal stock; others on milk flavored with honey, saffron, and sweet wine. A soup from Germany was composed of sliced onions fried in oil; crushed ginger, cinnamon, cloves, and saffron marinated in vinegar; crushed blanched almonds; hot water and beaten eggs. *Soupe au pain,* bread soup, was made with a base of sugar and white wine, ornamented with egg yolks, perfumed with a few drops of rose water, to which thick slices of bread, soaked in broth, fried in oil, and sprinkled with sugar and saffron, were added.

The oldest known English cookbook, *The Forme of Cury* (Old English for cooking), compiled about 1390 by the cooks of King Richard II, included a few soup recipes made with meat, onions, and poultry, strongly seasoned with spices, herbs, and condiments. The earliest recipe for cabbage soup, *caboches in potage*, written in Medieval English and translated into modern English, was: "Take cabbages and quarter them, and boil in good broth with minced onions, whites of leeks slit and cut small, adding saffron, allspice, and salt."

From the earliest times and even up to the eighteenth century it was not easy to distinguish between gruels, brews, broths, potages (all words commonly used for soups), and soups. All were nourishing and usually thickened with grains or breads.

A potage or pottage could be anything from a thin broth to a thick stew. Some authorities indicate that the word derived from the Roman *potus* for broth or bouillon, which was taken from the verb *potare*, to drink. Others believe it came simply from the name of a large dish or pot. In France, however, the word *potage* was used for a large dish of meat or fish and vegetables until the eighteenth century, when it became customary to call a soup a *potage*.

In the above-mentioned *Forme of Cury*, soups were called *potages, soupes, soppes, soppys, broths*, and *brewis*. The English word *soup* evolved from the French *soupe*, which is of Germanic origin. It came directly from *sop* or *sopp*, the name for a piece of bread served or dipped in roast drippings, broth, or sometimes another liquid. Eventually the broth or liquid, as well as the bread, was called *sop* or *soupe*, and other ingredients were added.

In the cuisines of Europe there are still many similar words. In Austria, Denmark, Germany, and Norway, for example, the dish is *suppe*. In Spain and Portugal it is *sopa;* in Holland *soep;* and Sweden, *soppa*. The Italians use the word *zuppa* for some kinds of soup, and the French likewise designate one category as *soupe*, a heartier dish than the more frequently used *potage*.

Supposedly the number of *sops*, or pieces of bread, once served in a soup was taken by guests as an indication of their host's stinginess or generosity.

Sweet soups, flavored with honey or sugar, and perhaps spices, were popular in Europe for centuries and are still enjoyed in some northern European countries. The soups were either thin or thick. Some could be made with broth, milk, or fruit juice, and might include wine or beer. At one banquet the diners indulged in six sweet colorful soups that were ornately garnished.

There are many accounts of soups in gastronomic literature. Joan of Arc ate soups made of bread and broth or wine to give her strength before and after battle. In the time of Louis XI, ladies of the French court subsisted on broths drunk privately because they believed that chewing food would develop unattractive facial muscles.

In the mid-sixteenth century, an Italian princess, Catherine de Medici, married the French King Henry II and altered court dining habits considerably. She decreed that meals should be shortened to three courses. The first included, however, four to six soups (in addition to *pâtés* and fricassees).

Henry IV of France, well known for praising a chicken in a pot, was fond of a beef soup made with slivered beef and onions fried in fat, moistened with wine, covered with bread slices, spread with mustard, and then sprinkled with vinegar, sugar, and tomato sauce. Other favorite soups of the time were made with capons, partridges, pigeons, and cocks' combs.

Cooking became an art during the reign of Louis XIV, *Le Roi Soleil*, who introduced at his court the innovative protocol of serving dishes as separate courses. The Sun King himself began a dinner with a variety of soups, but it became the custom at court banquets to commence with two of them, one clear and one thick. However, in *Les Délices de la Campagne,* published in 1655, one of the King's cooks explained how to arrange a formal dinner: "The great fashion is to place four fine soups at the four corners of the table with four dish stands between each two, with four salt cellars placed near the soup tureen."

According to one tale, it was Louis XIV who ordered his cooks to create a clear soup in which he might see his countenance. To please him they created clear consommés.

During the eighteenth century it became very fashionable among high society to entertain with intimate suppers, *petite soupers,* that often began with a tureen of rich soup. In Paris, restaurants featuring soups began opening in large numbers. We are indebted to soups not only for the establishment of the first restaurant but for the word itself. In 1765 an enterprising soup vendor, one Boulanger, began advertising on his menu "magical" *restaurants* (restoratives or pick-me-ups). Not only was his business successful but his soups became the rage of Paris.

Over the years as gastronomy became even more refined, so did the preparation of soups. During and after the sixteenth century, talented French cooks led the way by evolving the art of soup-making, taking the craft to heights theretofore unknown. Ever since, French culinary creations, including soups, have starred on international menus and French or French-trained chefs have set culinary styles. They no longer prepared soups by merely combining foods, but devised stocks, sauces, and seasonings that enhanced soup flavors and gave them new refinement and distinction. These would become standard fare wherever royal and other distinguished personages dined around the world.

The great chefs brought French cuisine to maturity during the eighteenth century. Very important to the improvement and increasing interest in soups and other fare was the growing number of cookbooks published then by both chefs and others interested in gastronomy. Ever since man learned to write, people have been fascinated with recording favorite recipes and giving culinary advice, and books on gastronomic subjects were among the first written. They began appearing in increasing numbers and with greater detail during the 1800s.

One of the most talented French chefs, Marie-Antoine Carême, "cook of kings and king of cooks," created interesting soups for the royal personages and other notables that he served. From his menus and books we know his dinners began with two, four, and sometimes eight *potages* that included a wide variety of garnished consommés and such creations as cucumber soup *à la hollandaise*, Madeira-flavored turtle soup, and sundew soup, Polish style.

An eccentric gourmet, Anthelme Brillat-Savarin, who left a glorious monument to the art of good eating in his book *Physiology of Taste*, was very fond of soups. "A rich soup; a small turbot; a saddle of venison; an apricot tart; this is a dinner fit for a king," he wrote. A soup he made and recommended as a marvelous cure-all, "worthy of the table of a connoisseur," was prepared with an old rooster, prime beef, onions, carrots, parsley, butter, sugar candy, and ambergris (a grayish, waxy substance, secreted by sperm whales and used in making perfumes).

A noted Parisian host and author, Grimod de la Reyniere, aptly described soup: "It is to a dinner what a portico or a peristyle is to a building; that is to say, it is not only the first part of it, but it must be devised in such a manner as to set the tone of the whole banquet, in the same way as the overture of an opera announces the subject of the work."

In *Le Grand Dictionnaire de Cuisine,* a lifetime effort of the noted author and amateur cook, Alexandre Dumas, foods and cookery are described with a personal touch. He was particularly fond of bouillon consommés, crab and crayfish bisques, bouillabaisse, and soups made with chicken and almonds, beer, onions, cherries, tomatoes, and shrimp, as well as one called "wooden leg," made with beef shinbone cut one foot long, one hen, two partridges, veal, vegetables, and bread. His favorite, however, was a rich creamy almond soup prepared by his mistress. As a prelude to dinner, Dumas relished three platefuls of this soup.

The famous French chef, Auguste Escoffier, introduced notable changes in the preparation and presentation of soups and wrote extensively about them. He customarily dined, however, on a light meal of soup with a sprinkling of rice, and fruit.

It was Escoffier who probably best described the role of soups at dinner when he said they should perform like "an overture in a light opera [divulging] what is to be the dominant phrase of the melody throughout." He also wrote that "Soup puts the heart at ease, calms down the violence of hunger, eliminates the tensions of the day, and awakens and refines the appetite."

Cooks in other European nations also created excellent soups, which were generally hearty and robust. Northern Europeans relished thick, hot soups made with peas, poultry, pork, root vegetables, and cabbage as well as cold ones made with fruit, beer, and wine. Eastern Europeans also favored a wide variety of similar soups, but many of those dishes were flavored with mushrooms, sour cream, vinegar, and dill. On the other hand, southern Europeans became noted for their seafood, pasta, rice, and vegetable soups, which were richly seasoned with herbs and piquant flavorings.

The British have long dined on substantial grain, poultry, meat, seafood, and vegetable soups, such as oxtail, Scotch broth, hodgepodge, and Mulligatawny. The names of the Scottish soups were as imaginative as their ingredients. Powsowdie is sheep's head broth; skink, a vegetable-beef soup; feather fowlie, a creamy chicken soup; nettle kail, a cockerel, nettle, and oat soup; and bawd bree, a hare soup.

Many of the European soup recipes were eventually brought to America. But the early development of New World soups was quite different from that of Europe.

The Aztecs, Mayas, and Incas prepared interesting basic soups with such native foods as turtles, wild game, and poultry, beans, corn, potatoes, squashes, pumpkins, and manioc, as well as avocados, tomatoes, and other fruits. The creations were well-seasoned with lime or lemon juice, hot peppers, and herbs. Many of the early soups still survive in Latin America and the Caribbean. Others were introduced later by Spaniards, Portuguese, other Europeans, and Africans.

North American Indians made simple but nourishing soups with greens, flowers, roots, and leaves of wild plants, sunflower seeds, nuts, beans, pumpkins, seafood, and the meat of wild animals, seasoned with native herbs and other foods.

Early settlers in North America would have been lost without soups. On their historic voyage the Pilgrims subsisted primarily on soups prepared in large pots suspended from the overhead beams of the *Mayflower*. In their first homes the capacious black kettles, filled with hearty soups and hung over a fire in the hearth, provided necessary nourishment and warmth. Later the soup pots simmered on the black iron stoves. Nothing was easier to make without great expense than soup, and seemingly every edible food went into the pot.

New Englanders made lavish use of nature's bounty of fish, shellfish, and wild game to make rich soups and chowders. Vegetables, fresh and dried, greens, and herbs went into seasonal soups.

Most early American housewives prepared broths or hot liquids in which meat, poultry, or fish had been boiled, to drink as snacks or in times of illness. Some of these dishes were plain and served with dried breads; some were flavored with vegetables, herbs, or flower petals. Those made with several greens and herbs in the spring were favored as tonics.

European settlers learned from the Indians how to make a concentrated essence of soup, the bouillon cube of the time, which was most convenient to use whether in the home, at sea, or while traveling. Portable soup, soup in-his-pocket, or pocket soup, as it was called, was made with a complicated recipe requiring housewives to boil large quantities of veal or beef stock (and pigs' trotters), which was reduced, pressed, cut in flat pieces, and dried. If kept in a dry place, the soup would last for years. It was evidently very effective and nourishing. One Virginia traveler wrote, "If you should faint with fasting or fatigue, let a small piece of this glue melt in your mouth and you will find yourself surprisingly refreshed."

In northern locales soups were commonly frozen in large wide-mouthed kettles and hung in cold back pantries to be used during winter months. Chunks could be easily chopped off and heated with the required amount of water.

Many "economical" soups are mentioned in early American cookbooks. Included among the recipes were those for Old-Fashioned Scrap Soup, Poor Man's Soup, Cheap Soup, Soup Maigre, Common Soup, and Nutritious Soup for the Laborious Poor.

Many of the favorite soups of the 1800s required tedious preparation, but cooks must have considered it worth the trouble. Cookbooks give lengthy instructions for making mutton, partridge, squirrel, oxtail, hare or rabbit, pigeon, venison, duck, eel, catfish, and green turtle soups. For some it was necessary to dress and clean the ingredients before they were cooked.

Some soups called for large quantities of ingredients and unusual foods. One recipe for a soup called "Cow-heel" began: "Take four pounds of lean mutton, three of beef and two of veal; cut them across and put them into a pot, with an old fowl, and four or five slices of lean ham." *The Williamsburg Art of Cookery* has a recipe for snail broth requiring twenty fresh garden snails and thirty frogs.

One of the most popular soups, served like other special ones in the family tureen, was Mock Turtle or Calf's Head Soup, made with a whole calf's head and pig's feet. After boiling, one had to follow complex instructions to make the well-seasoned dish. One cookbook author wrote about the soup: "This has been well called the 'king of soups,' and is actually more delicious than the real turtle soup. . . . If the directions be closely followed, the result is sure to be satisfactory. . . . "

Over the years Americans created many soups that were associated with various cities and regions. They are still relished. Among them are Philadelphia's pepper pot, Maryland's turtle soup, Louisiana gumbos, New England chowders, Charleston she-crab soup, Down East pea soup, Southern bisques, San Francisco's cioppino, and Pennsylvania Dutch chicken-popcorn, pretzel, noodle, and cider soups.

In America the nineteenth and early twentieth centuries were eras of great eating and dining. Nearly everything was home-made, and soup played a significant role in the daily menu. Cooks had stockpots and soup kettles in which they made stocks, consommés, bisques, and rich cream soups. Just about every household had a handsome soup tureen from which soups were proudly ladled into wide plates or two-handled bowls. Robust soups were ever available for breakfasts, mid-day dinners, and suppers.

When convenience foods became readily available and homemakers could buy canned, dehydrated, and frozen soups, as well as bouillon cubes, canned beef broth, chicken broth, and consommé in abundance, the interest in making homemade soups lessened.

But, thankfully, fashions in gastronomy change, and now, marvelous pots of soup, the old favorites of our forefathers and those from around the world, once again hold places of honor on our tables. There are also many soups, hot or cold, clear or creamy, simple or hearty, that can be made without great effort by combining several canned soups or convenience foods in the same kettle. Soups can be easily prepared with electric blenders and food processors.

The increasing popularity of internationally-inspired soups is a universal phenomenon. Now creative cooks everywhere can harvest the riches of the world's treasury of soup-making skills, making soup-eating an exquisite pleasure for everyone who sits at your table.

Basic Soup Data

To Make a Good Soup

Shopping Tips: Necessary ingredients for soups will, of course, vary according to the recipe. One general rule applies to the selection of all: the finer the quality of foods and liquids, the better the dish. This does not necessarily mean the most expensive items, but you should take time to select fresh food that is in prime condition. There are substitutes available for broths, stocks, and bouillon, but those made from scratch will add more flavor to the dish. If wine or other flavorings are used, they too should be of good quality.

Many of the cuts of meat used for these dishes are often among the less tender and less expensive, such as beef shank, neck, shin, brisket, short ribs, flank, and chuck; veal breast, shoulder, and shank; pork loin and shoulder; and lamb breast, neck, shoulder, and riblets. A great many soups are made with inexpensive fresh and canned vegetables, grains, dried legumes, chicken, and fish.

Most of the essential ingredients can be easily found in supermarkets and neighborhood groceries. But for some soups it may be necessary to go to a specialty food store or foreign market for certain items.

Equipment for Preparing and Cooking soups

An excellent assortment of equipment is readily available to help you prepare and cook soups. Most kitchens already have the necessary items. Some are essential; others are helpful but not necessary. A few must be considered luxuries.

Soup Pots: Soups can be cooked in large saucepans, kettles, Dutch ovens, or pots, with a cover. The size will vary according to the recipe and number of servings. Because soups are cooked on top of the stove over direct heat and usually for some time, the utensil should be sturdy and made of heavy-gauge material in which food will not scorch. It should have a flat and thick bottom and be able to retain heat.

Stockpots: A tall and narrow stockpot with medium-gauge metal sides, a heavy bottom, and a good set of handles is the best utensil for making stocks. The narrowness of the pot allows only a small surface area for evaporation, and the height forces the liquid to bubble up through the layers of food. Stockpots range in size from four quarts to over fifty quarts. A ten to sixteen quart size is adequate for the average home kitchen.

In France a tall and narrow cooking pot called a *marmite* is usually made of earthenware, but sometimes of metal. It is glazed inside so that it will not absorb fat and unglazed outside so that it will absorb heat readily. It is excellent for making stocks and is the traditional utensil for preparing the classic *petite marmite.*

Electric Blender: An electric blender is an excellent timesaver for chopping, blending, grating, and puréeing many soup ingredients. Some soups can be partly or wholly prepared in a blender.

Food Processor: A food processor is a great aid in slicing, chopping, cutting, shredding, grating, and puréeing soup ingredients. Some soups can be partly or wholly prepared in a processor. It is an excellent aid to facilitate preparation of most soups.

Food Mill: Because it does not destroy the texture of foods, a hand-cranked food mill with perforated discs for ricing and medium or fine puréeing is superb for making many soups.

Mortar and Pestle: A mortar and pestle made of the same material are useful for grinding herbs and spices and some mixtures to be added to soups.

Wooden Spoons: Wooden spoons are especially good for stirring hot soups and stocks; they don't conduct heat and the handle never gets hot. Neither will they scratch the cooking utensil or discolor the food.

Ladles: Perforated and solid ladles are useful for adding some foods to soups, for removing some foods from soups, and for serving soups.

Skimmers: Fine-meshed skimmers are useful for removing scum that rises to the tops of stocks and soups.

Tasting Spoon: A tasting spoon is useful to taste stocks and soups for seasoning. It will not transmit heat, burn the tongue or affect the flavor of the soup.

Additional Equipment: These utensils are necessary or desirable for most home kitchens: cutting knives, cutting board, kitchen forks, stirring and slotted spoons, kitchen scales, vegetable brush, vegetable parer or peeler, measuring cups and spoons, grater and shredder, can or jar opener, beater or whisk, funnel, colander, kitchen and poultry shears, kitchen bowls, portable timer, and strainers.

Seasoning Soups

The soups in this international collection are seasoned with a wide variety of herbs, spices, aromatic vegetables, condiments, wine, or other flavorings. These items are most important for successful soups. It's wise, therefore, to know the characteristics of the various seasonings and how they should be used.

"Season to taste" is a vague but realistic direction, since seasonings truly are primarily a matter of personal preference. What may be pleasing to one person may be distasteful to another. It's virtually impossible to prescribe exact amounts of seasonings that will suit everyone.

When employing seasonings with which you are unfamiliar, it's best to use them in small quantities. Seasonings should enhance the natural flavor of foods, not overpower them. Never overseason a soup when you begin cooking it, since flavors intensify during the process; too much seasoning will damage the taste. Besides, you can always add more seasoning just before serving.

Many of the soups in this book are designed to conform as closely as possible to the tastes prevalent in their places of origin. Some Oriental soups are liberally flavored with soy sauce, fresh ginger, or exotic spices. Sour cream and dill are featured in several Eastern European soups, while chilies and coriander enhance Latin American creations. You may wish to alter some of the seasonings by using lesser amounts, such as one rather than two cloves of garlic or a smaller quantity of onions. That's your option. You should also know that some flavorings vary in strength according to their brand. This is especially true of curry powder and soy sauce.

The amount and type of seasoning depends on not only the

kind of soup but also its place on the menu. In general, first-course soups are blander than main-course soups. When serving soups, consider the dishes to follow and do not, for example, serve a mint-flavored soup with an entrée of lamb and mint sauce.

Chilled and frozen soups must be checked and corrected for seasoning before serving, because the cold temperature will cause some of the flavoring to have been lost.

Herewith some helpful data about specific seasonings.

Herbs For Soups

The fresh and dried leaves of aromatic plants have been used to flavor soups since the earliest days of cookery, and a wide and varied selection of herbs is available to all of us to use for adding subtlety and distinction to our favorite soups.

Herbs for soups should be selected with care and caution. Certain herbs marry well with certain foods, for example, basil with tomatoes and tarragon with chicken. Herbs with similar characteristics may be used interchangeably. Some herbs have particular appeal in certain regions or countries. Dill is highly regarded in Northern Europe, and coriander is a great favorite in Latin America.

It is best to use only one herb in a soup if that herb has an outstanding flavor. However, you can combine a strongly-flavored herb with others of mild flavor. The amount you should use requires some discretion; begin by adding a little, and increase according to personal taste. Some herbs are added to the soup during the cooking and some are added at the end of the cooking. Never season two dishes of the meal with the same herbs.

Fresh herbs, particularly those in their prime, will add great flavor and color to soups. But dried herbs are good substitutes and are generally available to the average cook. Remember, however, that dried herbs are stronger than fresh herbs. As a general rule, ⅓ to ½ teaspoon of dried herbs may be used for each tablespoon of fresh herbs. The flavor of dried herbs deteriorates in storage, so older herbs have less flavor than those recently purchased or dried.

Sprigs of fresh or dried herbs are often tied together in a "bouquet" or put in a small cheesecloth bag before adding them to soups; that way it's easy to remove the herbs before serving. A *bouquet garni,* or varied bouquet, basic to French cooking, includes three or four different herbs according to the kind of soup. The most popular combination is bay leaf, parsley, and thyme, but some cooks include basil, celery leaves, chervil, chives, rosemary, savory, and/or tarragon. *Fines herbes,* or fine herbs, are a combination of fresh herbs suitable for flavoring soups and traditionally include chervil, chives, parsley, and tarragon.

Some of the better-known herbs that are commonly used to season soups are listed below:

Basil: The aromatic leaves of this plant of the mint family have a licorice or clovelike flavor. Basil has a special affinity for tomato soups, but it will enhance bean, beef, carrot, cauliflower, cucumber, pea, potato, poultry, seafood, and turtle soups. There are many varieties of basil, such as sweet basil, lemon basil, purple basil, and curly or Italian basil.

Bay Leaf: The dried aromatic green leaves of this evergreen shrub have a strong, pungent flavor that will lend an interesting taste to chowders and bean, beef, cabbage, lamb, poultry, sauerkraut, seafood, and tomato soups.

Borage: The oval, grayish-green leaves, with a cucumberlike fragrance and taste, are excellent additions to cabbage, cauliflower, cucumber, green pea, and spinach soups. It may take the place of parsley.

Burnet: The young, tender leaves with a distinct and delicate flavor are good additions to asparagus, beet, celery, cucumber, and mushroom soups.

Celery Leaves: The yellowish-green leaves of celery, with a pungent, sweet flavor, are especially good additions to chowders and cream, meat, seafood, and vegetable soups.

Chervil: The delicate green leaves, with a parsleylike flavor, will enhance asparagus, chicken, cucumber, sorrel, and spinach soups. They also make a good soup garnish.

Chives: The young, slender, tubular leaves, with a delicate onion flavor, are excellent additions to asparagus, bean, cauliflower, cucumber, potato, sorrel, and spinach soups. They are a good soup garnish, especially for cold soups.

Coriander Leaves: The aromatic, flat coriander leaves of the parsley family, with a sage-lemon flavor, are good additions to bean, pea, lentil, fish, chicken, fruit, meat, and sauerkraut soups, and may be used in the same way as parsley, although they have a stronger flavor. They are sold by the bunch in Italian, Latin American, and Oriental markets, and are also called Chinese parsley, *cilantro* or *culantro*.

Dill: The fresh and dried leaves (dillweed) give an appealing, pungent flavor to avocado, bean, chicken, cucumber, fish, pea, potato, tomato, and yogurt soups. They also make a good soup garnish, particularly for cream, seafood, and cold soups.

Fennel: The fresh leaves and stalks of fennel, a member of the parsley family, have a licorice flavor and are aromatic additions to cabbage and fish soups.

Lemon Balm: The almost round, dark-green leaves, with a lemon smell and flavor, are a good garnish for cream and cold soups.

Lovage: The pale-green leaves of lovage, a member of the

parsley family, have a strong celery flavor and may be used sparingly in the same soups to which celery is added.

Marigold: The bright golden, fresh or dried petals of this attractive garden flower will add a subtle flavor to fish chowders and chicken and vegetable soups.

Marjoram: The light-green, oval leaves, with a fragrant odor and spicy sagelike taste, are good additions to avocado, bean, clam, onion, potato, poultry, spinach, and turtle soups. Marjoram is also available ground.

Mint: An herb grown in many varieties, mint has an aromatic, sweet, and refreshing flavor and a cool aftertaste. It is a good addition to carrot, cucumber, fruit, green pea, split pea, and yogurt soups. It is also a good soup garnish.

Oregano: The strong, aromatic leaves of oregano, a member of the mint family, impart an interesting flavor to bean, beef, cabbage, chicken, eggplant, pork, spinach, tomato, and zucchini soups. It is also called wild marjoram.

Parsley: A delicate, mild green herb of the carrot family, parsley is grown in many varieties, of which the two best known are curly and flat-leafed, or Italian, parsley. It is the best known and most widely used of all herbs and can be used in almost any soup. It is also a popular soup garnish.

Rosemary: A fragrant, aromatic, strong, sweet herb of an evergreen shrub of the mint family with leaves like pine needles. Rosemary should be used sparingly since a little goes a long way. If used fresh, the leaves should be chopped, and if dried, they should be crushed or crumbled. The herb is a good addition to chicken, lamb, pea, pork, potato, spinach, and turtle soups.

Sage: The gray-green, aromatic leaves of this plant of the mint family have a pleasant, slightly bitter flavor. They may be used sparingly in fish chowders and cheese, chicken, meat, and some vegetable soups. Sage is available either whole or ground.

Savory: This member of the mint family comes in two varieties: summer savory and winter savory. The latter is more pungent and should be used sparingly. Savory leaves have a particular affinity for bean, pea, and lentil soups, and may be used in cabbage, onion, and vegetable soups.

Sorrel: The large, pale-green leaves of sorrel, grown in many varieties both wild and cultivated, have a lemonlike sour or tart taste. They may be used to make some soups and may be added to soups made with other greens. Sorrel is also called sour grass and dock.

Tarragon: The pointed, dark-green leaves have a slight licorice flavor and are good additions to asparagus, chicken, mushroom, potato, seafood, tomato, and veal soups.

Thyme: This member of the mint family with small, silvery-green leaves lends an aromatic and slightly pungent flavor to fish chowders, and beet, cucumber, fish, lentil, and tomato soups.

Watercress: The round, shiny dark-green leaves have a slightly peppery flavor and are especially good for making cream soups. Watercress is a good flavoring for fish chowders and potato and vegetable soups, and is a good soup garnish.

Spices For Soups

Spices from the barks, roots, buds, or fruits of aromatic plants grown primarily in the tropics have long been favorite seasonings. Some of them are used to flavor soups; most of them should be used sparingly. Most are available whole and ground. Because spices lose their flavor quickly, they should be bought in small quantities and kept in tightly-sealed jars. Some of the better-known spices that are good in preparing soups are listed below:

Allspice: This dried, hard, dark-brown berry of an evergreen tree has a fragrant, pungent flavor that resembles a blend of cloves, cinnamon, and nutmeg—hence its name. Allspice can be used sparingly in fruit, green pea, meat, and some vegetable (squash, sweet potato, and turnip) soups. Also called Jamaica pepper, pimento, and Jamaica pimento. Available whole and ground.

Cassia: The light-reddish bark of cassia, from an evergreen tree, has a sweet, pungent flavor similar to cinnamon, and is often called cinnamon and sold as such. It may be used to flavor the same soups as cinnamon. Available in buds and sticks or ground.

Cayenne: This hot, red powder, made from the dried ripe fruit of several capsicum peppers, gives piquancy and zest to soups. It may be used sparingly in cauliflower, cheese, chicken, cream, green bean, meat, shellfish, squash, and tomato soups.

Cinnamon: The dark, reddish-brown inner bark of an evergreen tree, which has a strong, sweet flavor, may be added sparingly to fruit, meat, and vegetable soups. Available in sticks and ground.

Cloves: The dried, unopened buds of an evergreen tree of the myrtle family have a reddish-brown color and a penetrating sweet flavor. Cloves are used to stud onions for flavoring soups and may be used sparingly in asparagus, bean, beef, carrot, meat, squash, sweet potato, and tomato soups. Available whole and ground.

Cumin: The dried, yellowish-brown fruit or seed of a plant of the parsley family has an earthy, strong flavor. It can be used sparingly to flavor bean, cabbage, cheese, lentil, meat, potato, and tomato soups. Available whole and ground.

Filé Powder: A Creole seasoning made from dried ground sassafras leaves that is used primarily to flavor and thicken gumbos.

Ginger: The pungent, spicy root of the ginger plant has a flavor slightly reminiscent of lemon. It can be used to flavor bean, carrot, cauliflower, chicken, fruit, lamb, onion, pork, and potato soups. Available ground, cracked, and whole.

Mace: The brownish-orange outer shell of nutmeg has a flavor similar to nutmeg but is more potent and of lighter color. Mace can be used like nutmeg but in lesser quantity. It can be used to flavor chicken, cream, fruit, mushroom, oyster, and vegetable soups made with sweetly-flavored vegetables. Available ground.

Nutmeg: The seed of the nutmeg tree has an appealing aromatic and slightly bitter flavor. It can be used to flavor broccoli, carrot, cauliflower, chicken, lamb, mushroom, spinach, split pea, and veal soups. Available ground, or whole to be freshly grated.

Paprika: The appealing orange-reddish powder made from a variety of ground dried peppers has a slightly sweet taste. The flavor and color depend on the selection of peppers. Hungarian paprika is the most highly regarded. Paprika can be used sparingly to flavor cheese, chicken, meat, fish, potato, and other vegetable soups. It is also a popular soup garnish.

Pepper: The world's most widely used spice is available in two varieties. Both derive from the dried berries of an East Indian woody vine. Black pepper, available whole as peppercorns, or ground, employs the whole berry. It can be used in almost all soups. White pepper is the ground, milder inside of the berry. It can be used interchangeably with black pepper but in larger quantity. Its special use is to flavor soups of light color for which the dotted appearance of black pepper is undesirable.

Saffron: This orange-yellow spice, made from the dried stigmas of the saffron crocus, has a slightly bitter flavor and is used in soups to add color as well as flavor. It is the world's most expensive spice, and only a very small amount is used in each soup. It can be used in chicken and some shellfish soups. Available whole and ground.

Turmeric: This aromatic ground root of a plant of the ginger family has a beautiful yellow color and slightly bitter flavor. It is an important ingredient of curry powder and prepared mustard. It can be used to flavor fish, poultry, meat, and tomato soups.

Seeds For Soups

Cooks have always used the seeds of herbs and spices for flavoring soups. Today's varied and interesting selection from around the world is widely available both whole and ground. Here's a list of some of the better-known seeds.

Anise Seed: The greenish-gray seeds of the anise plant have an aromatic, sweet licorice flavor. They are good flavorings for fruit and seafood soups.

Caraway Seed: The highly aromatic, tiny brown dried seeds of the caraway plant add flavor to beet, cabbage, carrot, cheese, mushroom, pork, potato, sauerkraut, and zucchini soups.

Cardamon Seed: The dark-brown dried seeds of a plant of the ginger family are encased in three-sided creamy-white, pithy pods. Cardamon has an unusual, pungent aroma. The seeds are appropriate for fruit and meat soups.

Celery Seed: The small, aromatic light-brown dried seeds of celery taste rather like the plant itself. Cabbage, cauliflower, cheese, corn, fish, potato, sauerkraut, and tomato soups are appropriate dishes for these seeds.

Coriander Seed: The little yellowish-brown dried seeds of the coriander plant have a flavor that is a blend of sage and lemon. The seeds are good flavorings for bean, fruit, pea, lentil, meat, and vegetable soups.

Cumin Seed: The tiny yellowish-brown dried seeds of the cumin plant taste slightly bitter. They can be used to flavor bean, cabbage, cheese, lentil, meat, potato, and tomato soups.

Dill Seed: The aromatic, pungent green dried seeds of dill have a distinctive, refreshing flavor. These seeds are traditionally used for bean, beet, cabbage, carrot, cauliflower, cheese, cucumber, fish, green pea, potato, sauerkraut, shellfish, and tomato soups.

Fennel Seed: The tiny, sand-colored dried seeds of the fennel plant have an appealing, light licorice flavor. They are right for cheese, fish, mushroom, pork, potato, sauerkraut, and seafood soups.

Mustard Seed: The pungent, light or dark dried seeds of the mustard plant have an appealing peppery flavor. They are a good flavoring for beet, broccoli, cabbage, cucumber, poultry, meat, sauerkraut, and vegetable soups.

Sesame Seed: The tiny white and black dried seeds of the sesame plant have an appealing rich, nutty flavor similar to that of almonds. They are good additions to some soups, particularly those from the Orient.

Some Ingredients and Seasonings for Soups

Celery Salt: A mixture of finely milled celery seed and salt is useful to impart the flavor of celery to soups.

Curry Powder: A ground seasoning of several pungent spices can be used to flavor beef, chicken, lamb, mushroom, potato, shellfish, and tomato soups.

Chili Powder: A powdered blend of dried ground chili pepper pods, which may or may not contain other herbs and spices. It can be used to flavor cheese, meat, shellfish, tomato, and some vegetable soups.

Coconut Milk: This is a white liquid made by grating and squeezing fresh cococut. It is used to thicken and flavor some Southeast Asian and Caribbean soups.

Fat: Any of a large variety of greasy or oily substances such as butter, margarine, chicken fat, lard, shortening, or oils can be used for sautéing foods to be included in soups. Butter and margarine have more flavor than the others.

Garlic: A member of the lily family, garlic is related to the onion. Its humble bulbous roots are made up of tiny sections, called "cloves," held together by a film of white skin. Garlic has long been an important soup seasoning in many countries, and there are many garlic soups. Its strong and pungent flavor and aroma have been either highly prized or strongly disliked since man began using it.

Dried garlic is sold loose, in strings, or packaged. It should be firm and plump with unbroken outer skin, and small green stems should not have begun to form. To use garlic, break off a clove from the bulb and remove the outer skin. Chop, mince, or put it through a garlic press before you add it to a soup. Garlic is also available powdered or flaked and in the form of garlic salt or juice.

Whether or not you use garlic in soups is something you'll have to decide for yourself. It should be used, whether whole, cut in half, chopped, or crushed, with great care and discretion. A little garlic can be very potent. The dishes preceding, accompanying or following the soup should also be considered. For example, a garlic-flavored soup is not appropriate before a specially seasoned entrée or delicacy.

Ginger Root: A gnarled or knobby brown root that, when peeled and sliced, shredded, or grated, imparts an interesting flavor and aroma to some soups, particularly those from the Orient. It is sold in Oriental food stores and some supermarkets.

Leek: This vegetable is the most delicately flavored of all the members of the onion family and is a very important ingredient of many soups including the famous Scoth cock-a-leekie. Only the white part of the leek is used, and it should be washed thoroughly to remove all dirt in the leaves.

Lemon: This oval, yellow citrus fruit has a delectable acid juice and an oily peel or rind that are good additions to several soups. Lemon juice is available canned, bottled, and frozen, but freshly-squeezed juice is best. Choose firm lemons that are heavy for their size and without any green tinges. Squeeze just before using to prevent loss of flavor and vitamin C content.

Mushrooms: Light tan or white cultivated mushrooms and wild varieties, sometimes called "field mushrooms," are frequently used to make and flavor soups. Many of the best European and Oriental mushrooms can be bought at specialty or foreign grocery stores, either in cans or dried. Dried mushrooms have a dark, shriveled appearance and a very concentrated flavor. A few will go a long way, but they are particularly recommended for soups. European varieties come in various shades of yellow or brown, whereas most of the dried mushrooms from the Orient are black. To prepare, wash them in cold water and then soak 20 to 30 minutes in lukewarm water to cover. Use a nonmetal container with a top.

Olive Oil: The oil extracted from olives has a light, appealing flavor and is used in many soups, particularly those from Mediterranean countries. It is best to use a good quality oil.

Onion: This well-known vegetable is the bulb of an herb of the lily family; it has a pungent odor and taste. There are innumerable varieties of onions, such as chives, leeks, scallions, shallots, types of red, white, and yellow onions, and lesser-known kinds, that are used in soups. The onion is the most universally used vegetable and flavoring agent for soups. Onion powder and onion salt are also used to flavor soups.

Salt: This widely-used seasoning is an important addition to most soups but should be added with caution. Add sparingly at the beginning of cooking; the flavor will intensify during the cooking. Check the seasoning just before serving. As a general rule, use one teaspoon salt to one quart soup.

Salt Pork: Any fat cut of pork preserved in salt is an excellent seasoning for shellfish chowders and bean, cabbage, green bean, pea, pork, potato, and sauerkraut soups.

Sour Cream: This thick, smooth cream with an appealing tangy flavor has long been used to add zest to beet, cabbage, meat, mushroom, potato, and tomato soups. It is also a popular soup garnish.

Soy Sauce: This pungent, salty brown liquid made from fermented soybeans, salt, and other ingredients is of Asian origin but is widely used in America as a seasoning. Salt is usually not used with soy sauce because that liquid is already salty.

Tabasco Sauce: A drop or two of this hot pepper sauce adds zest to some soups, particularly those made with tomatoes.

Tomatoes: Tomatoes of many varieties, colors, and shapes are popular soup ingredients. If good fresh tomatoes are available, use them. If not, canned tomatoes do very well. Remove any stem ends and peelings. Tomato juice, paste, puree, and sauce are also used frequently to make soups.

Wine: Small amounts of sherry, Madeira, and dry red and white wines add flavor to some soups. Some soups are also made with wine as a prime ingredient. Don't oversalt soups to which wine is added. Add wines to hot soup shortly before serving. Do not boil after adding wine.

Worcestershire Sauce: This piquant, dark-brown sauce, originally made in England, is used as a seasoning in some soups, particularly those made with meats.

Yogurt: The tangy, semisolid cultured milk called yogurt is used to make a variety of hot and cold soups. It is best to use unflavored yogurt, which can be made in the home or purchased.

Serving Soups

Soup is superb for every occasion. In this book you will find an international selection that will meet your needs for everyday and company dining. Elegant, light soups to whet the appetite make appealing appetizers or first courses. More substantial creations are excellent one-dish meals for supper or dinner. Fruit soups can serve as desserts, and soups are good for breakfast, brunch or luncheon.

In the Orient, people enjoy soups for breakfast and as between-meal snacks. Both the Chinese and French serve soups as palate cleansers between the courses of lengthy meals. Europeans and Middle Easterners drink soup in the wee hours of the morning as a restorative after a night of revelry.

Any soup you serve must be in perfect harmony with the rest of the menu if there are other dishes or courses. With a spicy entrée, serve a lightly seasoned first-course soup and vice versa. Cream soups do not go well with main courses that include cream sauces. Do not serve tomato or spinach soups if these foods are included in other dishes. Consider the color as well as the flavor for contrasts.

All soups should be served at the proper temperature, steaming if the soup is supposed to be hot, and chilled if it is supposed to be cold. A few, like the well-known French potato-leek cream soup or consommé Bellevue, are excellent either hot or cold. Tepid soups have little appeal

It is important to serve soups attractively. They may be served in a wide variety of dishes, depending on the type of soup and its role on the menu. While there are specially designed wide-shallow soup plates and two-handled bowls or cups for soups, usually part of luncheon or dinner sets, there are also other good dishes. Cups or mugs are ideal for soups that will be served as appetizers or snacks. Pretty glasses or stemware can be used for light or cream soups. Heatproof soup bowls or cups that can go from the oven to table are essential for soups with broiled or baked toppings.

Some soups may be served directly at the table from large containers. You can ladle some soups from the pot in which they were cooked. If the soup is fairly thin, a pitcher is a good dispenser. A chafing dish can double as a warmer and server. An attractive bowl, casserole, or jar may also serve as a good container. The most elegant way to serve a soup, however, is from an attractive tureen with a capacious interior. As Alice discovered in Wonderland:

> Beautiful soup, so rich and green
>> Waiting in a hot tureen!
> Who for such dainties would not stoop?
>> Soup of the evening, beautiful soup.

Freezing Soups

Most of the soups in this book can be satisfactorily frozen. In fact, in some cases the cook may wish to double or triple the recipe so that what is not needed immediately can be put in the freezer.

In order to save room in the freezer, it is preferable to freeze concentrated soups, since additional liquid can be added later. Stocks and broths can be boiled down to concentrates and, when cooled, poured into freezer trays and frozen. The cubes can then be stored in plastic bags and used as needed.

For soups that are to be frozen, be careful not to overcook them; remember that each will undergo additional cooking when reheated. It may be advisable to shorten the specified time by five to ten minutes.

Soups to be frozen should be cooled quickly and thoroughly and then put into appropriate containers, leaving at least an inch at the top to allow for expansion. Most soups may be stored in the freezer up to six months.

It is best to add some foods to soups after they have been defrosted and reheated. Among them are dumplings, pasta, and such vegetables as potatoes, green peas, lima beans, or corn. If a liquid is to be thickened with *beurre manié*, add this also after the soup is reheated and just before serving.

Frozen soups must be checked and corrected for seasoning after reheating; some of the flavoring will have been lost during the freezing.

A frozen soup can be thawed at room temperature and reheated. You may also put it in a saucepan or kettle and heat slowly, turning the frozen block occasionally to hasten defrosting, while stirring frequently to break up the frozen pieces. Stir well to restore smoothness.

Bouillons, Broths, and Stocks

Many soup recipes call for the use of bouillons, broths, or stocks. These terms are often used interchangeably, since all are produced by the same basic cooking procedure—simmering solid foods in seasoned liquid, usually water. The primary distinction, however, is that bouillons and stocks are richer and more concentrated, the solid ingredients having been cooked to the point of discard, whereas broths are cooked for a shorter period and the aim is not to extract all the goodness from the ingredients, which are sometimes served in the broth.

The classic French stock, *fumet* or *fond de cuisine* (foundation of cooking), is the soul of a good soup. To make stock in the manner of a French chef requires considerable time and effort, skill, and large quantities of foods that are cooked in huge stockpots. Some stock recipes call for pounds and pounds of meat, poultry, and other foods and gallons of water; which are simmered for several hours. This type of cookery isn't practical in the average home. You can, however, make manageable amounts of stock and have a flavorful liquid that can be used as the beginning of a soup. It may be used in a few days or may be stored in small quantities in the freezer and used as needed.

There are a number of methods of making soup stocks, and no two will give the same results. Classic stocks include brown (made with meat), white (made with veal or poultry or both), fish, and vegetable.

For each stock the meat, game, poultry or fish together with flavoring vegetables and seasonings are simmered very slowly in water to achieve a very rich concentrated base. Poultry requires less time than meat or game, and fish takes less time than poultry.

To make a good stock you must start with good fresh ingredients which contain the necessary elements required for the stock. Fresh uncooked beef or game is best for brown stock. The flesh of older animals contains more flavor than that of younger ones. Red meats yield more taste than white meats. Cooked meat, unless it is leftover roast beef, is not recommended. Shinbone and neck both include substances that make excellent stocks.

Bones that are disjointed or cracked are a most important addition to stocks, as their glutinous matter or marrow lends necessary strength and richness to the stock and causes it, when cold, to jell. Too great a proportion of bones, however, makes the stock too gluey. While leftover cooked bones are sometimes used, they should not be combined with raw bones in the same stock. Use one or the other.

For a veal or white stock it is best to have some veal knuckle and meat from the neck, as well as chicken feet or calves' feet, to provide a gelatinous quality. Chicken stock can be made with a stewing chicken or bony parts of chicken and should include, if possible, the gizzards or feet for the gelatin. A good fish stock can be prepared with white-fleshed fish and/or trimmings. Fresh vegetables are preferable for vegetable stock, although leftover scraps can also be used.

Meats for stocks should always be put with cold water in a kettle and allowed to simmer very slowly on the lowest possible heat so that the essence of the ingredients is slowly and thoroughly imparted to the liquid. Long, slow cooking is essential to the making of a good stock.

Stocks can also include flavorful vegetables and seasonings to be added according to taste and availability. They supply nutrients as well as flavor. These ingredients are added after the liquid has been brought to a boil and skimmed.

After cooking, the remnants of the solid ingredients should be discarded and the remaining liquid must be strained and properly degreased or skimmed. In some cases it is also clarified.

Recipies for a few stocks follow.

Brown Stock

2 pounds marrow bones, cracked
4 pounds shin or neck of beef, cut in small pieces
3 quarts cold water
½ cup chopped celery
½ cup scraped, diced carrots
½ cup chopped onion
1 bay leaf
3 sprigs parsley
¼ teaspoon dried thyme
¼ teaspoon dried marjoram
6 whole cloves
8 peppercorns, bruised
1 tablespoon salt

Brown stock will have a richer color if the bones and/or meat are browned first. There are two methods of doing this. One is to put the cracked bones into a preheated 450° oven about 25 minutes, turning once or twice, until well browned. Then put into a large kettle with other ingredients. The other method is to scrape the marrow from the bones and put it in a large kettle. Then the marrow is heated and half the pieces of meat browned in it. Add bones, remaining meat, and water. Put over moderate heat and bring slowly to a simmer. With a spoon or skimmer take off all foaming scum that has risen to the top. Add remaining ingredients and bring very slowly to a simmer. Leave over very low heat, partly covered, about 3 hours, until all possible goodness has been extracted from ingredients. Stir occasionally while simmering. When cooking is finished, strain liquid and degrease it. This may be done by letting stock settle for about 5 minutes and then removing fat with a spoon, skimmer or paper towel. Alternatively, the stock can be kept in the refrigerator until the fat hardens. Then it may be lifted or scraped off the top. Refrigerate or freeze. Makes over 2 quarts.

White Stock

Substitute cracked veal bones and veal knuckles or shank meat for marrow bones and beef in above recipe. Omit marjoram and thyme for a more delicate stock.

Chicken Stock

A well-flavored chicken stock can be made with a cut-up stewing chicken, two fryers, or bony chicken parts such as necks, backs, and wings. Desirable additions are chicken feet and gizzards, both of which have a gelatinous quality and thus add body to the stock. You'll find it worthwhile to make homemade chicken stock; it's superior to any commercial product. These two good recipes are easy to prepare:

Chicken Stock I

This is a rich stock. The addition of a few chicken feet and necks will make a full-bodied stock.

1 stewing chicken, 4 to 5 pounds, cut up
2 quarts water
1 medium-sized carrot, scraped and quartered
1 large onion, peeled and quartered
1 leek, white part only, cleaned and sliced (optional)
2 whole cloves
1 bay leaf
¾ teaspoon dried thyme
2 teaspoons salt
10 peppercorns, bruised

Put chicken, with feet and necks if available, into a stockpot or kettle. Add water and slowly bring to a boil. Remove any scum. Add remaining ingredients and reduce heat. Cook very slowly, covered, about 3 hours. Remove chicken and strain mixture through cheesecloth. Cool and chill in the refrigerator until fat hardens on surface. Lift off fat and strain again. Store, covered, in refrigerator up to four days or pour into containers and freeze. Makes about 2 quarts.

Note: When chicken is cool enough to handle, remove and discard skin and bones. Cut meat into bite-size pieces and use for salad, hash, or other dishes.

Chicken Stock II

5 pounds bony chicken parts (necks, wings, backs)
3 quarts water
1 medium-sized onion, peeled and chopped
1 stalk celery with leaves, chopped
1 bay leaf
½ teaspoon dried thyme
3 parsley sprigs

2 teaspoons salt
10 peppercorns, bruised

Put chicken parts into a stockpot or kettle. Add water and slowly bring to a boil. Remove any scum. Add remaining ingredients. Reduce heat and simmer, covered, 2½ to 3 hours, until meat falls off bones. Remove and discard* chicken and bones and vegetables. Strain liquid. Cool and chill in refrigerator until fat hardens on surface. Lift off fat. Store, covered, in refrigerator up to four days or pour into containers and freeze. Makes about 2 quarts.

*Although there's not much chicken on the bony parts, cooks who are very economy-minded often pick the wing bones and freeze the meat for later use.

Fish Stock

A good fish stock *(fumet de poisson)* can be made simply with white-fleshed fish and its bones and trimmings (head, tail, and skin) or only the fish trimmings, with flavoring vegetables, aromatic herbs, and water. A dry white wine will give additional flavor. You can use any white-fleshed fish such as cod, flounder, or haddock, but avoid those with strong flavors such as mackerel or salmon unless they are to be used in the soup.

2 pounds white-fleshed fish with trimmings, or only
  trimmings
2 quarts water
1 cup dry white wine (optional)
1 medium-sized carrot, scraped and chopped
1 bay leaf
2 whole cloves

4 parsley sprigs
½ teaspoon dried thyme
1 teaspoon salt
10 peppercorns, bruised

Put all ingredients into a stockpot or kettle. Bring slowly to a boil and skim. Reduce heat and simmer, uncovered, 30 minutes if fish is used and 20 minutes if only trimmings are used. Remove from heat and strain. Store stock, covered, in refrigerator up to three days or pour into containers and freeze. Makes about 2 quarts.

Note: The stock can be served simply garnished with chopped fresh parsley, a dash of cayenne, or a spoonful of lightly salted whipped cream, if desired.

Vegetable Stock

This is one recipe for vegetable stock. Substitute other vegetables such as tomatoes, mushrooms, or parsnips, if desired.

¼ cup butter or margarine
2 medium-sized onions, peeled and chopped
2 large carrots, scraped and chopped
1 medium-sized white turnip, peeled and chopped
1 stalk celery, diced
2 cups shredded lettuce
2 whole cloves
1 bay leaf
6 sprigs parsley
½ teaspoon dried thyme
½ teaspoon salt (or more, if desired)
10 peppercorns, bruised
6 cups water

Heat butter or margarine in a large kettle. Add onions, carrots, turnip, celery, and lettuce. Cook slowly, covered, 20 minutes, stirring frequently. Add remaining ingredients and slowly bring to a boil. Reduce heat and cook slowly, covered, 1½ hours. Skim occasionally during cooking. Strain and cool. Store in refrigerator up to one week. Or pour into containers and freeze. Makes about 1½ quarts.

Clarifying Stock

The object of clarifying stock is to remove any cloudiness and make the liquid sparkling clear or transparent and thus enhance its appearance. The process also further concentrates the flavors and improves the taste.

There are two common methods of clarifying stock. One involves the addition to the liquid of lean raw beef, diced vegetables, and an egg white and shell. This makes a richer stock.

The easiest method requires the simple addition of an egg white and shell to the stock. Before starting the process, be sure the stock has been thoroughly degreased and that the utensils to be used are perfectly clean and free of any grease.

For each quart of stock allow one slightly beaten egg white and one broken-up shell. Put the stock, egg white, and shell into a large saucepan. Bring very slowly to a simmer. Do not boil. Continue simmering 10 to 15 minutes. The egg whites attract the cloudy particles in the stock and form a scum on top during the simmering.

Remove the saucepan from the heat and let stand 30 minutes. Push the scum to one side, ladle the liquid from underneath, and strain through double cheesecloth placed over a saucepan. If the broth is still cloudy repeat the process.

Stock Substitutes

If homemade stocks are not available, you can use commercial substitutes; many varieties are available in stores. Canned, powdered, and cubed concentrates are easy to store, easy to use, and will keep indefinitely. While most are good products, they will never provide the body and flavor that distinguish home-made stocks.

Condensed beef broth, also called bouillon, is strained but not clarified and is highly concentrated. It is usually diluted with water, half and half, but can be used at full strength. Although much cheaper than the homemade product, the bouillon has a fairly strong flavor and is quite salty.

Condensed chicken broth is usually rather sweet and not nearly so good as the beef broth. Most powdered and cubed products are over-seasoned, particularly with salt.

Concentrated products are not recommended for long, slow cooking; they will make the dish too salty.

Although I'm not aware of any commercial fish bouillon on the market, clam juice is a good substitute.

Clear Soups

Thin clear soups, based on broths, bouillons, and consommés, are seasoned liquids of varying strength and flavor, and make ideal first courses for luncheons and dinners. Some are also excellent as snacks or pick-me-ups. The international repertoire is extensive and fascinating to explore.

In Western cuisines there are innumerable varieties of clear soups, with names often used interchangeably for soups which are similar. The names notwithstanding, these clear soups are often not exactly the same.

A broth is the weakest of the above-mentioned soups. It is a light liquid given some flavor and substance by having one or more solid foods simmered in it for a short time. Broths can be served by themselves, or with foods cooked in them or added to them. They can also be used as bases for other soups.

One of the best known English and American broths is called beef tea, a hot beverage made with beef and water generally cooked in a closed jar or bottle in a hot water "bath." It, like reliable chicken broth, has long been treasured as a between-meal stimulant or refresher during illness.

While some broths are called bouillons and vice versa, a true bouillon is a strained, strong liquid made by extracting flavors and goodness from various foods, especially meats, poultry, or fish, with seasonings, by long, slow simmering. Bouillons can also be made with vegetables, herbs, or cereals as prime ingredients. The word *bouillon* comes from the French *bouillier*, meaning "to boil."

Bouillon, in various forms, has long been enjoyed all over the world. Asians still relish flavorful and attractively garnished bouillons and broths made with seafood, poultry, mushrooms, vegetables, and seaweed.

Italian *brodo*, served with such enrichments as eggs, rice, or pasta in various forms, is a daily staple in the home and on restaurant menus. *Brodo classico*, classic bouillon, is the basis of a more elaborate soup made with characteristic flavorings and garnishes. As a first course, Austrians and Germans are fond of rich beef, veal, and chicken bouillons garnished with small dumplings, filled pastries, noodles, shredded pancakes, marrow slices, eggs, or farina.

The French have long been devotees of bouillon, which they drink as a stimulant as well as a soup. Cooks prepare one special variety with four kinds of meat and poultry for wedding and holiday meals. A particular favorite is *bouillon aveugle*, which is garnished with little "eyes" or spots of fat. Also relished are the bouillons from *petite marmite* and *pot-au-feu*. Since about 1860 a fast-food restaurant serving soups and light meals has been called a *bouillon* in France.

When a bouillon is made clear and sparkling by the process of clarifying (first chapter, see Basic Soup Data) it is called a consommé. The word comes from the French *consommer* meaning "to complete" or "to perfect."

There are two basic kinds of consommé. One, called *con-sommé simple,* is actually a flavorful strained bouillon. The other, called double consommé, is a rich concentrated bouillon that has been clarified to remove all extraneous elements and is thus further concentrated. This classic consommé is a luxury soup, expensive and difficult to make in the home because its production requires great skill and considerable time. It is very rich, absolutely clear, and should be of good color. It is always delightful and a perfect introduction to an elaborate meal, or one of many courses, as it clears the palate and stimulates the appetite.

There are hundreds of varieties of consommé. Some old cookbooks list as many as two hundred. Most of those created in the nineteenth century by French chefs for Continental banquets are culinary curiosities rarely prepared today.

Many of the classic consommés were named after performers and famous personalities, such as Adelina Patti, Grimaldi, Princess Alice, Xavier, and Yvette. Most consommés, however, are named to indicate the kind of garnish. *Argenteuil* indicates cooked asparagus tips; *brunois,* a mixture of vegetables; *Crécy,* carrots; *cheveux d'ange,* cooked vermicelli; *Royale,* small cubes or fancy shapes of royal custard; *Saint Hubert,* game and mushrooms; and Windsor, eggs and cream.

Consommés can be simply garnished with fresh herbs, lemon slices, julienne strips of raw or cooked vegetables, croutons, cooked rice or pasta, tapioca, slivered almonds, chopped watercress, eggs, diced chicken, whipped cream, and the like. But there are also those prepared for banquets with such elaborate garnishes as birds' nests, sturgeon marrow, quail strips, puréed chestnuts, plover eggs, *foie gras* stuffed *profiteroles,* cocks' combs, truffled chicken *quenelles,* and boned and stuffed chicken wings.

Some consommés are flavored and made fragrant with fortified wines, essence of truffles, mushrooms, or vegetables, or simply with lemon juice and grated lemon peel.

Hot consommé should be served very hot in warm two-handled cups or small bowls with appropriate spoons.

If cold, consommé forms a jelly and is called *consommé en gelée*. It is usually simply garnished. A familiar version is *consommé madrilène*, described in the chapter for cold soups.

In addition to homemade consommé, good consommé is available either plain or condensed in several brands. Some cooks improve the flavor of canned consommés by simmering them with mushrooms, onions, leeks, or other vegetables, herbs, or dry white wine. They may also be enriched with the addition of sherry or Madeira.

Two clear soups that appear frequently on international restaurant menus but are rarely made in the home today are oxtail and green turtle (see chapter on exotic soups).

One can easily and quickly prepare simple clear broths with store products. Combine, for example, half and half portions of clam broth and beef consommé, tomato juice and celery broth, beef bouillon and tomato juice, chicken broth and orange juice, beef bouillon and chicken broth, tomato juice and grapefruit juice, or mushroom bouillon and chicken broth.

Here's a round-the-world clear soup sampler.

Spanish Royal Soup

This attractively garnished clear soup, called *sopa real*, is traditionally served in Spain as a first course for luncheon or dinner. It is truly royal.

2 hard-cooked eggs, chopped
½ cup minced smoked ham

¾ cup finely chopped white meat of chicken
6 cups rich beef stock or bouillon
½ cup dry sherry
2 tablespoons chopped fresh parsley (optional)

Divide eggs, ham, and chicken among six soup bowls. Heat beef stock or bouillon to boiling. Remove from heat and add sherry. Pour at once into each bowl. Sprinkle with parsley. Serves 6.

Italian Soup With Poached Eggs

This well-known Italian soup, called *zuppa alla Pavese*, originated in Pavia, Lombardy. According to legend, the broth was created in 1525 for Francis I, King of France, when, after losing the battle of Pavia and while pursued by the victorious Spaniards, he stopped at a peasant's home and asked for food. Francis was so pleased with the humble dish that he termed it "a king's soup."

6 cups chicken broth
12 small thick slices crusty white bread
2 to 3 tablespoons butter or margarine
6 poached eggs
½ cup grated Parmesan cheese

Put chicken broth into a medium-sized saucepan and bring to a boil. Keep hot. Meanwhile, fry bread quickly in melted butter or margarine until golden brown on all sides. Put two slices into each of six soup bowls. Carefully put a poached egg into each soup plate over the bread. Sprinkle with cheese. Pour hot broth over eggs. Serve at once. Pass with additional cheese, if desired. Serves 6.

Indonesian Garnished Chicken Broth

In Indonesia a soup called *soto* is a tart, spicy broth tasting of lemongrass and garlic and including several garnishes such as noodles, vegetables, hard-cooked eggs, and seasonings. The most popular is *soto ajam*, chicken soup, and is prepared in many versions. This is one of them. Indonesians serve the soup with other dishes of the meal.

> *1 large onion, peeled and chopped*
> *2 tablespoons salad oil*
> *5 cups chicken broth*
> *1 teaspoon grated fresh ginger root*
> *1 or 2 garlic cloves, crushed*
> *1 tablespoon fresh lemon juice*
> *½ teaspoon pepper*
> *1 cup small pieces of cooked chicken*
> *1 cup thinly sliced celery or scallions*
> *2 hard-cooked eggs, chopped*

Sauté onion in heated oil in a small skillet until tender. Keep warm. Put chicken broth into a large saucepan. Add ginger root, garlic, lemon juice, and pepper. Bring to a boil. Reduce heat and cook over moderate heat, covered, 10 minutes. Put some of the chicken, celery or scallions, and eggs into each of six hot soup bowls. Fill with hot chicken broth. Sprinkle the top with sautéed onions. Serves 6.

Greek Egg-Lemon Soup

This refreshing soup, called *avgolemeno*, is a good first course for an informal dinner.

6 cups chicken broth
1/3 cup uncooked long-grain rice
Salt, pepper to taste
3 egg yolks
Juice of 2 lemons

Put chicken broth into a large saucepan and bring to a boil. Stir in rice. Reduce heat and cook slowly, covered, about 15 minutes, until rice is tender. Season with salt and pepper. Beat egg yolks until creamy in a small bowl. Add a few spoonfuls of hot broth and the lemon juice. Beat until light and creamy. Slowly stir into soup and leave on low heat only a few minutes, long enough for the soup to thicken. Do not boil or the mixture will curdle. Serve at once and do not reheat. Serves 4 to 6

Chinese Clear Soups

In China light and delicious clear soups are eaten at the end of the meal or between courses as refreshers or palate cleansers. The soups are made with clear, concentrated rich broths which are very flavorful. They may contain many kinds of vegetables, alone or in combination; shredded meats, poultry, or seafood; shredded greens; stuffed dumplings; bean curd cubes; or eggs. The typical soups below are easy and quick to prepare.

Chinese Egg-Drop Soup

2 eggs
6 cups rich chicken broth
1 cup shredded spinach leaves, washed and drained
1 tablespoon soy sauce (optional)

Beat eggs in a small bowl until light and creamy. Bring chicken broth to a boil in a large saucepan. Add spinach leaves. Pour in eggs and simmer several seconds, until cooked. Remove from heat at once and serve. Season with soy sauce, if desired. Serves 6.

Chinese Cabbage Soup

½ chicken breast, skinned, boned, and cut into thin strips
6 cups rich chicken broth
1 tablespoon soy sauce (optional)
*1 medium-sized head Chinese cabbage, cleaned and torn
 into 2-inch pieces*
Pepper to taste

Put chicken, chicken broth, and soy sauce into a large saucepan. Cook, covered, over medium heat 5 minutes. Add cabbage and cook, covered, about 5 minutes longer, until cabbage is tender but still crisp. Season with pepper. Serves 6.

Chinese Pork-Vegetable Soup

4 scallions, with some tops, sliced
1 cup raw carrots, cut in strips
1 cup celery, cut in strips
2 tablespoons peanut oil
6 cups chicken or beef broth
1 cup cooked pork, cut in thin strips
1 cup watercress or shredded spinach
2 tablespoons soy sauce
⅛ teaspoon pepper

Sauté scallions, carrots, and celery in heated oil in a large saucepan for one minute. Add broth and bring to a boil. Add remaining ingredients and cook slowly, covered, 5 minutes. serve at once. Serves 6.

Chinese Black Mushroom Soup

12 medium-sized dried black mushrooms
8 cups beef bouillon
½ cup minced scallions, with some tops
½ cup sliced bamboo shoots
1/3 cup sliced water chestnuts
2 to 3 tablespoons soy sauce
Pepper to taste

Soak mushrooms in lukewarm water to cover in a small bowl for 20 minutes. Drain, retaining liquid. Cut mushrooms in thick slices. Heat bouillon to boiling in a large saucepan. Add mushrooms with liquid, scallions, bamboo shoots, and water chestnuts. Reduce heat and simmer, covered, 30 minutes. Add soy sauce, the amount according to taste, and pepper. Remove from heat. Serves 8.

Roman Egg Soup

This specialty of Italy is named *stracciatella*, little rags, because the ingredients floating in the broth form small flakes.

2 eggs at room temperature
1 tablespoon all-purpose flour
2 tablespoons freshly grated Parmesan cheese

1 tablespoon chopped fresh parsley (optional)
4 cups chicken broth
Salt, pepper to taste

Beat eggs with a fork or whisk in a small bowl until light and creamy. Stir in flour, cheese, and parsley. Heat broth until just boiling. Stir in egg mixture and simmer, mixing constantly with a fork or whisk about 2 minutes, or until small flakes form in the soup. Season with salt and pepper. Serve at once. Do not reheat. Serves 4.

Luncheon Tomato Bouillon

2 cups tomato juice
2 cups beef bouillon
1 tablespoon fresh lemon juice
1 teaspoon Worcestershire sauce
Dash Tabasco sauce
1 teaspoon sugar (optional)
Salt, pepper to taste
2 tablespoons chopped fresh dill or parsley

Combine ingredients, except dill or parsley, in a medium-sized saucepan and bring to a boil. Reduce heat and cook slowly 5 minutes. Serve garnished with dill or parsley. Serves 4 to 6.

Portuguese Chicken Broth

Canja, or chicken broth, is a Portuguese national dish prepared in many versions. Typical additions to the flavorful broth are ham and rice, but eggs, onions, chestnuts, almonds, or other foods are also sometimes added to it. The broth is made tangy with lemon juice and is attractively garnished with mint.

½ cup chopped smoked ham
6 cups rich chicken broth
½ cup long-grain rice
Salt, pepper to taste
¼ cup fresh lemon juice
6 tablespoons chopped fresh mint

Put ham and chicken broth into a large saucepan. Bring to a boil. Stir in rice. Reduce heat and cook slowly, covered, about 20 minutes, until rice is tender. Season with salt and pepper. Add lemon juice and remove from heat. Serve in soup bowls garnished with mint. Serves 6.

Thai Lemony Chicken Soup

In Thailand soups called *tom yum* are light and clear and are made with a chicken or fish stock highly seasoned with aromatic and spicy foods such as chilies, lemongrass, and pungent herbs. These soups may also include such other ingredients as shrimp, chicken, pork, or mushrooms. They are traditionally eaten with or after other dishes of the meal. This recipe is an adaptation.

6 cups chicken broth
1 garlic clove, crushed
½ teaspoon ground coriander
2 bay leaves
¼ teaspoon crushed red peppers or ½ teaspoon cayenne
2 tablespoons fresh lemon juice
2 lemon slices
½ chicken breast, cooked and cut into shreds
3 medium-sized mushrooms, cleaned and slivered
4 scallions, cleaned and sliced, with some tops

Combine chicken broth, garlic, coriander, bay leaves, red

peppers or cayenne, and lemon juice, and slices in a large sauce-pan. Bring to a boil. Reduce heat and cook slowly, covered, 10 minutes. Add chicken and mushrooms and cook 5 minutes longer. Spoon into soup bowls and serve garnished with scallions. Serves 6.

Czech Beef Bouillon With Liver Dumplings

This traditional soup, called *polevka s jatennime*, is a favorite first course for luncheon or dinner.

> *1 pound beef chuck or soup meat, cubed*
> *6 cups water*
> *1 small carrot, scraped*
> *1 small onion, peeled and chopped*
> *4 sprigs parsley*
> *1 leek, white part only, cleaned and sliced*
> *2 tablespoons chopped celery leaves*
> *1½ teaspoons salt*
> *¼ teaspoon pepper*

Put all ingredients into a kettle. Bring to a boil. Skim well. Reduce heat and cook slowly, covered, 2 hours. Skim again. Strain bouillon. Reheat bouillon and drop in liver dumplings (recipe below). Cover and cook until dumplings rise to the surface, about 10 minutes. Spoon dumplings into large soup bowls and pour bouillon over them. Serves 6.

Liver Dumplings

> *½ pound beef liver*
> *2 tablespoons butter or margarine, softened*

1 garlic clove, crushed
½ teaspoon grated lemon rind
Salt to taste
Dash pepper, dried marjoram, and ground allspice
2 eggs, slightly beaten
About 1¼ cups fine dry bread crumbs

Grind liver or chop fine. Mix with butter, garlic, lemon rind, salt, pepper, marjoram, and allspice. Mix in eggs. Stir well. Add bread crumbs, enough to make a stiff mixture. Form into small balls. Leave at room temperature one hour. If not stiff enough, add more bread crumbs.

Korean Egg Soup

In Korea a favorite soup called *kook* is made with a basic flavorful broth to which are added cubed bean curd, eggs, stuffed dumplings, or sliced vegetables. This is one of the best.

8 cups beef bouillon
2 to 3 tablespoons soy sauce
1 garlic clove, crushed
1 tablespoon sesame oil
6 scallions, cleaned and sliced, with some tops
Pepper to taste
3 eggs

Put bouillon into a large saucepan and bring to a boil. Add soy sauce, garlic, sesame oil, scallions, and pepper. Mix well. Reduce heat and cook, covered, 10 minutes. Beat eggs with a fork or whisk in a small bowl until light and creamy. Pour quickly into soup and cook, stirring, until eggs are just firm. Serve at once. Serves 8.

Polish Barszcz

This flavorful clear beet soup has been served hot in Poland for centuries at Christmas and Easter dinners, and is eaten cold at the traditional harvest festival. There are many varieties of the soup, which can be made with vegetable or meat broth and can be either clear or with several ingredients. The foundation for the true *barszcz* is a tart ferment called *kwas*, made from sour rye bread and beets. The clear soup can include such foods as cooked potatoes, sliced sausages, cooked meat, or filled pastries, and may be garnished with sour cream. The special version served on Christmas Eve called *barszcz Wigilijny* usually includes *uszka*, "little ears," of dough stuffed with mushrooms.

4 or 5 dried mushrooms
4 large beets
4 cups beef bouillon
½ cup liquid from canned pickled beets
1 teaspoon sugar
Salt, pepper to taste

Soak mushrooms in lukewarm water to cover in a small bowl for 20 minutes. Squeeze dry and slice. Reserve liquid. Wash beets; peel and chop fine. Put in a large saucepan with mushrooms, reserved liquid, and bouillon; bring to a boil. Lower heat and cook slowly, covered, about 35 minutes, until vegetables are tender. Strain. Mix liquid with pickled beet liquid, sugar, salt, and pepper; heat. Serves 4.

Note: Add wine vinegar or lemon juice, about 1 tablespoon, for a stronger flavor.

Japanese Clear Soups

In Japan a clear soup is called *suimono* and is made with the national soup stock, *dashi,* to which various garnishes can be added. *Dashi* is indispensable to Japanese cookery, used as a liquid ingredient for many dishes as well as a soup base. It is made from dried bonito flakes and seaweed. The stock or broth should be clear and light. Garnishes added to the stock can be just about anything, such as eggs, greens, bean curd, seafood, poultry, or vegetables. Each food is artistically cut into a design and often two or three of them are arranged in the soup to depict a "scene." A *suimono* is always attractive as well as delectable and is served as the first course of a meal. *Dashi* can be made in the home with Japanese seasonings. It can also be purchased in small envelopes and easily made by boiling the ingredients in hot water. Here's a recipe for *dashi* and three soups that are made with it. The Japanese ingredients can be purchased in Oriental or specialty food stores.

Japanese Soup Stock (Dashi)

1 inch square Kombu *(seaweed)*
5 cups water
1 cup flaked Katsvobushi *(dried bonito)*

Rinse any sand from *Kombu.* Pour into water and bring to a boil. Add *Katsvobushi* and remove from heat. Let stand two minutes. Strain through cheesecloth. Use plain or season with 1 teaspoon soy sauce and 2 teaspoons salt. Makes about 5 cups.

Japanese Chicken Soup

8 slivers or bite-size pieces raw white chicken
½ cup soy sauce
4 scallions, cleaned and sliced, with some tops
4 fresh mushrooms, cleaned and thinly sliced lengthwise
1 small piece ginger root
3 cups dashi

Combine chicken and soy sauce in a small saucepan. Boil two minutes, until tender. Remove from pan. Divide chicken, scallions, and mushrooms among four soup bowls. Heat *dashi* to boiling. Press juice from ginger root with a garlic press and add one or two drops to each bowl. Pour hot *dashi* into each bowl. Serve at once. Serves 4.

Japanese Bean Curd Soup

4 teaspoons bean curd (tofu)
4 1-inch strips fresh spinach
3 cups dashi

Put one teaspoon bean curd and one strip spinach into each of four soup bowls. Heat *dashi* to boiling and pour into the bowls. Serve at once. Serves 4.

Japanese Gingered Shrimp Soup

6 cups dashi *or chicken broth*
1½ tablespoons minced ginger root
1 teaspoon ajinomoto (monosodium glutamate)
12 medium-sized shrimp, cleaned and shelled
6 medium-sized raw onion rings

Combine *dashi* or chicken broth, ginger root, and *ajinomoto* in a large saucepan. Bring to a boil. Reduce heat and simmer 5 minutes. Add shrimp and simmer 5 more minutes. Put two shrimp and one onion ring into each of six soup bowls. Pour *dashi* or broth mixture into each bowl. Serves 6.

Swiss Mushroom Consommé

¾ pound fresh mushrooms
3 tablespoons butter or margarine
8 cups beef bouillon
⅛ teaspoon freshly grated nutmeg
Salt, freshly ground pepper to taste
1 cup dry sherry
2 tablespoons minced scallions, with some tops, or chopped fresh parsley

Rinse mushrooms quickly or wipe them with wet paper toweling to remove any dirt. Cut off any tough stem ends. Sauté in butter or margarine in a large saucepan for 2 minutes. Add bouillon, nutmeg, salt, and pepper. Bring to a boil. Reduce heat and cook over moderate heat 10 minutes. Add sherry and scallions or parsley and leave over moderate heat long enough to heat through. Serves 8.

Consommé Bellevue

This chicken-clam soup, served garnished with whipped cream, is a traditional dish of Philadelphia.

3 cups chicken broth
3 cups clam juice
Dash cayenne

Salt to taste
4 tablespoons lightly salted whipped cream

Put chicken broth, clam juice, cayenne, and salt into a large saucepan. Bring to a boil. Reduce heat and simmer, covered, over moderate heat 5 minutes. Serve in heated soup bowls garnished with a dollop of whipped cream. Serves 6 to 8.

Consommé Julienne

This is an attractive easy-to-prepare soup.

½ cup sliced scallions, with some tops
1 tablespoon butter or margarine
2 tablespoons tomato paste
4 cups beef consommé
Salt, pepper to taste
1 cup cooked vegetables (carrots, green beans, celery, green peppers), cut into julienne
2 cups cooked and drained small pasta (alphabets, pastina)

Sauté scallions in heated butter or margarine in a large saucepan until tender. Stir in tomato paste. Add consommé and bring to a boil. Reduce heat and cook slowly, covered, 10 minutes. Season with salt and pepper. Mix in vegetables and pasta. Leave over medium heat long enough to heat through. Serves 4.

Bisques
and Cream Soups

Rich and flavorful bisques and cream soups are aristocratic delicacies made with an amazing variety of inviting ingredients. While they are usually served as first courses for dinner, many are superb as luncheon entrées.

Bisque, the French term for a very rich creamy soup that is highly seasoned, has been made traditionally with shellfish, but fish, meat, puréed vegetables, or fruits may also be used.

The bisques created in France between 1700 and 1750 were quite different from those we know today. They were more like stews and were prepared with all sorts of poultry and game, such as pigeons, quail, rabbits, and squab, and were cooked with a thick bread crust.

One recipe for a 1758 bisque described it as a quail soup with a crayfish garnish. Over the years bisques became lighter and richer with a base of shellfish, particularly lobsters, shrimp, crabs, and crayfish.

59

Bisques have long been regarded as very stylish preparations to be served at elegant meals or banquets. Victorians and Edwardians were very fond of bisques and often enjoyed more than one kind for dinner. In Alexander Dumas' *Dictionary of Cuisine,* bisque is described as "the most royal of royal dishes" and "a food for princes and financiers."

Bisques were introduced to America from England, and colonial cooks began making the soups with the abundant bounty of native seafood such as clams, crabs, crayfish, lobsters, oysters, salmon, scallops, shrimp, and trout. Subsequently, bisques made with avocados, mushrooms, tomatoes, and other ingredients became popular.

Although American bisques are now made in many variations, each should be well-flavored, often with wine or brandy, and enriched with egg yolks and cream. Some are served with fancy garnishes.

The preparation of an authentic French shellfish bisque in the traditional manner requires so much time and expertise that it is usually made only by restaurant chefs or expert cooks. The procedure begins with the sautéing of a blend of cut-up vegetables, or *mirepoix,* and raw shellfish in their shells to extract maximum flavor and color. Additional cooking steps produce one of the world's most wonderful culinary creations, which is cooked and strained after wine, brandy, seasonings, stock, rice, cream, and butter have been added.

Cream soups are made in several variations. Many are prepared with a white *roux* or Bechamel sauce that includes butter, flour, broth or stock, and light cream, as well as a purée of meat, poultry, seafood, or vegetables, and seasonings. Others do not include the *roux* but are thickened with such binders as puréed rice, grated potatoes, or raw egg yolks.

The richest cream soups are called *velouté,* or velvet, which describes their characteristic texture. They are generally composed of a rich chicken or veal stock, basic purée, and seasonings, and are thickened at the end of cooking with a liaison of egg yolks, heavy cream, and butter. Some well-known varieties are Bagration (meat), Lucullus (chicken), Saint Hubert (pheasant), and Santé (potatoes and sorrel).

Many of the cream soups that were created by French chefs and which became popular in Europe and America still appear on international menus and take the name of their principal ingredient, such as *crème de volaille* (chicken) or *crème de poissons* (fish). Among the hundreds of others, many are named for personalities or the type of garnish, ranging from *crème Agnes Sorel* and *à la Louise* to *Xavier* and *Zingari*.

Colonial Americans were fond of cream soups for everyday and entertaining; among their favorites were herb-flavored asparagus, celery, corn, green bean, green pea, spinach, and watercress. They also made many kinds of stylish chicken and rich almond soups for special occasions. Southerners especially favored cream of peanut and pumpkin soups.

The roster of ingredients used in cream soups expanded considerably over the years to include just about every kind of food, including bread, cheese, cereals, frogs' legs, nuts, rabbits, stone crabs, and tripe.

The international repertoire of cream soups includes those from Russia and the Middle East made with sour cream and yogurt, those from the Orient and Polynesia made with coconut milk, and dishes from northern Europe made with buttermilk. The Spanish and Portuguese are fond of rich shellfish and tomato cream soups.

Each cream soup should be light and smooth with no trace of flour or thickening agent. It should also be distinctive in flavor and well-seasoned with perhaps the addition of a little onion and/or other flavorings that enhance the taste of the basic ingredients. Many cream soups are served with decorative garnishes that contrast in color and texture with the soup and which are appropriate to its primary ingredient.

Here are some fine recipes for bisques from France and America and for cream soups from around the world.

New England Clam Bisque

This easy-to-prepare bisque is made with canned minced clams. It is a good supper dish.

> *3 tablespoons minced onions*
> *1½ tablespoons butter*
> *1½ tablespoons all-purpose flour*
> *2 cans (7½ ounces each) minced clams, cleaned*
> *¼ teaspoon celery salt*
> *1 teaspoon salt*
> *⅛ teaspoon pepper*
> *3 cups light cream*
> *1 cup heavy cream*
> *3 tablespoons chopped fresh parsley*

Sauté onions in heated butter in a large saucepan. Add flour and cook slowly, stirring, 1 or 2 minutes. Add clams with liquid, celery salt, salt, and pepper. Simmer, stirring occasionally, 5 minutes. Meanwhile, scald the creams. Add to clam mixture and leave over low heat 1 or 2 minutes to blend flavors. Serve at once garnished with parsley. Serves 4 to 6.

Chesapeake Oyster Bisque

This traditional Eastern Shore specialty is an excellent weekend luncheon dish.

> *1 pint shucked standard oysters with their liquor*
> *1 small onion, peeled and minced*
> *2 small stalks celery, minced*
> *3 tablespoons butter*
> *3 tablespoons all-purpose flour*

4 *cups light cream*
1 *teaspoon salt*
⅛ *teaspoon pepper*
3 *tablespoons chopped fresh parsley*
Dash paprika

Heat oysters in their liquor but do not boil. Drain; reserve liquor. Chop oysters. Sauté onion and celery in heated butter in the top of a double boiler over simmering water until tender. Add flour and cook slowly, stirring, 1 or 2 minutes. Gradually add cream, stirring, and cook until smooth and thickened. Add oysters and liquor, salt, pepper, and parsley. Leave on stove long enough to heat through. Serve at once garnished with paprika. Serves 4.

Louisiana Crayfish Bisque

Crayfish bisque or *bisque d'ecrevisse,* based on small, succulent freshwater crayfish caught in southern Louisiana bayous and swamps, is a famous dish of New Orleans and the nearby Cajun country. The bisque is dark and thick and is made aromatic with the intriguing flavors of crayfish, vegetables, herbs, and spices. Bright-red crayfish heads, stuffed with bread crumbs, seasonings, and minced crayfish, float in the bisque. The stuffing is traditionally scooped or sucked out and the empty shells placed around the rim of the soup bowl. Because the bisque requires crayfish and a great deal of labor and skill, it is not easy to prepare in the home kitchen unless you live in Louisiana. Below, however, is a traditional recipe for bisque. Use shrimp as a substitute for crayfish, if you like.

Put crayfish meat and shells (previously cooked alive in boiling water) into a large kettle with cooking water. Add 1 onion, chopped, 1 garlic clove, minced, 1 carrot, 3 or 4 stalks celery, 2 or

3 sprigs parsley, 1 bay leaf, 2 cloves, a little dried thyme, a little mace or nutmeg, and bring to a boil. Add rice, about ½ cup for 4 dozen crayfish. Boil until rice is well cooked. Press all through a sieve, mashing shells and pressing them through, to achieve a thick purée. Thin with oyster liquor and return to the heat. Taste and season. Meanwhile, remove heads from several large crayfish and empty and clean. Prepare a stuffing with minced onion, bread moistened with milk, an onion, chopped and sautéed in butter, salt, pepper, minced parsley, thyme, and bay leaf. Put stuffing into head shells, dot with butter, and bake. Put stuffed heads in a soup tureen and pour bisque over them. Serve with croutons. Serves 6-8.

Fresh Tomato Bisque

This is a good bisque to prepare in the summer with vine-ripened fresh tomatoes.

> 3 *cups peeled, seeded, and chopped ripe tomatoes*
> 2 *tablespoons minced onion*
> 1 *bay leaf*
> ¼ *teaspoon celery seed*
> 2 *whole cloves*
> 1½ *teaspoons salt*
> ¼ *teaspoon pepper*
> ¼ *cup butter*
> ¼ *cup all-purpose flour*
> 3 *cups light cream*

Combine tomatoes, onion, bay leaf, celery seed, cloves, salt, and pepper in a medium-sized saucepan. Cook, uncovered, 15 minutes, stirring frequently. Purée in a food mill or processor. Melt butter in a large saucepan. Stir in flour and cook slowly, stirring, about 2 minutes. Gradually add cream, stirring while adding, and cook slowly, stirring, until smooth and thickened. Meanwhile, heat strained tomato mixture and add, stirring, to hot cream sauce. Leave on low heat about 5 minutes, long enough to heat through and blend flavors. Serves 4 to 6.

Oregon Salmon Bisque

This bisque can be served as an entrée with sandwiches for a luncheon.

> *1 small onion, peeled and minced*
> *2 tablespoons butter*
> *2 tablespoons all-purpose flour*
> *1 can (1 pound) tomatoes, undrained and chopped*
> *¼ teaspoon dried rosemary or thyme*
> *1½ teaspoons salt*
> *⅛ teaspoon pepper*
> *1 can (1 pound) red or pink salmon, cleaned and flaked*
> *3 cups light cream or milk, scalded*
> *¼ cup dry sherry*

Sauté onion in heated butter in a large saucepan until tender. Add flour and cook slowly, stirring, 2 minutes. Add tomatoes, rosemary or thyme, salt, and pepper, and cook slowly, stirring frequently, for 10 minutes. Add salmon and its liquid and cream or milk. Leave over low heat 5 minutes to blend flavors. Remove from heat and stir in sherry. Serves 6 to 8.

French Shrimp Bisque

This is a classic recipe for making traditional bisque with raw unshelled shrimp.

2 *shallots, minced*
¼ *teaspoon minced garlic*
2 *small carrots, scraped*
2 *sprigs parsley*
8 *cups water*
1 *cup dry white wine*
1½ *teaspoons salt*
¼ *teaspoon pepper*
2 *dozen raw, unshelled shrimp*
¼ *cup butter*
¼ *cup brandy*
1 *egg yolk*
1 *teaspoon cornstarch*
½ *cup heavy cream*
Dash cayenne

Combine shallots, garlic, carrots, parsley, water, ½ cup wine, salt, and pepper in a kettle. Simmer, covered, 30 minutes. Remove from heat and strain. Keep hot. Sauté shrimp in heated butter in a large skillet on all sides for 1 or 2 minutes. Heat brandy and pour over shrimp. Ignite and let burn off. Add ½ cup wine. Cook 10 minutes, until shrimp turn red. Remove from heat and cool. Shell shrimp, reserving shells; clean and mince shrimp. Pound shells in a mortar with a pestle or grind and put through a sieve. Mix with minced shrimp. Blend egg yolk with cornstarch and add some of hot strained broth. Cook slowly, stirring constantly. Add shrimp and remaining broth. Cook slowly, stirring, until thickened and smooth. Mix in cream and cayenne and serve at once. Serves 4.

Southern Sherried Lobster Bisque

This delectable lobster bisque includes mushrooms and is flavored with sherry.

¾ *pound fresh mushrooms*
¼ *cup minced onion*
6 *tablespoons butter*
3 *tablespoons all-purpose flour*
5 *cups chicken broth*
⅛ *teaspoon dried marjoram*
1 *teaspoon salt*
⅛ *teaspoon pepper*
1 *tablespoon fresh lemon juice*
1½ *cups cooked lobster, cubed*
1½ *cups light cream*
1/3 *cup dry sherry*

Wash mushrooms quickly or wipe with wet paper toweling to remove any dirt. Remove stems from caps. Set aside caps; chop stems, discarding any tough ends. Sauté onion in 3 tablespoons heated butter in a large saucepan. Add flour and cook slowly, stirring, 2 minutes. Add chopped mushroom stems, chicken broth, marjoram, salt, and pepper. Simmer, covered, 25 minutes. Strain mixture, pressing mushrooms to release their juices. Pour into a large saucepan. Meanwhile, slice mushroom caps and sauté in remaining 3 tablespoons butter and lemon juice for 3 minutes in a small skillet. Add, with lobster and cream, to strained liquid. Leave over low heat 1 or 2 minutes to blend flavors. Remove from heat and stir in sherry. Serves 8.

Potage Bonne Femme

This is a well-known basic French potato-leek soup which is versatile as a soup base. You may add other vegetables or herbs to it.

4 *large leeks*
1 *medium-sized onion, peeled and diced*

> *3 tablespoons butter*
> *4 large potatoes, peeled and diced*
> *4 cups water or chicken broth*
> *2 teaspoons salt*
> *2 cups hot milk*
> *2 tablespoons chopped fresh chervil*
> *6 to 8 toasted slices crusty French bread*

Remove green tops and roots from leeks. Wash well to remove all sand; wipe dry; dice. Sauté leeks and onion in 2 tablespoons heated butter in a large saucepan until tender but do not brown. Add potatoes, water or broth, and salt. Bring to a boil. Reduce heat and cook slowly, covered, about 35 minutes, until potatoes are tender. Add hot milk, remaining 1 tablespoon butter, and chervil. Ladle into soup plates over slices of toasted bread. Serves 6 to 8.

Potage Parmentier

This variation of *potage bonne femme* is named for the French horticulturist Antoine-Auguste Parmentier, who made the potato popular in France during the late 1700s. Many French dishes that include potatoes are named for him.

> *4 large leeks*
> *1 medium-sized onion, peeled and diced*
> *3 tablespoons butter*
> *4 large potatoes, peeled and diced*
> *3 cups hot water*
> *2 teaspoons salt*
> *3 cups hot milk*

Remove green tops and roots from leeks. Wash well to remove all sand; wipe dry; dice. Sauté leeks and onion in 2 tablespoons butter in a large saucepan until tender but do not brown. Add potatoes, water, and salt. Bring to a boil. Reduce heat and cook slowly, covered, about 35 minutes, until potatoes are tender. Purée in a food mill, blender, or food processor. Put in a large saucepan. Add hot milk and remaining 1 tablespoon butter. Leave over low heat about 3 minutes. Serve garnished with chopped chives, if desired. Serves 6 to 8.

Note: A richer soup can be made with a final addition of two beaten egg yolks and ½ cup heavy cream. Do not boil.

Crème Crécy

This French soup called *crème* or *purée* Crécy is named for a little town in France where excellent golden carrots are grown. Any dish which incorporates the word Crécy in its name includes carrots as a primary ingredient or a garnish.

 1 *medium-sized onion, peeled and chopped*
 3 *tablespoons butter*
 3 *cups scraped, diced carrots*
 4 *cups chicken broth or water*
 ¼ *cup uncooked long-grain rice*
 1 *teaspoon salt*
 ¼ *teaspoon white pepper*
 1 *cup light cream*

Sauté onion in 2 tablespoons butter in a large saucepan until tender. Add carrots, chicken broth or water, rice, salt, and pepper. Cook slowly, covered, 40 minutes, or until carrots are tender. Purée in a food mill or processor. Return purée to kettle and bring slowly to a simmer. Add cream and remove from heat. Add remaining 1 tablespoon butter. Serve garnished with chopped fresh parsley, if desired. Serves 6 to 8.

Potage Saint Germaine

This traditional green pea soup should be made only with fresh green peas.

3 cups shelled fresh green peas
1 small onion, peeled and minced
3 lettuce leaves, shredded
1 small carrot, scraped and diced
2 sprigs parsley
5 cups chicken broth
1 cup light or heavy cream
Salt, pepper to taste
2 tablespoons butter
2 teaspoons chopped fresh mint

Combine peas, onion, lettuce, carrots, parsley, and chicken broth in a large saucepan. Cook over medium heat, covered, 15 minutes, until peas are tender. Purée in a food mill or processor. Return to saucepan. Add cream, salt, and pepper. Slowly heat to simmering. Remove from heat and add butter. Serve garnished with mint. Serves 6.

Lady Curzon Soup

One of the great specialty soups of German and some other Continental restaurants is an appealing turtle soup flavored with curry powder and sherry. No one seems to know why the soup was named for Lady Curzon or whether she created it. Lady Curzon was an American married to Lord Curzon, Viceroy of India at the beginning of the century. The soup, however, is not served in India or England. It appears in many variations, prepared sometimes with thick or clear turtle soup or such substitutes as clam or mussel broth. The soup is always very rich and is served in special small cups similar to a demitasse. This recipe is one variation that is served in Frankfurt, Germany.

4 cups clear turtle soup
½ teaspoon curry powder
2 tablespoons minced mushrooms
1 egg yolk
2 tablespoons heavy cream
1 tablespoon dry sherry or Madeira
2 tablespoons grated Parmesan cheese

Put soup into a medium-sized saucepan. Add curry powder and mushrooms and simmer 5 minutes. Blend egg yolk and heavy cream in a small bowl. Add a little hot soup and mix well. Remove soup from heat and mix in egg-cream mixture. Beat until creamy. Stir in sherry or Madeira. Pour into heatproof small cups and sprinkle with cheese. Put under broiler until top is golden brown. Serves 6.
Note: Omit cheese and top with whipped cream sprinkled with minced fresh parsley, if you prefer.

Chinese Velvet Corn-Chicken Soup

This is a modern version of a classic Chinese soup that is made with canned cream-style corn. You will find that the soup has a refreshing and different flavor.

½ chicken breast, skinned, boned, and minced
3 cups chicken broth
1 teaspoon salt
1 can (about 8 ounces) cream-style corn
1 tablespoon cornstarch

2 *tablespoons water*
2 *egg whites, slightly beaten*
¼ *cup minced cooked ham*

Put minced chicken, chicken broth, and salt into a medium-size saucepan. Bring to a boil. Add corn, stirring constantly, and bring again to a boil. Mix in cornstarch, dissolved in water, and cook over medium heat, stirring, until thickened and clear. Remove from heat and quickly stir in egg whites. Mix well and serve at once in a tureen or soup bowls garnished with ham. Serves 4.

Australian Cream of Scallop Soup

This is a good luncheon or supper soup.

1 *pound sea scallops*
2 *tablespoons butter or margarine*
3 *tablespoons all-purpose flour*
6 *cups light cream or milk*
2 *teaspoons anchovy paste*
1 *tablespoon fresh lemon juice*
1½ *teaspoons salt*
½ *teaspoon pepper*

Remove any shell particles from scallops and wash. Chop and set aside. Melt butter or margarine in a large saucepan. Add flour and cook slowly, stirring, 2 minutes. Gradually add cream or milk, stirring while adding. Add anchovy paste, lemon juice, salt, and pepper. Cook slowly, stirring, until thickened and smooth. Add scallops and cook over low heat, covered, about 5 minutes, until scallops are cooked. Serves 6.

African Cream of Peanut Soup

The peanut, called a groundnut in Africa, is used to make many good soups. This one is flavored with red pepper.

1 small onion, peeled and minced
2 tablespoons peanut oil or butter
2 tablespoons all-purpose flour
4 cups chicken broth
½ teaspoon ground red pepper
½ teaspoon salt
¼ teaspoon pepper
1 1/3 cups ground salted peanuts
1 cup light cream

Sauté onion in heated oil or butter in a medium-sized saucepan until tender. Add flour and cook slowly, stirring, 2 minutes. Gradually add broth, stirring while adding. Add seasonings and cook slowly, stirring frequently, 5 minutes. Add peanuts and cream and leave on stove long enough to heat through. Serves 4.

Boula-Boula

This well-known American soup, made with turtle soup and puréed fresh green peas, has a confusing name. Some people believe it comes from the famous Yale song. One culinary authority states that the soup originated in the Seychelles. Although the soup was popularized as a favorite of President and Mrs. John F. Kennedy, boula was served at the White House much earlier, when Martin Van Buren was President. There are now many recipes for the soup, but it is best made with fresh green peas. This is the recipe of White House chefs during the Kennedy administration.

2 cups freshly shelled green peas
Salt
1 tablespoon butter
White pepper to taste
2 cups canned green turtle soup
1 cup dry sherry
½ cup lightly salted whipped cream

Cook peas in lightly salted boiling water until tender, about 10 minutes. Drain; purée or whirl in a blender. Reheat. Add butter, salt, and pepper to taste. Mix in turtle soup and sherry; blend well. Heat just to boiling. Pour soup into heat-proof serving cups or bowls. Top each with a spoonful of whipped cream. Put under heated broiler until topping is delicately golden brown. Serves 4.

Indonesian Curried Coconut Cream Soup

This traditional spicy soup includes spinach and Chinese cabbage.

1 small onion, peeled and minced
1 garlic clove, crushed
2 tablespoons peanut oil or butter
1 tablespoon curry powder
½ teaspoon ground coriander
¼ teaspoon pepper
3 cups chicken broth
1 cup shredded spinach
1 cup shredded Chinese cabbage
1 cup coconut milk

Sauté onion and garlic in heated oil or butter in a medium-size saucepan until tender. Add curry powder, coriander, and pepper and cook 1 minute. Add chicken broth and bring to a boil. Mix in spinach, cabbage, and coconut milk. Reduce heat and cook slowly, uncovered, 5 minutes. Serves 4.

Iraqi Cream of Almond Soup

The sweet almond, closely related to the peach, has long been a primary ingredient of soups in many parts of the world including the eastern Mediterranean where the almond originated. One of the best-known almond soups is *Potage à la Reine,* made with chicken and almond milk and enjoyed in England and America. This is a good basic almond soup.

2/3 cup blanched almonds
¼ cup heavy cream
2 tablespoons butter or margarine
2 tablespoons all-purpose flour
1½ cups chicken broth
2 cups light cream
Salt, pepper to taste (optional)

Chop or crush almonds as fine as possible, preferably in a mortar with a pestle. Combine with heavy cream in a small bowl. Heat butter or margarine in a medium-sized saucepan. Add flour and cook slowly, stirring, 2 minutes. Gradually add chicken broth, stirring, and cook slowly, stirring, until thickened and smooth. Add cream, salt, and pepper and leave on stove long enough to heat through. Mix in almonds and cream just before serving, garnished with watercress, if desired. Serves 4.

Connecticut Cream of Onion Soup

This is an old-fashioned favorite soup in Connecticut, where it has been savored since Colonial times.

> 2 *medium-sized onions, peeled and sliced*
> 3 *tablespoons butter or margarine*
> 2 *cups water*
> 2 *tablespoons all-purpose flour*
> 1½ *teaspoons salt*
> ¼ *teaspoon pepper*
> *Dash grated nutmeg*
> 2 *cups hot light cream*

Sauté onions in heated butter or margarine in a large saucepan until tender. Add water and cook slowly, covered, 15 minutes. Mix some of the hot liquid with flour in a small bowl; blend well. Stir into hot liquid, mixing well with a whisk. Add salt, pepper, and nutmeg. Cook slowly, stirring, 5 minutes. Mix in hot cream. Remove from heat. Serve with croutons, if desired. Serves 4.

French Crème de Champignons Potage

This cream of mushroom soup is an elegant first course for a company dinner.

> 1 *pound fresh mushrooms*
> 5 *tablespoons butter or margarine*
> 1 *tablespoon fresh lemon juice*
> 1½ *teaspoons salt*
> ¼ *teaspoon pepper*
> 2 *tablespoons minced shallots or scallions*
> 3 *tablespoons minced onions*

2 tablespoons all-purpose flour
6 cups chicken broth
1 bay leaf
2 sprigs parsley
Dash cayenne
¾ cup heavy cream

Wash mushrooms quickly or wipe with wet paper toweling to remove any dirt. Pull stems from caps. Cut off any tough ends from stems; chop finely. Slice caps. Sauté sliced caps in 2 table-spoons heated butter or margarine and lemon juice in a large saucepan 3 minutes. Add salt and pepper. Remove to a plate. Melt remaining 3 tablespoons butter in a saucepan. Add shallots and onions and sauté until tender. Add chopped mushroom stems; sauté 2 minutes. Mix in flour and cook over low heat, stirring constantly, 2 minutes. Gradually add chicken broth, stirring while adding. Add bay leaf, parsley, and cayenne. Cook over very low heat, stirring frequently, 15 minutes. Strain, press-ing mushrooms with a spoon to release all juices. Return strained liquid to saucepan. Add sautéed sliced mushrooms and cream. Leave on stove long enough to heat through. Serves 4 to 6.

Dutch Cream of Cheese Soup

This well-seasoned cheese soup is a good supper dish. Serve with toasted crusty French bread.

4 thin slices bacon, chopped
¼ cup butter or margarine
1 medium-sized onion, peeled and minced
2 tablespoons tomato paste
1 teaspoon sharp prepared mustard
1 teaspoon Worcestershire sauce

⅛ teaspoon paprika
2 teaspoons salt
¼ teaspoon pepper
4 cups rich chicken broth
2 cups shredded Edam or Gouda cheese
2 cups hot light cream

Fry bacon in a large saucepan until almost crisp. Pour off fat. Add butter or margarine and melt. Add onion and sauté until tender. Mix in tomato paste, mustard, Worcestershire sauce, paprika, salt, and pepper. Mix well. Cook 1 or 2 minutes to blend flavors. Add chicken broth and bring slowly to a boil. Reduce heat and cook slowly, covered, 30 minutes. Add cheese and continue to cook over low heat, stirring, until melted. Add cream and mix well. Remove from heat and serve at once. Serves 6 to 8.

Caribbean Coconut Soup

This unusual soup is made with grated coconut and flavored with curry powder.

8 ounces freshly grated coconut from 1 medium-sized coconut or 2 cans (4 ounces each) moist sweet shredded coconut
4 cups beef bouillon or chicken broth
1 tablespoon cornstarch
1 teaspoon curry powder
1 cup cold milk
½ cup heavy cream
Salt, pepper to taste

Combine coconut and bouillon or broth in a medium-sized saucepan. Cook slowly, covered, 30 minutes. Strain, pressing to extract all liquid. Discard coconut. Put liquid into a saucepan. Combine cornstarch, curry powder, and milk; stir into coconut liquid. Cook slowly, stirring, until thickened and smooth. Add cream and season with salt and pepper. Serve hot or cold. Serves 4 to 6.

Maryland Cream of Crab Soup

Serve this rich soup as a first course for a holiday or company dinner.

> 1 *pound fresh lump crabmeat*
> ¼ *cup minced onion*
> ¼ *cup butter*
> 2 *tablespoons all-purpose flour*
> ¼ *teaspoon celery salt*
> 1 *teaspoon salt*
> ⅛ *teaspoon pepper*
> *Few drops hot sauce*
> 1 *cup vegetable bouillon*
> 4 *cups light cream*
> 3 *tablespoons chopped fresh parsley*

Remove any cartilage from crabmeat. Sauté onion in heated butter in a large saucepan until tender. Add flour and seasonings. Cook slowly, stirring, 2 minutes. Gradually add vegetable bouillon, stirring, and cook slowly 5 minutes. Add cream and cook slowly until thickened and smooth. Add crabmeat and parsley and leave on low heat long enough to heat through. Serves 6.

Venezuelan Cream of Pumpkin Soup

The gourdlike pumpkin has been used for centuries in Latin

American countries to make flavorful soups. The sweet orange-colored flesh is delectable and nourishing.

> 2 *tablespoons butter or margarine*
> 2 *tablespoons all-purpose flour*
> 1 *cup beef bouillon*
> 3 *tablespoons brown sugar*
> ¼ *teaspoon ground cinnamon*
> ¼ *teaspoon ground nutmeg*
> 1 *teaspoon salt*
> ⅛ *teaspoon pepper*
> 2 *cups mashed cooked or canned pumpkin, drained*
> 2½ *cups light cream*
> 2 *egg yolks, lightly beaten*

Melt butter or margarine in a large saucepan. Stir in flour and cook, stirring, 2 minutes. Gradually add bouillon, stirring, and cook slowly until thickened and smooth. Add remaining ingredients, except egg yolks, and mix well. Simmer, covered, 15 minutes. Spoon some of the hot mixture into egg yolks. Return to soup. Simmer 1 or 2 minutes. Remove from heat and serve at once. Serves 6.

Charleston She-Crab Soup

Crab bisque, a famous specialty in South Carolina's Low Country since the early 1880s, is better known as she-crab soup as it includes the female crab's roe, which enhances the flavor. The she-crab is in such demand in Charleston that street vendors still announce when they are in supply by going through the streets calling: "Shee Craib! Shee Craib!" The soup is properly served by placing one tablespoon of sherry in a soup bowl, adding the hot soup, and topping it with whipped cream sprinkled with paprika or finely chopped parsley.

1 *small onion, peeled and minced*
2 *tablespoons butter*
1 *teaspoon all-purpose flour*
2 *cups milk*
2 *cups light cream*
2 *cups cleaned lump crabmeat*
¼ *pound crab roe*
⅛ *teaspoon ground mace or nutmeg*
½ *teaspoon salt*
⅛ *teaspoon pepper*
1/3 *cup dry sherry*

Sauté onion in heated butter in top of a double boiler over simmering hot water. Blend in flour; mix until smooth. Gradually add milk and cream, stirring while adding. Then add crabmeat, roe, mace or nutmeg, salt, and pepper. Cook slowly 20 minutes, stirring occasionally. Remove from heat. Spoon sherry into soup bowls and pour soup over it. Serve at once garnished with a dollop of whipped cream, sprinkled with paprika, if desired. Serves 4 to 6.

Note: If you do not have crab roe, put one crumbled hard-cooked egg yolk in bottom of each soup bowl before adding soup.

German Cream of Asparagus Soup

In Germany this soup is traditionally made with the highly prized white asparagus called *spargel*, but green asparagus can be a good substitute.

1 *pound fresh white or green asparagus*
2 *teaspoons sugar*
Salt to taste
1 *cup light cream*

2 tablespoons butter, softened
2 tablespoons all-purpose flour
2 egg yolks, lightly beaten
Freshly ground pepper and grated nutmeg to taste
3 tablespoons chopped fresh parsley

If white asparagus is used, it must be peeled from just below the tip to the base. For green asparagus, trim off the scales and any tough stalk ends. Wash well and cut into 1-inch pieces, reserving the tips. Put 5 cups water into a kettle and bring to a boil. Add asparagus pieces and sugar, and season lightly with salt. Reduce heat and cook slowly, covered, about 12 minutes, until asparagus is tender. Cook tips separately in salted boiling water to cover until tender. Drain tips and set aside. Put cooked asparagus pieces and liquid through a sieve or whirl in a blender until smooth. Heat in a large saucepan. Add cream. Combine butter and flour in a small bowl until smooth and form into tiny balls. Drop into the soup and cook slowly, stirring, until thickened. Mix two or three tablespoons of the hot soup with egg yolks and return mixture to kettle. Add asparagus tips, pepper, and nutmeg. Season with salt. Leave on stove only a few minutes, stirring. Serve garnished with parsley. Serves 6.

Czech Cream of Cauliflower Soup

The cauliflower, a variety of cabbage with a delicate flavor, is highly prized by Czech cooks, who use it in a number of delectable dishes, including soups.

1 medium-sized head cauliflower
2 cups water
Salt
2 tablespoons fresh lemon juice

2 *tablespoons butter or margarine*
2 *tablespoons all-purpose flour*
1 *bay leaf*
½ *teaspoon dried thyme*
¼ *teaspoon pepper*
3 *cups light cream*
2 *tablespoons chopped fresh parsley*

Wash cauliflower and cut off stem and tough outer leaves. Put in a kettle with water, 1 teaspoon salt, and lemon juice. Cook, uncovered, 5 minutes. Cover and cook another 15 minutes. Drain, reserving liquid. Cut cauliflower into small pieces. Melt butter or margarine in a large kettle and stir in flour. Cook 2 minutes. Gradually add cauliflower liquid and cook slowly, stirring, until thickened and smooth. Add bay leaf, thyme, salt to taste, pepper, and cream. Cook slowly, stirring, until smooth and thickened, about 10 minutes. Add cauliflower and cook another 5 minutes. Remove and discard bay leaf. Serve garnished with parsley. Serves 6 to 8.

Cream of Vegetable Soup

This basic cream soup can be made with just about any kind of vegetable ranging from artichokes to zucchini. The vegetable can be freshly cooked or leftover, and should be puréed in a food mill, electric blender, or food processor. Typical seasonings include onions, lemon juice, and herbs (one or two that are appropriate for the particular vegetable, such as basil for tomatoes, thyme for carrots, and mint for green peas).

1 *small onion, peeled and minced*
3 *tablespoons butter or margarine*
3 *tablespoons all-purpose flour*

1½ teaspoons salt
⅛ teaspoon pepper
3 cups light cream or milk or combination of cream and chicken broth
2 cups puréed vegetables
1/3 cup heavy cream (optional)
Parsley, chives, hard-cooked egg, or croutons (optional)

Sauté onion in heated butter or margarine in a medium-sized saucepan until soft. Do not brown. Add flour, salt, and pepper. Cook slowly, stirring, 2 to 3 minutes. Gradually add cream, stirring, and cook slowly until thickened and smooth. Add vegetables and cook slowly, stirring frequently, a few minutes to blend flavors. Add heavy cream and mix well. Serve garnished with chopped parsley or chives, chopped hard-cooked egg, or croutons, if desired. Serves 4 to 6.

Chicken Velouté

This is a flavorful, rich chicken soup, a good dinner first course.

½ cup minced onion
4 tablespoons butter
3 tablespoons all-purpose flour
2 cups rich chicken broth
4 cups light cream
1 teaspoon salt
⅛ teaspoon white pepper
Dash cayenne
½ cup heavy cream
2 egg yolks, beaten

Sauté onion in heated butter in a large saucepan until tender. Add flour and cook slowly, stirring, 2 minutes. Gradually add chicken broth, stirring, and cook slowly several minutes, until thickened and smooth. Add light cream, salt, pepper, and cayenne. Cook slowly, stirring, several minutes. Spoon some of hot soup to mix with heavy cream and egg yolks. Mix well and return to soup. Leave over low heat, stirring, a few seconds, until rich and creamy. Remove from heat and serve at once. Serves 4 to 6.

Chilled and Jellied Soups

There is nothing more refreshing and satisfying than a chilled or jellied soup on a hot day. In recent years these appealing cold soups have become popular staples in America for summer dining. But you can also serve them at any time of the year. A cold soup is superb as a first course before a highly-seasoned dinner entrée, or may be enjoyed with a sandwich or salad for luncheon or supper.

Cold soups are time-tested fare. Those made with fresh or dried fruits and berries date back thousands of years. Soups based on yogurt have been enjoyed since Biblical times in the Balkans and the Middle East. Cold beet and other vegetable soups, as well as those made with buttermilk, sour cream, ale, or beer, long have been enjoyed in Eastern and Northern Europe. Even the currently popular Spanish *gazpacho* was created centuries ago.

One gastronomic tale gives credit for the popularity of more refined cold soups to King Louis XIV of France. Afraid that he might be poisoned while dining, the King had a retinue of tasters to sample each soup before he partook of it. Thus, many soups were cool by the time they reached him. On one occasion, so the story goes, the angry monarch demanded that the tepid soups be returned to the kitchen and chilled. Thereafter, cold soups were often served at the royal table and became popular in France.

Chilled soups were introduced into England by the French in the late 1700s and shortly thereafter began appearing on tables in the American South as the first course of the mid-day dinner. Among those mentioned in early American cookbooks are gazpacho, and cold peanut, pumpkin, and cucumber soups.

An extensive assortment of unusual cold soups is available to the modern cook. Clear beef and chicken soups including vegetables and herbs are old favorites. Smooth and velvety cream soups, made with the summer bounty of fresh vegetables, are superb. To a cream base you can add puréed avocados, broccoli, chicken, cucumbers, green peas, mushrooms, potatoes, tomatoes, or watercress. Sour cream and yogurt will enhance many of the soups.

There are also the well-known vichyssoise, borsch (also borsht), minted split pea and green pea, almond, dilled potato, Senegalese, lemony avocado, curried asparagus, and sherried black bean soups, among others.

The Danes make a cold beer soup that includes rye bread, sugar, and grated lemon rind. In Alaska a favorite soup is made with cranberries, orange juice, and whipped cream. The English are devotees of ale soups. Cold wine soups are enjoyed in northern Europe, and cider soups have long been popular in France and America.

Cold soups made with fresh and dried fruits and berries are prepared in many countries in fascinating variety. Middle Easterners, for example, use several fruits, but especially cherries and apricots, cooked with spices. Russians and Poles are partial to cold berry soups that are well-seasoned with spices, tart juices, and sour cream. Hungarians prepare a thick wine-flavored apple soup that includes heavy cream.

In the Caribbean and Latin America there are flavorful soups featuring such fruits as papaya, citrus, avocado, breadfruit, banana, passion fruit, pineapple, and mango.

Nowhere are fruit soups more appreciated than in Northern Europe; a wide variety are served there as a first course or a dessert at luncheon or dinner, and sometimes for breakfast. These colorful and tart soups may include sour cherries, plums, apples, roses, currants, or any kind of berry, which are cooked to a purée, flavored with spices, fruit juices, and/or wine, sweetened, and slightly thickened with cornstarch or flour. Some are garnished with whipped cream, or crumbled macaroons or other cookies.

Scandinavian immigrants to America, who settled in the Midwest and Northwest, found a bounty of many fruits to use in their native soups. The Pennsylvania Dutch also made cold fruit soups for supper. A simple but good one is prepared with pieces of white bread, covered with berries and sugar, and topped with cold milk.

All cold soups should be well-seasoned, as chilling diminishes the strength of salt, herbs, and spices.

Jellied soups, including consommés, are essentially a combination of plain gelatin with a rich standard beef or chicken broth, bouillon, or other liquid. Sometimes solid foods are added. The soups should be well-laced with such seasonings as citrus juice, vinegar, sherry, Worcestershire sauce, grated onion, herbs, or spices.

The procedure for making a cold and sparkling jellied soup is easy. Gelatin, allowing about one tablespoon for two cups of liquid, is first soaked in a small amount of cold liquid, then dissolved in a larger amount of hot liquid. The proper amount of gelatin is important, as too much will make the soup too stiff. If solid foods are added to the soup, they should be added when it is part chilled.

After cooling, the soup is refrigerated for several hours in order to jell. When ready to serve, the soup is usually lightly stirred with a fork to break up the solid mixture.

The refreshing quality of cold soups is absolutely dependent upon their being thoroughly chilled and served very cold, because a long chilling mellows the flavor. They should remain in the refrigerator until ready for use and be served in cold dishes. Some soups benefit from the addition of shaved ice or ice cubes just before serving. An attractive way to serve a cold soup is to place each bowl on a bed of crushed ice.

Chilled and jellied soups should be served in attractive small bowls or cups and garnished to complement both the color and flavor of the soup. Pleasing garnishes include chopped fresh herbs, chives or scallions, diced raw vegetables, whole berries, dollops of whipped cream or sour cream, chopped hard-cooked eggs, thin slices of lime or lemon, or sprigs of watercress, mint, or parsley.

Cold soups make ideal appetizers or first courses. Some may even include alcohol and are served as pre-meal beverages. Fruit soups are not only excellent curtain-raisers for some meals but may be served as unusual desserts.

This collection of cold soups includes both old favorites and more innovative creations.

Spanish Gazpacho

This familiar cold soup is a dish of humble origin; it was created in Spain centuries ago. The name derives from the Arabic for "soaked bread," as the soup was sopped up with chunks of bread. Among the many versions of gazpacho some

still include bread. While the best-known recipes specify tomatoes and green peppers, brought to Spain from the New World
by Columbus and added to the soup soon thereafter, not all
gazpachos include these vegetables. A Malaga gazpacho, *ajo
blanco con uvas*, white garlic with grapes, has almonds as a basic
ingredient. This recipe is typical of the gazpacho served in
Seville.

> 3 cups coarsely chopped peeled ripe tomatoes
> 1½ cups coarsely chopped peeled cucumbers
> 1 large green pepper, cleaned and chopped
> 2 cloves garlic, minced
> ½ cup water
> 1/3 cup olive oil
> 3 tablespoons wine vinegar
> ½ cup soft bread cubes
> Salt, pepper to taste
> Garnishes: Finely chopped cucumbers, scallions, and crou-
>   tons

Combine ingredients, except garnishes, in a bowl; chill. Serve
in chilled soup bowls. Pass garnishes. Serves 6.

Danish Cold Buttermilk Soup

This sweet buttermilk soup, served with whipped cream floating on top, is a favorite Danish summer soup. It has the unpro-
nounceable name of *Kaernemaelkskoldskaal*.

> 3 eggs
> 1/3 cup sugar
> Juice of 1 lemon
> 1 tablespoon grated lemon rind

1 *teaspoon vanilla extract*
6 *cups cold buttermilk*
1 *cup whipped heavy cream*

Beat eggs in a large bowl with an electric beater or whisk until light and creamy. Gradually add sugar, beating while adding. Add lemon juice and rind, vanilla, and buttermilk, two cups at a time. Continue to beat until light and smooth. Chill two hours or longer. Serve in chilled soup bowls garnished with spoonfuls of whipped cream. Serves 6 to 8.

Florida Chilled Avocado Potage

2 *medium-sized ripe avocados*
2 *tablespoons fresh lemon juice*
2 *large tomatoes, peeled and chopped*
3 *cups chicken broth*
¼ *cup finely chopped scallions, with some tops*
1 *teaspoon salt*
¼ *teaspoon pepper*

Cut avocados in halves lengthwise with a stainless-steel knife. Remove seeds. Cut off skin. Whirl avocados with lemon juice in a blender, covered, or mash to a smooth pulp with a fork in a large bowl. Combine with remaining ingredients in a large bowl and chill two hours or longer. Serve in chilled soup bowls garnished with paprika, if desired. Serves 4 to 6.

Crème Vichyssoise Glacée

When Louis Diat was a chef at New York's Ritz-Carlton Hotel in the 1920s he created a rich cold soup by adding cream to a cooled leek and potato potage he had known during his childhood near Vichy in France. Diat named the soup Vichyssoise and since then it has become an American classic. The soup appears often on restaurant menus as *Crème Vichyssoise Glacée*. This recipe is similar to Diat's original.

> 4 *large leeks, white parts only, well washed, cleaned, and thinly sliced*
> 1 *medium-sized onion, peeled and chopped*
> 3 *tablespoons butter*
> 5 *medium-sized potatoes, peeled and thinly sliced*
> 4 *cups chicken broth*
> 1½ *teaspoons salt*
> 1 *cup light cream*
> 1 *cup heavy cream*
> *White pepper to taste*
> *About 2 tablespoons finely chopped chives*

Sauté leeks and onion in heated butter in a large saucepan until tender. Add potatoes, chicken broth, and salt. Bring to a boil. Reduce heat and cook slowly, covered, about 30 minutes, or until potatoes are tender. Strain the broth. Purée vegetables in a food mill, blender, or food processor. Combine broth and purée in a large container. Add creams and season with pepper and more salt if needed. Chill several hours. Serve garnished with chives. Serves 8 to 10.

Jewish Cold Borsch (Borsht)

This variety of borsch sometimes includes beaten eggs that are added to the hot soup right after it is cooked and before cooling.

> 1 *bunch beets (about 5, or 1¼ pounds)*
> 1 *medium-sized onion, peeled and chopped*
> 4 *cups water*

1 *tablespoon sugar*
¼ *cup red wine vinegar or fresh lemon juice*
1 *teaspoon salt*
¼ *teaspoon pepper*
½ *cup dairy sour cream*

Remove tops from beets. Peel beets and shred. Put with onion and water in a large saucepan. Bring to a boil. Reduce heat and simmer, covered, 45 minutes. Add sugar, vinegar or lemon juice, salt, and pepper. Cool and pour into a large container. Chill several hours. Serve in chilled soup bowls garnished with a spoonful of sour cream. Serves 4 to 6.

Belgian Cold Broccoli Soup

This is a good luncheon soup.

1 *medium-sized onion, peeled and chopped*
2 *tablespoons butter*
4 *cups chicken broth*
2 *packages (10 ounces each) frozen chopped broccoli*
1 *teaspoon dillweed*
1½ *teaspoons salt*
½ *teaspoon pepper*
3 *tablespoons all-purpose flour*
1½ *cups light cream or milk*

Sauté onion in heated butter in a large saucepan until tender. Add broth and bring to a boil. Mix in broccoli, dillweed, salt, and pepper. Cook slowly, covered, about 12 minutes, until broccoli is tender. Stir a few spoonfuls of hot soup with flour to make a smooth paste. Stir into soup. Bring to a boil. Remove from stove and strain or whirl in a blender, covered. Combine with cream or milk in a large bowl and chill two hours or longer. Serves 4 to 6.

Russian Cold Meat-Vegetable Soup

This traditional cold tart soup called *okroshka* is a popular Russian warm-weather dish. It includes a variety of colorful ingredients. The flavoring for the soup is derived from *kvass*, a fermented and slightly alcoholic liquid made from grain. There is no real substitute for *kvass*, but some suggestions are given in this recipe.

> *1 cup diced cold cooked beef, ham, or veal*
> *1 medium-sized cucumber, peeled, seeded, and diced*
> *½ cup sliced scallions, with some tops*
> *2 hard-cooked eggs, chopped*
> *About ½ cup dairy sour cream*
> *4 cups apple cider, beer, or a mixture of 3 cups of beef*
>   *bouillon and 1 cup dry white wine*
> *2 teaspoons sharp prepared mustard*
> *1 teaspoon sugar*
> *Salt to taste*
> *3 tablespoons chopped fresh dill or parsley*

Combine meat, cucumber, scallions, and eggs in a large bowl. Mix together sour cream, cider or other liquid, mustard, sugar, and salt. Add to meat mixture. Stir to combine. Chill two hours or longer. Serve in chilled soup bowls garnished with dill or parsley. Serves 6.

California Chilled Avocado Soup

1 large or 2 small ripe avocados
1 teaspoon salt
1 clove garlic, crushed
2 tablespoons fresh lemon juice
¼ cup sliced scallions, with some tops
1 teaspoon chili powder
3 cups chicken broth
1 cup dairy sour cream or plain yogurt

Cut avocado or avocados in half lengthwise with a stainless-steel knife. Remove seeds. Cut off skin. Whirl in a blender, covered, or mash with a fork to a smooth pulp. Add next five ingredients and mix well. Turn into a large saucepan. Gradually add chicken broth and heat to boiling. Remove from heat and mix in sour cream or yogurt. Cool. Turn into a large bowl and chill two hours or longer. Serve in chilled soup bowls garnished with an avocado slice, if desired. Serves 4 to 6.

Cold Yogurt Soups

Versatile cold soups made with yogurt, cucumbers, seasonings, and sometimes other foods, are long-time favorites in the Balkans and Middle East. They are also eaten as appetizers and salads. These are recipes for three of the best cold yogurt soups.

Bulgarian Cold Walnut-Yogurt Soup

This flavorful soup is called *tarator.*

1 medium-sized cucumber, peeled, seeded, and diced
Salt

2 cups plain yogurt
1/3 cup chopped walnuts
1 or 2 cloves garlic, crushed
1 tablespoon red wine vinegar
2 tablespoons olive oil
2 tablespoons minced fresh dill
White pepper to taste

Put diced cucumber into a colander. Sprinkle with salt. Leave to drain 30 minutes. Combine with remaining ingredients in a container. Chill two hours or longer. Serve in chilled soup bowls with 2 or 3 ice cubes in each. Serves 4.

Iranian Garnished Cold Yogurt Soup

This colorful yogurt soup includes raisins, scallions, and hard-cooked eggs.

1 medium-sized cucumber, peeled, seeded, and diced
Salt
3 cups plain yogurt
1/3 cup seedless raisins or currants
1/3 cup chopped scallions, with some tops
2 hard-cooked eggs, chopped
3 tablespoons chopped fresh parsley
2 tablespoons chopped fresh mint or dill

Put diced cucumber into a colander. Sprinkle with salt. Leave to drain 30 minutes. Combine yogurt, raisins or currants, scallions, eggs, parsley, and diced cucumbers in a large bowl. Chill two hours or longer. Serve in a large bowl or chilled individual soup bowls garnished with mint or dill. Serves 6.

Armenian Minted Yogurt Soup

This mint-flavored yogurt soup includes radishes and scallions.

> *1½ cups peeled, seeded, and diced cucumbers*
> *Salt*
> *3 cups plain yogurt*
> *1 cup sliced red radishes*
> *1/3 cup chopped scallions, with some tops*
> *3 tablespoons white vinegar*
> *2 tablespoons olive oil*
> *1 teaspoon sugar*
> *1/3 cup chopped fresh mint*
> *1½ teaspoons salt*
> *¼ teaspoon white pepper*

Put diced cucumbers in a colander. Sprinkle with salt. Leave to drain 30 minutes. Combine with remaining ingredients in a large bowl. Chill two hours or longer. Serve in a large bowl or individual chilled soup bowls. Serves 6.

Billi-Bi

This elegant creamy cold mussel soup is called billi-bi or billi-by. It was created by a chef at the famous Ciro's in Paris in 1925 and was named for a customer who wanted only the soup's broth and not the mussels. This version is by Jean-Pierre Goyenvalle, owner of Le Lion D'Or, a fashionable French restaurant in Washington, D.C.

> *1 small onion, peeled and chopped*
> *4 shallots, peeled and minced*

1 *tablespoon sweet butter*
4 *pounds mussels, scrubbed and cleaned*
1½ *cups dry white wine*
2 *cups heavy cream*
2 *egg yolks*
Salt, white pepper to taste

Sauté onion and shallots in heated butter in a large kettle. Add mussels and white wine. Bring to a boil. Cook, covered, over moderately high heat until mussel shells open, about 7 minutes. Add 1½ cups cream and bring just to a boil. Remove mussels with a skimmer and reserve. Combine egg yolks with remaining ½ cup cream in a small bowl. Slowly add broth, stirring constantly. Return to kettle and cook over low heat, stirring, until hot. Do not boil. Season with salt and pepper. Strain through a fine sieve and chill. Serves 6.
Note: The mussels can be used for cold *hors d'oeuvre*, seafood *au gratin*, or as a garnish for a fish course.

Southern Chilled Pumpkin Soup

1/3 *cup finely chopped onion*
2 *tablespoons butter or margarine*
2 *cups mashed cooked or canned pumpkin, drained*
2½ *cups chicken broth*
⅛ *teaspoon ground cloves*
½ *teaspoon ground nutmeg*
⅛ *teaspoon pepper*
½ *teaspoon salt*
1 *cup light cream or milk*
½ *cup heavy cream*

Sauté onion in heated butter or margarine in a large saucepan until tender. Add pumpkin, chicken broth, spices, and salt. Stir thoroughly to blend well. Bring to a boil. Reduce heat and add light cream or milk. Cook slowly, covered, stirring occasionally, 15 minutes. Stir in heavy cream and remove from heat. Cool. Chill two hours or longer. Serves 4 to 6.

Texas Cold Buttermilk-Cucumber Soup

This flavorful cold soup is a treasured luncheon dish in Texas. It is made with, or without, the addition of cooked shrimp.

> 1 *medium-sized firm cucumber, peeled, seeded, and diced*
> *Salt*
> 4 *cups cold buttermilk*
> 2 *teaspoons sugar*
> 2 *teaspoons prepared mustard*
> 1 *tablespoon minced fresh dill*
> ½ *pound small shrimp, cooked and shelled (optional)*
> 2 *tablespoons minced chives*

Put diced cucumber in a colander. Sprinkle with salt. Leave to drain 30 minutes. Combine buttermilk, sugar, mustard, dill, and 1 teaspoon salt in a large bowl; blend well. Add diced cucumber and shrimp. Chill two hours or longer. Serve in chilled soup bowls garnished with chives. Serves 6.

Polish Garnished Cold Beet Soup

This traditional Polish cold soup called *chlodnik* is made with a number of ingredients that may vary considerably but generally include beets, cucumbers, scallions, radishes, sour cream, and dill. When crayfish are in season they are also included. The soup should have a tart flavor. Some versions are made with a fermented liquid, sour milk or cream, or juice of pickles. The soup is always served with colorful garnishes.

> 1 *bunch beets with leaves (about 5, or 1¼ pounds)*
> 6 *cups water*
> *Salt*
> 1 *medium-sized cucumber, peeled, seeded, and diced*
> 6 *red radishes, cleaned and sliced*
> 6 *scallions, with some tops, cleaned and sliced*
> 2 *tablespoons fresh lemon juice*
> 2 *cups dairy sour cream*
> 1 *dill pickle, minced (optional)*
> ¼ *cup minced fresh dill*
> *Pepper to taste*
> 1 *lemon, thinly sliced*
> 2 *hard-cooked eggs, chopped*
> 12 *cooked large shrimp, cleaned, shelled, and halved*

Scrub beets and carefully wash the leaves. Leave beets whole and do not peel. Put into a kettle with the water. Salt lightly. Bring to a boil. Reduce heat and cook slowly, covered, until tender, about 35 minutes, depending on the size. Drain; reserve liquid. Peel and chop beets. Mince leaves finely. Combine in a large bowl or container with reserved liquid, cucumber, radishes, scallions, lemon juice, sour cream, pickle, and 3 tablespoons dill. Season with salt and pepper. Chill two hours or longer. Serve in a large bowl or individual chilled soup bowls garnished with lemon slices, eggs, shrimp, and remaining 1 tablespoon dill. Serves 6 to 8.

Israeli Cold Sorrel Soup

Sorrel, also called sour grass or dock, is an ancient green or herb with an acetic sour flavor; it is used frequently in Jewish cuisine. Sorrel is valuable for its high vitamin-A content. This soup takes its name, *schav*, from the Yiddish word for the plant.

½ pound fresh sorrel leaves
1 medium-sized onion, peeled and minced
4 cups water
1 teaspoon salt
1 teaspoon fresh lemon juice
2 tablespoons sugar
2 egg yolks
4 tablespoons dairy sour cream

Remove stems from sorrel and wash leaves well in warm water. Combine with onion, water, and salt in a large saucepan. Bring to a boil. Reduce heat and cook slowly, covered, 15 minutes. Add lemon juice and sugar and cook 5 minutes longer. Mix egg yolks with a fork until creamy in a small bowl. Stir in some of hot soup; mix well. Return to soup and leave over low heat, stirring, until thickened and creamy. Remove from heat and cool. Chill two hours or longer. Serve in chilled soup bowls garnished with sour cream. Serves 4.

Caribbean Avocado Vichyssoise

This avocado version of vichyssoise is popular in some Caribbean hotels.

1 medium-sized onion, peeled and chopped
2 tablespoons butter or margarine
2 medium-sized potatoes, peeled and sliced
4 cups chicken broth
2 teaspoons salt
2 small avocados
2 tablespoons fresh lemon juice
2 cups light cream
2 tablespoons minced chives

Sauté onion in heated butter or margarine in a large saucepan until tender. Add potatoes, chicken broth, and salt. Bring to a boil. Reduce heat and cook over moderate heat, covered, about 35 minutes, until potatoes are tender. Purée or whirl in a blender or food processor. Turn into a large saucepan. Cut avocados in halves lengthwise with a stainless-steel knife. Remove seeds. Cut off skin. Purée with lemon juice to a smooth paste. Add to soup. Mix well. Bring to a boil. Remove from heat. Turn into a large container and add cream. Cool. Chill several hours. Serve in chilled soup bowls garnished with chives. Serves 6 to 8.

Polish Apple Soup

The Poles are partial to tasty cold soups made with berries and fruit, sweetened with sugar, and flavored with spices, wine, and either sweet or sour cream. This is one of the best.

6 large apples, peeled, cored, and quartered
1 one-half-inch stick cinnamon
1 teaspoon grated lemon rind
4 cups water
½ cup sugar
½ cup dry white wine
1 cup dairy sour or heavy sweet cream
1/3 cup fruit jelly (optional)

Combine apples, cinnamon stick, lemon rind, and water in a large saucepan. Bring to a boil. Lower heat and cook slowly, covered, until apples are soft, about 12 minutes. Remove cinnamon stick. Purée in food mill, processor, or blender. Combine with sugar, wine, and cream in a large bowl. Chill two hours or longer. Serve in chilled soup bowls garnished with jelly, if desired. Serves 4 to 6.

Michigan Cherry Soup

This attractive soup can be made with either fresh or canned sour cherries.

1 can (1 pound, 4 ounces) sour red cherries
About 3½ cups water
3 tablespoons sugar
1 1-inch stick cinnamon
2 whole cloves
2 tablespoons cornstarch
2 tablespoons fresh lemon juice
½ cup dry red wine (optional)

Combine cherries with juice, 3½ cups water, sugar, cinnamon, and cloves in a large saucepan. Dissolve cornstarch in 2 tablespoons cold water. Add to cherry mixture. Cook over low heat, stirring constantly, until clear and thickened. Remove cinnamon stick. Put through a sieve or whirl in a blender or food processor. Turn into a large bowl. Add lemon juice. Chill two hours or longer. Stir in wine just before serving. Serve in chilled soup bowls. Serves 6.

Scandinavian Berry Soup

This colorful soup can be made with any kind of berry.

1 pint blueberries, blackberries, or raspberries
About 4 cups water
1 teaspoon grated lemon rind
1/3 cup sugar
⅛ teaspoon ground nutmeg
¼ teaspoon salt

2 *tablespoons cornstarch*
½ *cup heavy cream, whipped*

Combine berries, 4 cups water, and lemon rind in a large saucepan. Bring to a boil. Reduce heat and cook slowly, covered, until berries are soft, about 15 minutes. Put through a sieve or whirl in a blender or food processor. Put with sugar, nutmeg, and salt in a large saucepan. Dissolve cornstarch in 2 tablespoons cold water. Add to berry mixture. Cook, stirring constantly, until clear and thickened. Remove from heat and cool. Chill 2 hours or longer. Serve in chilled soup bowls garnished with whipped cream. Serves 6.

Jellied Herbed Soup

This jellied soup is flavored with herbs and sour cream or yogurt.

4 *cups chicken broth*
2 *envelopes (2 tablespoons) unflavored gelatin*
½ *teaspoon dried basil*
¼ *teaspoon dried thyme*
½ *teaspoon salt*
¼ *teaspoon pepper*
1 *cup dairy sour cream or plain yogurt*
2 *tablespoons fresh lemon juice*
Watercress or parsley

Put ½ cup cold chicken broth in a medium-sized saucepan. Sprinkle gelatin over it to soften. Let stand 2 to 3 minutes. Add remaining 3½ cups chicken broth, basil, thyme, salt, and pepper. Heat, stirring, until gelatin is dissolved. Bring just to boiling. Remove from heat and stir in sour cream or yogurt and lemon juice. Cool. Chill at least 4 to 6 hours, until thoroughly chilled and firm. Cut or break up with a fork into small cubes. Serve in chilled soup bowls or cups garnished with sprigs of watercress or parsley, if desired. Serves 4 to 6.

French Jellied Mushroom Potage

This fresh mushroom jellied soup is flavored with sherry.

½ pound fresh mushrooms, cleaned and finely chopped
1/3 cup fresh lemon juice
3 tablespoons minced chives
⅛ teaspoon grated nutmeg
1½ teaspoons salt
¼ teaspoon pepper
2 envelopes (2 tablespoons) plain gelatin
4 cups beef bouillon
3 tablespoons dry sherry
Watercress or parsley

Combine mushrooms, lemon juice, chives, nutmeg, salt, and pepper in a large bowl. Mix well and leave 30 minutes, mixing occasionally. Meanwhile, sprinkle gelatin over ½ cup cold beef bouillon in a large bowl to soften. Heat remaining bouillon to boiling. Remove from heat and add sherry. Pour over gelatin; stir until gelatin is dissolved. Cool. Chill until partially thickened. Stir in mushroom mixture. Mix well. Chill four hours or longer, until thoroughly chilled and firm. Cut or break up with a fork into small cubes. Serve in chilled soup bowls or cups garnished with sprigs of watercress or parsley, if desired. Serves 6.

Russian Jellied Beet Soup

This colorful soup is garnished with sour cream and caviar.

2 envelopes (2 tablespoons) unflavored gelatin
2 cups beet juice or liquid from canned beets
2 cups beef bouillon
1/3 cup chopped scallions, with some tops
1/3 cup finely chopped celery
¼ cup red wine vinegar
1 teaspoon dillweed
1½ teaspoons salt
¼ teaspoon pepper
6 tablespoons dairy sour cream
6 teaspoons red caviar

Sprinkle gelatin over ½ cup cold beet juice in a large bowl to soften. Heat remaining beet juice, bouillon, scallions, celery, vinegar, dillweed, salt, and pepper in a large saucepan to boiling. Cook over medium heat 5 minutes. Pour over gelatin and stir until gelatin is dissolved. Cool. Chill 4 hours or longer, until thoroughly chilled and firm. Cut or break up with a fork into small cubes. Serve in chilled soup bowls or cups garnished with a tablespoon of sour cream and a teaspoon of caviar on top of each cup of soup. Serves 6.

Caribbean Jellied Orange Potage

3 envelopes (3 tablespoons) plain gelatin
2 cups orange juice
4 cups chicken broth
2 whole cloves

6 orange slices
6 sprigs mint

Sprinkle gelatin over ½ cup cold orange juice in a large bowl to soften. Heat remaining 1½ cups orange juice, chicken broth, and cloves to boiling. Pour over gelatin and stir until gelatin is dissolved. Remove cloves. Cool at room temperature. Chill 4 hours or longer, until thoroughly chilled and firm. Cut or break up with a fork into small cubes. Serve in chilled soup bowls or cups garnished with an orange slice and mint sprig. Serves 6.

Consommé Madrilène

This well-known clear soup can be made with chicken or beef consommé flavored with tomato pulp or juice and served hot or cold or jellied. The name means in the style of Madrid, as tomatoes are associated with Spanish cooking. This version is handsomely garnished with sour cream and chives.

2 envelopes (2 tablespoons) unflavored gelatin
2 cups tomato juice
2 cups chicken or beef consommé
1 teaspoon grated onion
1 tablespoon fresh lemon juice
2 tablespoons dry sherry
1½ teaspoons salt
½ teaspoon pepper
½ cup dairy sour cream
1/3 cup finely chopped chives

Sprinkle gelatin over ½ cup cold tomato juice in a large bowl to soften. Heat remaining 1½ cups tomato juice, consommé, and onion to boiling. Pour over gelatin and stir until gelatin is dissolved. Strain mixture into a large bowl. Add lemon juice, sherry, salt, and pepper. Pour into six individual soup bowls or cups. Chill at least 4 hours or longer, until thoroughly chilled and firm. Serve garnished with a tablespoon of sour cream and a sprinkling of chives on top of each cup of soup. Serves 6.

Chowders
and Gumbos

Of America's most treasured soups, chowders and gumbos have such special appeal and lore that they merit a separate chapter. Many are hearty dishes that can serve as either a soup or a main dish. While Americans pride themselves on these particular dishes, other national cuisines include interesting versions of these soups.

Although chowders are regarded as typically American, the dishes are believed to have originated in France. The name was taken from a kind of large kettle or cauldron called a *chaudière*. Centuries ago villagers on the coast of Brittany began a tradition of celebrating the return of the fishing fleet by preparing a community fish soup with the fleet's catch and other foods in a *chaudière*.

How the soup became a New England staple is not certain. Perhaps English settlers who had known a version of the dish called *chowter* or *chouder* brought it to Plymouth Colony. Or Breton fishermen may have introduced the custom of making a *chaudière* in Newfoundland and from there it wandered down the Atlantic coast to New England, where it became known as chowder. During the first hard years the early settlers lived primarily on fish, supplemented by corn, so quite naturally the first chowders were made with these foods. Gradually, coastal cooks also began to include other seafood, such as clams, scallops, oysters, mussels, shrimp, lobsters, and eel. Before long, inland cooks adopted chowders and made them with beans, parsnips, other vegetables, chicken, and to a lesser extent, meat and game. There was even a good egg chowder. Potato chowders did not appear until the early 1800s.

The first American recipes for chowders reveal that they were more like stews than soups. They specified layers of salt pork, fish, onions, and soaked crackers that, after being seasoned with salt and pepper or other flavorings, and covered with boiling water, were simmered slowly until cooked.

What later evolved as the traditional New England or Yankee chowder was a thick soup made with salt pork, onions, potatoes, milk, and one or more primary foods, usually seafood or vegetables.

Salt pork was probably first used as a filler and to enrich the soup, but it was later considered an essential ingredient because of the flavor it imparted to the chowder. Cooks have never seemed to agree, however, on whether the pork tidbits, fried crisp to render all the fat, should be left in the finished chowder or removed.

Recipes stipulate that the milk be rich. This was when it was thick and creamy, whole and fresh from the farm; later, a combination of half milk and half light cream or evaporated milk was used.

Although chowder is traditionally made only with simple seasonings, merely salt and pepper, and perhaps a few flakes of chopped parsley, recipes for chowders in early English and American cookbooks called for numerous seasonings such as wine, vinegar, lemon juice, catsup, beer, butter, herbs, and spices.

Traditionalists maintain that chowders should not be thickened with flour. Early versions, however, included a special crackerlike bread or unsalted crackers. An old recipe directed: ". . . and have ready some pilot bread, soaked in water, and throw them into your chowder five minutes before taking off." Unsalted crackers, called in New England common or Boston crackers, are still used in chowders by some cooks, but most often they are split or crumbled and added to the finished dish. Another reason for not thickening chowders is that many of them contain potatoes, which will sufficiently bind the mixtures.

Although most cookbooks do not mention it, chowders will be better if they are aged or mellowed. In years past they were left at the back of the stove for several hours before being served. Some people preferred to eat chowders two or three days after the soup was cooked. Perhaps the easiest method is to let the chowder rest at room temperature for a few hours and then to reheat it slowly. A chowder should never be cooked very long and never allowed to boil.

The oldest and most popular chowder was made with fish. Although probably every kind of fish was used at one time or another to make the soup, early Americans preferred a firm, non-oily, white-fleshed fish such as cod, haddock, or sea bass. Recipes also called for tautog (blackfish) and porgie. Usually the fish was cut up into large pieces with bones included, although a whole fish was sometimes used.

Daniel Webster, the noted New Hampshire statesman, was a devotee of fish chowder, and in one recipe for it, which bears his name, he recommended "for a large fishing party." It stipulates that you begin with ". . . a cod of ten pounds, well cleaned, leaving on the skin. Cut into pieces one and a half pounds thick, preserving the head whole." The fish was arranged in layers with sliced salt pork and potatoes, sprinkled with salt and pepper, and boiled in water to which milk and crackers were later added.

Fish chowder was also made in some homes with cods' heads and salted codfish, which had to be freshened by soaking in cold water several hours before simmering gently in boiling water with salt pork, onions, and potatoes. These were inexpensive staple winter soups. Smoky chowders were made with smoked fish, including finnan haddie. Portuguese settlers flavored their chowders with garlic, tomatoes, and herbs. French-Canadians added bay leaves, thyme, and perhaps celery.

New England fish chowders varied greatly from place to place, with such differences as the size of the fish pieces, cubed or sliced potatoes, the addition of hot or cold milk, and the use of salt pork and thickeners. A proper fish chowder, however, should have a thin broth, genuine fish flavor, and be served in a wide soup plate.

As pioneers moved across the country, chowder cookery went with them, and fish chowders were prepared with freshwater fish and, eventually, those from the Pacific Ocean. In the South well-seasoned chowders featured catfish or hogfish. There were also grouper, mullet, and mackerel chowders. Along the Gulf Coast flavorful chowders were made with red mullet, red snapper, pompano, and sheepshead. Midwesterners prepared chowders with whitefish, pickerel, herring, perch, trout, buffalofish, and walleyed pike. In the Far West good chowders starred salmon, ocean perch, lingcod, rockfish, sablefish, and tuna.

American cooks also created a diverse variety of rich corn chowders, which were eaten throughout the year. In the summer the soups were made with green or freshly-cut corn. Some cooks also included the cobs for additional flavor. Otherwise, home-canned whole or cream-style or dried corn was used. In New England the dish was a simple preparation made at first with salt pork, onions, and water. Later versions included potatoes and cream or milk. In other areas cooks flavored the chowders with tomatoes, herbs, spices, or other seasonings. There was also a succotash chowder made with corn and beans. Some Southerners added peanuts to their corn chowder.

America's most famous chowder is made with clams. The preparation of this soup has been controversial for over 200 years and has inspired an amusing literature on the subject. "A New England clam chowder made as it should be, is a dish to preach about, to chant praises and sing hymns and burn incense before. To fight for . . . It is 'Yankee Doodle' in a kettle," wrote Joseph C. Lincoln.

The Indians taught the early settlers how to dig and clean clams and the tribal ritual of the clambake which traditionally begins with at least two bowls of clam chowder. Clam chowder was one of the first soups prepared by the Pilgrims and became a great favorite of early Americans. Now there are many versions.

Although New England clam chowder was made to suit the individual taste of the cook making the dish, it became established as a combination of clams, milk, salt pork, onions, and potatoes.

Three kinds of clams were popular: large, hard-shelled quahogs (from an old Indian name); soft-shelled steamers; or medium-sized, hard-shelled quahogs, frequently called "bay clams." The latter were preferred because of their succulence and flavor.

As chowder became more popular in the Mid-Atlantic states, milk and cream were entirely replaced by broth, and other foods were added to the original recipe. Strangest of these to New England's "white clam purists" was the addition of tomatoes, as well as carrots, celery, peppers, and parsley. Down Easterners in Maine once became so incensed about the inclusion of tomatoes in chowder that a bill was introduced in the legislature to outlaw their addition forever. A Portland newspaper editor made caustic reference to tomato-flavored chowder, calling it a "Red Menace" and urged that it be banned from New England. Cooks in Rhode Island and Connecticut, however, uphold this recipe, commonly called Manhattan clam chowder.

There have even been debates about the manner of serving clam chowder. One *Boston Globe* editorial decreed that "The right way to serve a genuine New England clam chowder is in a bowl or a junior-size bucket, at least ten inches in diameter and at least two or three inches deep. . . . The diner should eat two or three helpings, then be assisted to a chair or bed. A teacup full of chowder is merely an aggravation."

Cooks in other locales made chowders with the many kinds of clams found along American shores. The Pacific coast has some thirty varieties, including the razor clam, Pismo clam, large mud clam, and geoduck, which make flavorful chowders. In Florida good coquina, trading clam, and donax chowders are served.

There are simply too many chowders to enumerate. Herman Melville in *Moby Dick* must have thought so too. For in his famous article about this soup he wrote: "Fishiest of all fishy places was the Try Pots, which well deserved its name; for the pots there were always boiling chowders. Chowder for breakfast, and chowder for dinner, and chowder for supper, till you began to look for fishbones coming through your clothes."

Gumbo, the most distinctive and beloved of Creole dishes, is one of the few truly original creations in American cookery. It also defies classification. To some it is a soup, to others a stew. It's even been called a chowder or a bouillabaisse. A gumbo isn't really either liquid or solid.

It is easy to get into a heated argument about what comprises a proper gumbo, and there certainly is no definitive recipe. A gumbo, according to the Creoles, can be made with any food you have or can get. An old saying goes: "The Creole puts everything into Gumbo except the Creole." Gumbos can be made with virtually any sort of food: shrimp, crabs, crayfish, oysters, chicken, sausage, ham, frogs' legs, rabbits, squirrels, wild duck, catfish, muskrats, vegetables, or greens. One of the simplest is *chou* (cabbage) gumbo. There are pure gumbos starring only shrimp, chicken, or oysters. Some include several foods.

Gumbos exist in countless forms throughout the American South, and there are also some Caribbean versions. They are particularly prized, however, in and around New Orleans, in Louisiana's Cajun country, and along the Gulf Coast from Mobile, Alabama to Galveston, Texas.

All gumbos, with the exception of some vegetable varieties, must include either *filé* powder or okra, which thicken and flavor the dish. Among gumbo devotees, there are those who differ over which is the best. Whatever the preference, there is one cardinal rule: never use both *filé* powder and okra.

The origin of gumbo is not certain. It's a marvelous combination of culinary contributions from the American Indians, Africans, and European settlers. The dish probably evolved when French emigrées, settling in southern Louisiana and weary of mundane New World foods, began seeking ways to improve their daily fare. Cooks created hearty soup-stews with the abundance of seafood from the nearby Gulf and bayous; the dishes were flavored with native herbs and vegetables.

The settlers, later called Creoles, learned from the Choctaw Indians that a particular seasoning would make their soup-stews distinctive. The Choctaws prized sassafras or laurel trees, which grew wild along the Gulf Coast, because all parts of the plants could be used in some way. The leaves, when dried, pounded in a mortar, and sifted through a hair sieve, formed a fine powder that had a pleasing and delicate flavor, somewhat like that of thyme, and it imparted a beneficial glutinous quality to thicken liquid dishes. Long ago the Choctaws packed the powder into canoes and paddled up the Bayou St. John to sell it, as well as other sassafras products, at the French Market in New Orleans.

Filé became the Creole word for the sassafras powder. It

derived from a French word meaning to spin or knit. This is exactly what the sticky seasoning does in any mixture containing water. The art of making a genuine *filé* gumbo depends on the judicious measuring and mixing of the powder into the gumbo to produce a savory, rich gravy or sauce.

Many connoisseurs regard a gumbo made with filé powder as superior to one made with okra because the former not only has a captivating subtle taste but requires more skill to prepare. The *filé* must be added slowly and in just the right amount, stirring all the while so that it won't become lumpy. It also must be added to the boiling liquid after it is removed from the heat and cannot be boiled again lest the gumbo become too bound, or stringy, and thus unpalatable.

Filé powder can be purchased in bottles in most grocery stores and can also be ordered from New Orleans' French Market, where it is still sold by surviving Choctaws. The best powder is made from pure sassafras leaves with no additions.

Besides *filé*, other foods were added to the early versions of gumbo. The Spaniards brought New World chile peppers, while blacks from Africa and the Caribbean added flavorful herbs and spices to gumbo.

A notable vegetable addition to gumbo was okra, a tapered, green seed pod of a native African plant belonging to the mallow family. It had a gooey, mucilaginous quality when cooked. The word *gumbo* or *gombo* probably derived from the name *kingombo*, used for okra in the West African nation of Angola.

Caribbean and Creole cooks found that okra pods could be used interchangeably with *filé* powder to thicken and flavor gumbos. Okra has long been called the "lazy man's *filé*," since it requires less care in cooking. To make gumbo *fevi*, lazy man's gumbo, okra is introduced at the beginning of the cooking to simmer with the other ingredients until the gummy substance no longer strings from the okra but has been absorbed by the liquid to make it smooth, rich, and flavorful. An okra gumbo should be cooked in a porcelain or enamelware pot because metal makes it "turn dark (or black) with rage."

In the South, okra is sometimes called "gumbo," "gombo," or "gumbo plant" because of its traditional association with the dish. "Gumbo" is also used as a slang expression meaning "everything or all together" implying that everything is in a pot. "Gumbo ya-ya" means everyone talking at once. "Okra gumbo" is redundant.

Years ago when okra was a seasonal vegetable, it was used only for summer gumbos. Now it is available fresh the year round, as well as frozen or canned, but true gumbo devotees use only tender fresh pods.

A genuine *filé* or okra gumbo is a satisfying, mystical dish with a slightly sweet taste, peppery sting, a strong aromatic flavor, and an appealing dark color. It takes a lot of practice to make a perfect gumbo, and most Southerners scoff at versions served in other locales.

An important aspect of making a gumbo is the proper preparation of the *roux*, consisting of flour and fat cooked together very slowly for a period at just the right temperature and properly stirred. Creole cooks maintain that you can detect when the *roux* is done by its odor, but its dark-brown color is also important. *Roux* can be prepared in large quantities and refrigerated. Prepared *roux* in bottles is sold in Louisiana and in some specialty food stores.

Nearly every Creole cook or gumbo devotee has a favorite recipe for this specialty, and many of the preparations remain "secret," known only to one person or family. New Orleans ladies once competed with each other in making and serving gumbos. A good gumbo was a matter of personal pride and tradition. One of the best places to enjoy a genuine gumbo is in a Creole home. Otherwise, it is best to go to New Orleans, Cajun, or other Southern cafes and restaurants that specialize in making gumbos. Spooned over hot, dry rice in a wide dish, a gumbo is one of the world's great culinary treats.

Many gumbos have colorful tales and legends attached to them, and a great deal has been written about them in Southern literature, especially in the annals of voodoo history. One of the earliest and best-known soups, *gumbo z'herbes* (a Creole contraction for *gumbo aux herbes*) was believed at first to have occult quality. It did not include meat and was made with at least "seven greens for good luck" as a Lenten dish. More recent versions have included sausage, ham, veal, or chicken and as many as fifteen greens and herbs. It is eaten any time of the year. I like this anonymous ditty about gumbo, which appears in a spiral-bound cookbook, *Favorite Recipes of The Lower Cape Fear*:

> It don't take no mumbo-jumbo
> Fo' to make dat soup or gumbo,
> Jes' you take whatever you got
> An' keep it simmerin' in de pot;
> Min', you gits up early to start it bilin',
> When it gits to de table you'll have 'em smilin'.

And now, here are some marvelous recipes for chowders and gumbos.

Maine Lobster Chowder

This is an elegant chowder for a company luncheon.

2 cups cut-up cleaned lobster
¼ cup butter
2 cups diced raw peeled potatoes

1 *small onion, peeled and minced*
1 *cup water*
2 *cups hot milk*
Salt, pepper to taste
Dash paprika

Cook lobster in heated butter in a small skillet 5 or 6 minutes. Set aside. Combine potatoes, onion, and water in a large saucepan. Cook slowly, covered, about 12 minutes, until potatoes are tender. Add hot milk, salt, pepper, paprika, and lobster. Cook about 1 minute to blend flavors. Serves 4.

Cape Cod Fish Chowder

This is a recipe for a traditional chowder.

1 *pound cod or haddock fillets*
¼ *cup diced salt pork*
1 *large onion, peeled and sliced*
2 *cups boiling water*
2 *cups diced raw peeled potatoes*
2 *cups hot light cream or rich milk*
Salt, pepper to taste
4 *unsalted soda crackers, split in halves*

Cut fillets into 1-inch pieces. Fry salt pork in a large saucepan to release all fat and until crisp. Add onion and sauté until tender. Pour in water; add potatoes. Cook slowly, covered, about 10 minutes, until potatoes are just tender. Add fish and continue cooking slowly about 8 minutes longer, until fish flakes easily and potatoes are tender. Add cream or milk, salt, and pepper. Serve in soup bowls over halved crackers. Serves 4.

Vermont Tomato-Corn Chowder

This chowder is made with butter or margarine rather than the traditional salt pork.

1 large onion, peeled and chopped
3 tablespoons butter or margarine
2 cups (or 1 pound can) tomatoes, undrained and chopped
1 bay leaf
Salt, pepper to taste
1 package (10 ounces) frozen corn kernels
3 cups milk
1 tablespoon sugar

Sauté onion in heated butter or margarine in a large saucepan until tender. Add tomatoes, bay leaf, salt, and pepper. Cook slowly, uncovered, 10 minutes. Mix in corn, milk, and sugar and continue cooking slowly about 10 minutes, or until corn is cooked. Serves 4.
Note: Substitute canned corn for the frozen, if you like, but cook only about 5 minutes.

Old-Fashioned Corn Chowder

Serve this chowder with warm corn bread and relish or pickles for a supper.

½ cup diced salt pork
1 large onion, peeled and chopped
2 cups boiling water
2 cups diced raw potatoes
2 cups corn kernels, fresh, frozen, or canned
1½ cups rich milk or 1 cup light cream and ½ cup milk

Salt, pepper to taste
4 unsalted soda crackers, split in halves

Fry salt pork in a large saucepan to release all fat and until crisp. Add onion and sauté until tender. Pour in water; add potatoes. Cook slowly, covered, about 10 minutes, until potatoes are just tender. Add corn and cook 5 minutes longer for fresh or frozen corn, 2 minutes for canned. Add milk, salt, and pepper and leave on the stove long enough to heat through. Serve in soup plates ladled over the crackers. Serves 4.

New Hampshire Parsnip Chowder

This is an old favorite chowder made with parsnips, which have a desirable sweetness if left in the ground until after the first frost.

½ cup diced salt pork
1 large onion, peeled and sliced
2 cups diced peeled potatoes
2 cups diced peeled parsnips
2 cups boiling water
Salt, pepper to taste
1 quart rich milk
2 tablespoons butter or margarine
2 tablespoons chopped fresh parsley

Fry salt pork in a large saucepan to release all fat and until crisp. Remove pork and reserve. Add onion and sauté until tender. Add potatoes, parsnips, and water. Bring to a boil. Season with salt and pepper. Lower heat and cook slowly, covered, about 30 minutes, or until vegetables are tender. Add milk and leave on stove long enough to heat through. Mix in butter or margarine and parsley. Return reserved pork to chowder. Serves 6.

Down East Clam Chowder

This is a flavorful luncheon or supper dish.

> *2 pounds (about 3½ dozen) medium-sized soft- or hard-shelled clams*
> *¼ pound salt pork, diced*
> *1 large onion, peeled and chopped*
> *2 medium-sized potatoes, peeled and cut into small cubes*
> *Salt, pepper to taste*
> *2 cups light cream or 1 cup evaporated milk and 1 cup milk*
> *4 unsalted soda crackers, split in halves*

Scrub clams under running water to remove any sand. Put into a large saucepan to which ½ inch water has been added. Steam, tightly covered, about 10 minutes, or until shells partly open. Strain broth through cheesecloth and reserve. Remove clams from shells, clean, and chop. Fry salt pork in a large saucepan to release all fat and until crisp. Add onion and sauté until tender. Add reserved broth and potatoes and cook until tender, about 10 minutes. Add clams. Season with salt and pepper. Pour in cream or milk and leave on stove long enough to heat through. Serve over crackers or leave to mellow in refrigerator, reheat, and serve when desired. Serves 4.

Eastern Shore Oyster-Corn Chowder

A good chowder for a late supper.

¼ pound salt pork, diced
1 medium-sized onion, peeled and chopped
1 pint shucked standard-sized oysters, with liquor
1 can (1 pound, 4 ounces) cream-style corn
2 cups milk
Salt, pepper to taste

Fry salt pork in a large saucepan to release all fat and until crisp. Remove pork. Add onion and sauté until tender. Add oysters and cook until edges begin to curl. Add corn and milk. Season with salt and pepper. Leave on stove long enough to heat through. Serves 4.

Midwestern Fish-Tomato Chowder

Prepare this tasty chowder with buffalofish or other white-fleshed fish fillets.

1 pound buffalofish fillets or other fish fillets
¼ cup chopped bacon
½ cup chopped onion
½ cup chopped green pepper
1 cup chopped celery with leaves
2 cups boiling water
1 cup diced peeled raw potatoes
¼ teaspoon dried thyme
Dash cayenne
Salt, pepper to taste
2 cups tomato juice

Cut fillets into bite-size pieces. Fry bacon until golden. Add onion, pepper, and celery. Sauté 2 or 3 minutes. Add water, potatoes, thyme, cayenne, salt, and pepper. Bring to a boil.

Lower heat and cook slowly, covered, about 10 minutes, until potatoes are just tender. Add fish and continue cooking slowly about 8 minutes longer, until fish is tender. Pour in tomato juice and leave on stove long enough to heat. Serves 6 to 8.

Cape Cod Portuguese-Style Fish Chowder

This is a well-seasoned supper dish. Some recipes call for a pinch of saffron which should be dissolved in boiling water and added to soup 5 minutes before cooking is finished.

1 large onion, peeled and chopped
1 tablespoon salad oil or shortening
2 large tomatoes, peeled and chopped
1 green pepper, cleaned and chopped
6 medium-sized potatoes, peeled and cubed
6 cups water
1 tablespoon wine vinegar
¼ teaspoon ground cumin
1½ teaspoons salt
¼ teaspoon pepper
2 pounds white-fleshed fish (haddock, cod, flounder), cut in chunks

Sauté onion in heated oil or shortening in a large saucepan until tender. Add tomatoes and green pepper; sauté 1 minute. Add potatoes, water, vinegar, cumin, salt, and pepper. Bring to a boil. Reduce heat and cook slowly, covered, 15 minutes. Add fish and continue cooking until fish and potatoes are tender, about 8 minutes. Serves 6.

Manhattan Clam Chowder

This nineteenth-century version of clam chowder is a scrumptious soup made with tomatoes, celery, and thyme.

1 pint clams
¼ cup chopped salt pork
1 medium-sized onion, peeled and minced
½ cup diced green pepper
1 cup chopped celery
3 large tomatoes, peeled and chopped
4 cups tomato juice or water
1 bay leaf
¼ teaspoon dried thyme
1 teaspoon salt
¼ teaspoon pepper
Dash cayenne
3 medium-sized potatoes, peeled and diced

Drain clams, reserving liquor; chop. Fry salt pork in a large saucepan until golden. Add onion, green pepper, and celery; sauté until onion is tender. Add tomatoes and sauté 1 minute. Add tomato juice or water, clam liquor, bay leaf, thyme, salt, pepper, and cayenne. Cook slowly, uncovered, 10 minutes. Add potatoes and cook about 15 minutes longer. Add clams and cook 2 or 3 minutes. Serves 6.

Northwestern Salmon Chowder

This is one version of several salmon chowders prepared in the Northwestern states.

1 pound salmon steaks or fillets
2 thin slices bacon, chopped

1 *medium-sized onion, peeled and chopped*
1 *green pepper, cleaned and chopped*
3 *cups boiling water*
2 *medium-sized potatoes, peeled and diced*
1 *can (8 ounces) whole-kernel corn, drained*
2 *cups hot milk*
½ *teaspoon dried thyme*
1 *teaspoon salt*
¼ *teaspoon pepper*
3 *tablespoons chopped fresh parsley*

Cut salmon into half-inch cubes. Fry bacon until crisp. Add onion and pepper and sauté 1 minute. Add water and potatoes. Cook slowly, covered, 10 minutes. Add salmon and continue cooking 10 minutes longer, until fish flakes. Add corn, milk, thyme, salt, and pepper and cook 1 or 2 minutes. Serve garnished with parsley. Serves 6.

Southern Shrimp Chowder

This is a delicious chowder for a weekend luncheon.

¼ *pound salt pork*
1 *cup chopped onion*
½ *cup diced green pepper*
3 *cups boiling water*
2 *cups diced raw peeled potatoes*
1 *can (1 pound) tomatoes, undrained and chopped*
1 *bay leaf*
1½ *teaspoons salt*
¼ *teaspoon pepper*
Dash cayenne
1½ *pounds cooked shrimp, shelled and cleaned*
3 *tablespoons chopped fresh parsley*

Fry salt pork in a large saucepan to release all fat and until crisp. Add onion and green pepper and sauté until tender. Pour in water; add potatoes, tomatoes, bay leaf, salt, pepper, and cayenne. Cook slowly, covered, about 15 minutes, until potatoes are tender. Add shrimp and parsley and continue cooking 3 to 4 minutes. Remove and discard bay leaf. Serves 6.

California Abalone Chowder

Abalone, the pink or red mollusk found in the Pacific Ocean off the coast of California, has a delicious clamlike meat that requires tenderizing before cooking. Tenderize the abalone by pounding it with a mallet or rolling pin. It makes a toothsome chowder.

¼ pound salt pork, diced
1 large onion, peeled and chopped
1 pound abalone, tenderized and diced
2 cups boiling water
2 medium-sized potatoes, peeled and diced
1 bay leaf
2 cups light cream or milk, heated
1 tablespoon butter
Salt, pepper to taste
3 tablespoons chopped fresh parsley

Fry salt pork in a large saucepan to release all fat and until crisp. Add onion and abalone and sauté until onion is tender. Pour in water; add potatoes and bay leaf. Cook slowly, covered, 15 minutes, until potatoes and abalone are tender. Add heated cream or milk, butter, salt, pepper, and parsley. Leave on stove 1 or 2 minutes to blend flavors. Remove and discard bay leaf. Serves 4 to 6.

French-Canadian Clam Chowder

This tasty version of clam chowder includes tomatoes and other vegetables.

¼ pound salt pork, diced
1 large onion, peeled and chopped
1/3 cup minced scraped carrots
1/3 cup minced celery
2 cups boiling water
2 cups diced raw peeled potatoes
1 can (1 pound) tomatoes, undrained and chopped
½ teaspoon dried thyme
2½ cups minced clams
Salt, pepper to taste

Fry salt pork in a large saucepan to release all fat and until crisp. Add onion, carrots, and celery. Sauté 5 minutes. Pour in water; add potatoes, tomatoes, and thyme. Cook slowly, covered, about 15 minutes, until potatoes are tender. Add clams. Season with salt and pepper. Cook another 5 minutes. Serves 4.

Key West Conch Chowder

Conch (pronounced "konk") is a food taken from a beautiful amber-colored spiral shell with a highly-polished pink, peach, and yellow, pearllike luster. The conch is native to the West Indies and also inhabits the water of the Florida Keys and the Bahamas. Conch meat makes a delicious chowder. Because conch has a tendency to be tough, it is usually tenderized by pounding with a mallet before using.

¼ pound salt pork, diced
1 large onion, peeled and chopped

2 *medium-sized tomatoes, peeled and chopped*
2 *medium-sized potatoes, peeled and chopped*
1 *bay leaf*
½ *teaspoon dried thyme or oregano*
2 *cups boiling water*
2 *cups ground or minced conch*
2 *cups evaporated milk or light cream*
Salt, pepper to taste
3 *tablespoons chopped fresh parsley*

Fry salt pork in a large saucepan to release all fat and until crisp. Remove pork pieces and set aside. Add onion and sauté until tender. Add tomatoes, potatoes, bay leaf, and thyme or oregano. Pour in water. Cook slowly, covered, about 10 minutes, until potatoes are just tender. Add conch and continue cooking about 10 minutes longer, until ingredients are tender. Add milk or cream, salt, pepper, and parsley. Leave on stove long enough to heat through. Remove and discard bay leaf. Return salt pork pieces to chowder. Serves 4.

Cajun Chicken-Oyster Gumbo

1 *broiler-fryer chicken, about 4 pounds, cut up*
Salt, pepper to taste
4 *tablespoons salad oil*
¼ *cup butter or shortening*
1/3 *cup all-purpose flour*
1 *large onion, peeled and chopped*
1 *cup chopped celery*
2 *large tomatoes, peeled and chopped*
1 *cup diced cooked ham*
1 *bay leaf*
½ *teaspoon dried thyme*

Salt, pepper to taste
4 cups boiling water
2 dozen shucked oysters with liquor
2 teaspoons filé powder

Cut chicken into 12 pieces. Sprinkle with salt and pepper. Fry on all sides until golden in 2 tablespoons heated oil and the butter or shortening in a heavy kettle. Remove chicken pieces with tongs to a plate. Add flour to drippings and brown very slowly to make a dark brown *roux*, about 30 minutes. Sauté onion and celery in 2 tablespoons heated oil in a small skillet. Add tomatoes, ham, bay leaf, thyme, salt, and pepper. Cook slowly 10 minutes. Add, with chicken pieces and water to *roux*. Cook slowly, covered, until chicken is tender, about 35 minutes. Add oysters and liquor. Cook 3 or 4 minutes longer. Remove and discard bay leaf. Remove from heat and add filé powder, stirring slowly to mix thoroughly. Serve over hot cooked rice in soup bowls. Serves 6 to 8.

Shrimp Gumbo Filé

7 tablespoons shortening or salad oil
1/3 cup all-purpose flour
1 large onion, peeled and chopped
1 or 2 cloves garlic, crushed
1/3 pound sausage, chopped
2 bay leaves
¼ teaspoon ground red pepper
½ teaspoon dried thyme
1½ teaspoons salt
¼ teaspoon pepper
2 cups boiling water
1 pound raw or fresh shrimp, shelled and deveined
2 teaspoons filé powder

Heat 5 tablespoons shortening or oil in a kettle. Gradually add flour, stirring, and brown very slowly to make a dark brown *roux*, about 30 minutes. Sauté onion and garlic in 2 tablespoons heated oil in a small skillet. Add sausage, bay leaves, red pepper, thyme, salt, and pepper. Cook 1 or 2 minutes. Add water and shrimp. Cook slowly, uncovered, until shrimp are bright pink, about 8 minutes. Remove from heat and add filé powder, stirring slowly to mix thoroughly. Serve over hot cooked rice in soup bowls. Serves 4.

Alabama Seafood Gumbo

1/3 cup all-purpose flour
5 tablespoons bacon drippings
2 medium-sized onions, peeled and chopped
2 cloves garlic, crushed
1 cup chopped celery
½ cup chopped green pepper
2 tablespoons salad oil
2 large tomatoes, peeled and chopped
1 can (8 ounces) tomato sauce
1 bay leaf
½ teaspoon dried thyme
1½ teaspoons salt
¼ teaspoon pepper
1 package (10 ounces) frozen cut-up okra, parboiled
4 cups boiling water
2 pounds medium-sized shrimp, shelled and deveined
1 pint shucked oysters with liquor
2 tablespoons Worcestershire sauce

Slowly brown flour in bacon drippings in a kettle to make a dark brown *roux*, about 30 minutes. Sauté onions, garlic, celery, and green pepper in heated oil in a medium-sized skillet until tender. Add tomatoes, tomato sauce, bay leaf, thyme, salt, and pepper. Cook slowly, uncovered, 10 minutes. Add to brown *roux*. Add okra and water and cook, covered, 25 minutes. Add shrimp, oysters, and Worcestershire sauce and continue cooking 7 or 8 minutes longer, until shrimp are bright pink, Remove and discard bay leaf. Serve over hot cooked rice in soup bowls. Serves 6 to 8.

Southern Catfish Gumbo

1 medium-sized onion, peeled and chopped
2 cloves garlic, crushed
1 medium-sized green pepper, cleaned and chopped
¼ cup salad oil
1 can (1 pound) tomatoes, undrained and chopped
2 cups boiling water
1 package (10 ounces) frozen cut-up okra, parboiled
½ teaspoon dried thyme
1 bay leaf
2 teaspoons salt
¼ teaspoon pepper
1 pound fresh or frozen catfish fillets, cut into 1-inch cubes.
Few drops hot pepper sauce.

Sauté onion, garlic, and green pepper in heated oil in a large saucepan until tender. Add tomatoes, water, okra, thyme, bay leaf, salt, and pepper. Cook slowly, covered, 25 minutes. Add fish cubes and hot pepper sauce. Continue cooking about 12 minutes longer, until fish is tender. Remove and discard bay leaf. Serve over hot cooked rice in soup bowls. Serves 4 to 6.

Creole Chicken-Okra Gumbo

1 broiler-fryer chicken, about 3 pounds, cut up
Salt, pepper to taste
About 9 tablespoons salad oil
1/3 cup all-purpose flour
2 medium-sized onions, peeled and chopped
1 cup chopped celery
2 large tomatoes, peeled and chopped
1 bay leaf
½ teaspoon ground thyme
3 sprigs parsley
2 cups sliced fresh okra or 1 package (10 ounces) frozen
   cut-up okra, parboiled
4 cups boiling water

Cut chicken into 12 pieces. Sprinkle with salt and pepper. Fry on all sides until golden in about 4 tablespoons heated oil in a kettle. Remove chicken pieces with tongs to a plate. Add enough oil to drippings to make 1/3 cup. Add flour and brown very slowly to make a dark brown *roux*, about 30 minutes. Sauté onions and celery in 2 tablespoons heated oil in a small skillet until tender. Add tomatoes, bay leaf, thyme and parsley. Season with salt and pepper. Cook 5 minutes. Add, with chicken, okra, and water, to *roux*. Cook slowly, covered, until chicken is tender, about 35 minutes. Remove and discard bay leaf and parsley. Serves 4 to 6.

Easy Shrimp Gumbo

2 cups sliced fresh okra or 1 package (10 ounces) frozen
   cut-up okra
1/3 cup salad oil or shortening

    6 scallions, with some tops, cleaned and sliced
    2 cloves garlic, crushed
    2 large tomatoes, peeled and chopped
    2 cups hot water
    2 bay leaves
    ½ teaspoon dried oregano or thyme
    Salt, pepper to taste
    1 pound raw or frozen shrimp, shelled and deveined
    Few drops hot pepper sauce

Fry okra in heated oil or shortening in a large saucepan until okra loses its gummy consistency, about 15 minutes. Add scallions, garlic, tomatoes, water, bay leaves, oregano or thyme, salt, and pepper. Cook slowly, covered, 20 minutes. Add shrimp and hot pepper sauce and continue cooking about 8 minutes, until shrimp are bright pink. Remove and discard bay leaf. Serves 4 to 6.

Mississippi Gulf Coast Okra Gumbo

    2 pounds fresh okra, rinsed and cut into ½-inch slices
    About 5 tablespoons salad oil
    2 medium-sized onions, peeled and chopped
    1 or 2 cloves garlic, crushed
    1 cup chopped celery
    1 cup diced cooked ham
    3 large tomatoes, peeled and chopped
    ½ cup chopped fresh parsley

Fry okra in about 3 tablespoons heated oil, uncovered, in a skillet until okra loses its gummy consistency, about 15 minutes. Meanwhile, sauté onions, garlic, and celery in 2 tablespoons heated oil in a large saucepan until tender. Add ham and tomatoes and cook 5 minutes. Add fried okra and as much water as desired and cook slowly, covered, about 25 minutes, until vegetables are cooked. Mix in parsley shortly before serving. Serves 4.

New Orleans Seafood Gumbo

4 tablespoons bacon fat or shortening
4 tablespoons all-purpose flour
1 cup chopped onions
1 cup chopped celery
About 2 tablespoons salad oil
1 pound fresh okra, rinsed and cut into ¼-inch slices
1 cup tomatoes, canned or fresh, peeled and chopped
3 cups hot water
1 cup tomato juice
1 bay leaf
½ teaspoon dried thyme
Salt, pepper to taste
2 cups small shrimp, shelled and deveined
1 cup cleaned crabmeat
1½ dozens shucked oysters with liquor
2 tablespoons chopped fresh parsley
Few drops hot sauce

Heat fat or shortening in a kettle. Gradually add flour, stirring, and brown very slowly to make a dark brown *roux*, about 30 minutes. Sauté onions and celery in 2 tablespoons heated oil in a medium-sized skillet until tender. Add okra and fry, uncovered, until it loses its gummy consistency, about 15 minutes. Add vegetables to *roux*. Then add tomatoes, water, tomato juice, bay leaf, thyme, salt, and pepper. Bring to a boil. Reduce heat and cook slowly, covered, 30 minutes. Add shrimp and cook 5 minutes. Add crabmeat, oysters with liquor, parsley, and hot sauce and cook 3 or 4 minutes. Remove and discard bay leaf. Serve over hot cooked rice in soup bowls. Serves 4 to 6.

Caribbean Okra-Fish Giambo

A Caribbean gumbo or giambo (pronounced "ghee-yam-bo") is prepared in several variations. This is one easy-to-make version.

¼ pound salt pork
2 tablespoons salad oil
2 large onions, peeled and chopped
1 or 2 cloves garlic, crushed
1 large green pepper, cleaned and chopped
2 small carrots, scraped and diced
2 stalks celery, chopped
1 cup tomatoes, canned or fresh, peeled and chopped
1 pound fresh okra, parboiled and sliced
½ teaspoon dried basil
2 tablespoons chopped fresh parsley
½ teaspoon ground red pepper
Salt, pepper to taste
3 to 4 cups tomato juice or water
1½ pounds red snapper or white-fleshed fish fillets, cubed
2 tablespoons fresh lime or lemon juice
12 medium-sized cooked shrimp, shelled and deveined

Fry salt pork to render all fat and until crisp in a kettle. Add oil and heat. Add onions, garlic, green pepper, carrots, and celery. Sauté 5 minutes. Add tomatoes, okra, basil, parsley, red pepper, salt, and pepper. Cook slowly, 10 minutes. Add tomato juice or water. Cook 10 minutes. Add snapper or other fish, and lime or lemon juice. Cook slowly, covered, about 8 minutes, until fish is tender. Serve over hot cooked rice in soup bowls garnished with shrimp. Serves 6.

Meat Soups

Many hearty varieties of meat soups can be served as one-dish meals. The earliest of these soups utilized bits of meat or game or split animal bones with clinging particles of meat, simmered in water. Later, legumes, vegetables and seasonings were added to the basic dishes. They were nutritious and could be prepared with whatever foods were available.

In the Middle Eastern cuisines most meat soups were made with mutton or lamb. All parts of the animal, including the head, innards, and feet, went into flavorful soups, enriched with such seasonings as garlic, lemon juice, herbs, greens, and yogurt. Legumes, vegetables, rice, or pasta are often added. Cooks prepare some of the rich soups for religious festivals and family celebrations. In Greece a beloved Easter soup, *mayeritsa*, is still made with lamb innards, scallions, fresh dill, and egg and lemon sauce. The Turks prepare a flavorful spiced lamb "wedding soup" and a rich tripe soup that is recommended as a "cure" in the wee hours of the morning after a night on the town.

141

Early European cooks made basic hearty soups with a wide variety of the meats and by-products of domesticated and wild animals. We have only to look at old European cookbooks to discover what could be done with whole or cut-up carcasses, calves' heads and brains, oxtails, giblets, liver, feet, and even udders. One soup was made with neat's foot, or cow heel, and was seasoned with sweet herbs and lemon juice. Another featured sheep's feet in a creamy liquid. Everything but the "oink" of the pig went into soups that might also include grains, legumes, vegetables, or dumplings. Soups made with veal, ox, or calf tripe were extremely popular. Meatball soups of many varieties are also old and popular dishes.

Creative European cooks relied on hearty meat soups for warmth and nourishment but were wise enough to make them also appeal to the palate. Each of the national cuisines features a number of praiseworthy favorites. One good Hungarian specialty called Shepherd's Wife Soup was made with cut-up shoulder of mutton, flavored with paprika and sour cream, to which noodles were added. Another was prepared with scraps of suckling pig, onions, herbs, paprika, lemon juice, and sour cream. Humble but flavorful dishes!

In European homes a great many of the hearty beef and pork soups have traditionally constituted meals in themselves. Notable among them are the numerous French soups made usually with beef—rump, breast, shin, or chuck—sometimes poultry or game, and vegetables, as well as the renowned *pot-au-feu* and *petite marmite*; the Austrian beef-vegetable soup called *Rindsuppe*; Swiss beef and dried-bean soups; Scottish lamb-barley soups; and Spanish *cocido* and *puchero*, thick soups or stews that may include many ingredients.

Early American meat soups were often adaptations of those prepared in Europe. But colonial cooks created several regional specialties with New World foods, notably the bounty of wild game. One old-time recipe for a squirrel soup directed: "Quarter your squirrels and stew them in salted water. After they are done add milk, mace, salt, pepper and butter 'to yr taste.'"

Colonists were very fond of soups made with calves' heads, innards, and especially tripe. The famous Philadelphia Pepper Pot, improvised during the harsh winter of 1777-8 at Valley Forge to sustain the disheartened troops, was first made with tripe, meat scraps, and peppercorns. "All hot! All hot! Pepper pot! Pepper pot! Makes back strong! Makes live long! All hot! Pepper pot!" were words of a song chanted by street vendors who sold the soup in Philadelphia during the 1800s. It is now widely available in cans.

Americans have always been fond of substantial beef soups, usually including vegetables. George Washington, Thomas Jefferson, and Dwight Eisenhower all wrote detailed recipes for their favorite versions of this soup. Ike's ended with the suggestion: "As a final touch, in the springtime when nasturtiums are green and tender, you can take a few nasturtium stems, cut them up in small pieces, boil them separately . . . and add one tablespoon of them to your soup."

There are also excellent Latin American, African, and Oriental meat soups. The international meat soups below are super.

Scotch Broth

The most traditional of all the Scottish soups is one called barley broth or Scotch broth, a beloved family dish made with mutton or lamb, barley, and vegetables. It is a good winter supper soup.

    2 pounds neck or breast of lamb, cut up
    2 quarts water
    Salt to taste
    4 peppercorns, bruised

½ cup pearl barley
1 cup diced carrots
1 cup sliced onions
1 medium-sized turnip, peeled and diced
3 tablespoons chopped fresh parsley

Put lamb into a large kettle. Add water and season with salt. Bring to a boil. Skim off any scum from top. Add peppercorns and barley. Cook slowly, covered, 2 hours. Take off stove and remove meat with tongs. When cool enough to handle, cut meat from bones and trim any fat from it. Return meat to kettle. Discard bones and fat. Add carrots, onions, and turnip. Bring to a boil. Lower heat and cook slowly, covered, 30 minutes, or until ingredients are cooked. Correct seasoning. Remove and discard peppercorns. Stir in parsley. Serves 6.

Dutch Pork-Vegetable Soup

The national soup of The Netherlands, *erwtensoep,* is made with green split peas, pork, and vegetables. Properly prepared, it should be so thick that a spoon can stand upright in the rich purée. It is best cooked the day beforehand, left overnight, and then reheated. A traditional accompaniment is pumpernickel.

2 cups (1 pound) split green peas, washed and picked over
3 quarts water
Salt to taste
2 large pigs' feet, cleaned and split
1 pound smoked bacon or pork in one piece
2 medium-sized leeks, white parts and 2 inches of green, cleaned and thickly sliced
4 medium-sized potatoes, pared and diced
1 medium-sized celery root, peeled and diced

Pepper to taste
½ pound frankfurters, sliced into ½-inch rounds

Put split peas, water, and salt into a large kettle and bring to a boil. Reduce heat and simmer, covered, 1 hour. Add pigs' feet and bacon and continue to cook 1 more hour. Add leeks, potatoes, celery root, and pepper and continue cooking another 30 minutes. Remove from heat and take out pigs' feet and bacon. Cut any meat from feet, discarding bones and skin. Cut bacon into slices. Return meat and bacon to kettle. Add frankfurter slices. Check seasoning. Reheat over a low fire or reheat the next day. Serves 8.

Austrian Beef-Vegetable Soup

The favorite Austrian soup is *Rindsuppe,* which serves several culinary roles. The meat and vegetables cooked in it can be taken out and served as a meal. The broth is then strained and clarified and used to enrich other dishes or is served by itself as a clear bouillon. Served as a bouillon, any of a number of characteristic garnishes are usually added. This recipe is one variation.

2 to 2½ pounds beef bones, cracked
3 pounds soup beef, chuck, or other beef
3 tablespoons butter or vegetable oil
3 quarts water
1 tablespoon salt
½ teaspoon pepper
1 large onion, thinly sliced
2 medium-sized leeks, white parts only, cleaned and thinly sliced
2 medium-sized carrots, scraped and thinly sliced
1 celery root, pared and cubed

3 *small turnips, pared and cubed*
2 *cups cut-up cauliflower*
4 *sprigs parsley*
2 *medium bay leaves*
½ *teaspoon dried thyme*

Scald bones and rinse in cold water. Wipe the meat dry. Melt butter or heat oil in a large kettle. Add meat and brown on all sides. Add bones, water, salt, and pepper. Slowly bring to a full simmer. Skim off any scum from top. Cook over very low heat, partly covered, 1½ hours. Again remove any scum from top. Add remaining ingredients and continue cooking until vegetables and meat are tender, about 1 hour longer. Remove and discard parsley sprigs and bay leaves. Take out meat and cut into bite-size pieces, discarding any bones and gristle. Return meat to soup. Serves 8 to 10.

South American Sopa de Albondigas

Meatballs, *albondigas,* are included in many different well-seasoned South American soups. This is one of them.

1 *pound lean ground beef*
1 *slice stale white bread*
1 *egg, beaten*
1 *clove garlic, crushed*
2 *tablespoons chopped fresh parsley*
½ *teaspoon dried oregano*
1½ *teaspoons salt*
¼ *teaspoon pepper*
1 *medium-sized onion, peeled and chopped*
1 *tablespoon vegetable oil*
2-3 *teaspoons chili powder*

1 *can (1 pound) tomatoes, undrained*
1 *can (6 ounces) tomato paste*
2 *quarts beef bouillon*

Put beef into a large bowl. Cover slice of bread with water in a small bowl. When soft, squeeze dry and break into small pieces. Add bread, egg, garlic, parsley, oregano, salt, and pepper to beef. Mix well to combine thoroughly. Shape into ¾-inch balls and set aside. Sauté onion in heated oil in a large kettle. Stir in chili powder and cook several seconds. Add tomatoes and break up. Stir in tomato paste and cook 1 minute. Add bouillon and bring to a boil. Drop meatballs into it. Lower heat and simmer, covered, about 45 minutes, until meatballs are cooked. Serves 8.

Moroccan Lamb Soup

In Morocco this flavorful soup, called *harira*, is a traditional dish eaten to break the strict religious fast of *Ramadan*. It is a good soup for any occasion.

1/3 *cup olive oil*
1 *large onion, peeled and chopped*
1½ *pounds neck and/or breast of lamb, cut up*
4 *medium-sized tomatoes, peeled and chopped*
1 *to 2 teaspoons crushed red pepper*
½ *teaspoon coriander seeds*
2 *teaspoons salt*
½ *teaspoon pepper*
2 *quarts water*
2 *cups cut-up vegetables*
½ *cup broken vermicelli or spaghetti*
½ *cup chopped fresh coriander or parsley*

Heat oil in a large kettle. Add onion and sauté until tender. Add lamb and brown on all sides. Mix in tomatoes, red pepper, coriander seeds, salt, and pepper. Cook 1 or 2 minutes. Add water and bring to a boil. Lower heat and cook slowly, covered, 1½ hours, or until meat is tender. Add vegetables 20 minutes and vermicelli or spaghetti 10 minutes before cooking is finished. Stir in fresh coriander or parsley just before serving. Serves 6 to 8.

Caribbean Pepper Pot

This highly-seasoned soup, made with meat and a wide variety of vegetables, is prepared in several variations throughout the Caribbean. This is one version.

¼ pound salt pork, diced
1½ pounds short ribs of beef, cut into 3-inch pieces
1½ pounds stew beef, cut into 2-inch cubes
3 quarts water
½ teaspoon dried thyme
1½ teaspoons salt
¼ teaspoon pepper
1 large onion, peeled and diced
2 cloves garlic, crushed
2 scallions, with some tops, cleaned and sliced
2 tablespoons salad oil
1 large green pepper, cleaned and chopped
1 package (10 ounces) fresh spinach, washed and trimmed
1 package (10 ounces) fresh kale, washed and trimmed
1 can (15½ ounces) okra, drained
4 medium-sized sweet potatoes, peeled and cubed
1 large tomato, peeled and cubed

Put salt pork and short ribs into a large kettle. Brown ribs in pork fat on all sides. Add stew beef and brown. Pour in water and slowly bring just to a boil. Skim. Add thyme, salt, and pepper. Lower heat and simmer, covered, 1 hour, occasionally removing any scum that rises to the top. While meat is simmering, sauté onion, garlic, and scallions in heated oil in a small skillet until tender. Add green pepper and sauté 1 minute. Remove from heat and set aside. After meat has cooked 1 hour, add sautéed vegetables and other ingredients to kettle. Continue to cook slowly, covered, about 30 minutes, until meat and vegetables are cooked. Remove from heat and take out short ribs. When cool enough to handle, cut off and discard any fat. Cube meat and return to kettle. Reheat, if necessary. Serves 8.

French Potée Lorraine

In French *potée* means a dish cooked in an earthenware pot, and this is generally a thick and substantial soup. The regional *potée* of Lorraine is made with pork, beans, and cabbage.

2 *cups (1 pound) dried kidney beans, washed and picked over*
12 *cups water*
1 *large onion, peeled and chopped*
4 *medium-sized carrots, scraped and chopped*
3 *medium-sized leeks, white parts only, cleaned and sliced*
2 *tablespoons bacon drippings or shortening*
1 *smoked boneless pork butt, about 2 pounds*
1 bouquet garni *(parsley, bay leaf, and thyme)*
1 *clove garlic*
3 *whole cloves*
4 *medium-sized potatoes, peeled and cubed*
4 *small turnips, pared and cubed*
3 *cups shredded green cabbage*
Salt, pepper to taste

Put beans and 6 cups water into a large saucepan and bring to a boil. Boil 2 minutes. Remove from heat and let stand, covered, 1 hour. Meanwhile, sauté onion, carrots, and leeks in heated drippings or shortening in a large kettle 5 minutes. Put pork butt in center of them. Add remaining 6 cups water, *bouquet garni,* garlic, and cloves. Bring to a boil. Lower heat and cook slowly, covered, 30 minutes. Add beans and liquid and continue cooking 1 hour. Add remaining ingredients and cook about 40 minutes longer, until ingredients are cooked. Take out pork and cut into slices or cubes. Serve separately or return to soup. Serves 10.

Korean Beef-Noodle Soup

This soup, or *kook,* is highly seasoned with characteristic Korean flavorings. It is a good luncheon dish.

>   *3 scallions, with some tops, sliced*
>   *1 clove garlic, crushed*
>   *2 tablespoons peanut or salad oil*
>   *½ pound lean beef, cut into tiny cubes*
>   *1 tablespoon sesame oil*
>   *3 tablespoons soy sauce*
>   *6 cups beef bouillon or water*
>   *½ teaspoon monosodium glutamate*
>   *Pepper to taste*
>   *1½ cups broken or very fine egg noodles*

Sauté scallions and garlic in heated oil in a large kettle until tender. Push aside and add beef. Brown on all sides. Add sesame oil, soy sauce, bouillon or water, monosodium glutamate, and pepper. Bring to a boil. Lower heat and cook slowly, covered, about 40 minutes, until meat is tender. While soup is cooking, boil noodles in salted water until just tender; drain. Add to soup and leave on stove long enough to heat through. Serves 6 to 8.

Gulyás Soup

The well-known Hungarian stew, *gulyás*, which means herdsman's pot, is a paprika-flavored dish of many variations. A thinner version is eaten as a soup. This is a good dish for a late evening supper.

4 medium-sized onions, peeled and chopped
2-3 garlic cloves, crushed
6 tablespoons lard or bacon drippings
3-4 tablespoons paprika
3 pounds beef chuck or round, cut into 1-inch cubes
2 large carrots, scraped and diced
2 large tomatoes, peeled and chopped
8 cups water
Salt, pepper to taste
4 medium-sized potatoes, peeled and cut into small cubes

Sauté onions and garlic in heated lard or drippings in a large kettle until tender. Stir in paprika and cook 1 minute. Add beef cubes, several at a time, and brown on all sides. Add carrots, tomatoes, water, salt, and pepper. Bring to a boil. Lower heat and simmer, covered, 1 hour. Add potatoes and continue cooking about 30 minutes longer, until ingredients are cooked. Serves 8 to 10.

Vietnamese Pho

The national soup of Vietnam is made with beef, noodles, and seasonings and is called *pho* or *po*. This is a modified version of the original recipe.

2 pounds soup bones
1 pound stew beef, cut into large cubes

1 *large onion, peeled and thinly sliced*
1 *clove garlic, crushed*
1 *tablespoon finely chopped fresh ginger*
½ *teaspoon crushed aniseed*
½ *teaspoon monosodium glutamate*
4 *cups water*
Salt, pepper to taste
¼ *pound Oriental or fine egg noodles*
6 *scallions, with some tops, sliced*
1 *teaspoon anchovy paste*
1 *teaspoon vinegar*
Ground red pepper or chili pepper to taste

Put soup bones and beef into a large kettle. Add onion, garlic, ginger, aniseed, monosodium glutamate, water, salt, and pepper. Bring to a boil. Lower heat and cook slowly, covered, 1½ hours. Remove from heat. Take out and discard bones. Take out meat and cut into small pieces. Return to kettle. Cook noodles in boiling water until just tender. Drain. Add with scallions to broth and beef. Combine remaining ingredients and stir into soup. Leave on stove 1 or 2 minutes. Serves 6 to 8.

Hungarian Hangover Soup

Hungarians drink this flavorful sauerkraut soup to alleviate the aftereffects of imbibing too liberally. Thus, the very popular soup is called "hangover" or "tippler's" soup.

1 *large onion, peeled and chopped*
¼ *cup bacon fat or shortening*
1 *tablespoon paprika*
3 *cups finely chopped sauerkraut, drained*
1 *clove garlic, crushed*

½ *pound smoked sausage, sliced*
Salt, pepper to taste
6 *cups water*
1 *tablespoon all-purpose flour*
3 *tablespoons chopped fresh dill*
1 *cup sour cream at room temperature*

Sauté onion in heated fat or shortening in a large kettle until tender. Add paprika and cook several seconds. Add sauerkraut and sauté, mixing with a fork, 1 minute. Add garlic, sausage, salt, and pepper. Mix well. Add water. Bring to a boil. Reduce heat and cook slowly, covered, 30 minutes. Stir flour and dill into sour cream. Stir into soup and cook slowly, stirring, 1 or 2 minutes. Serves 6.

Bulgarian Meatball-Rice Soup

This is a tartly-flavored soup enriched with yogurt.

¾ *pound lean ground beef*
1 *small onion, peeled and minced*
1 *teaspoon dillweed*
2 *eggs*
1 *clove garlic, crushed*
1 *teaspoon salt*
¼ *teaspoon pepper*
All-purpose flour
6 *cups beef bouillon*
1/3 *cup uncooked long-grain rice*
Juice of ½ lemon
2 *tablespoons chopped fresh dill or parsley*
1 *cup plain yogurt*

Combine beef, onion, dillweed, 1 egg, garlic, salt, and pepper in a large bowl. Mix to combine ingredients thoroughly. Shape into small balls, about ¾-inch. Dredge lightly in flour. Set aside. Heat bouillon to boiling. Drop in meatballs; add rice. Lower heat. Cook slowly, covered, until rice is tender and meatballs are cooked, about 35 minutes. Combine lemon juice, remaining egg, and dill or parsley. Add some of hot soup and beat until creamy. Return to soup and mix well. Leave on low heat 1 minute. Serve with a spoonful of yogurt in each dish. Serves 6 to 8.

Petite Marmite

Petite Marmite, or small pot, is a favorite French soup made with meat, chicken, and vegetables. It is a specialty in Parisian restaurants and is often eaten as a clear broth garnished with toasted crusty bread sprinkled with grated cheese, with the meat and vegetables served separately. The name derives from the pot, a *marmite,* in which the soup is traditionally cooked and served.

> 2 *medium-sized onions, peeled and sliced*
> 2 *tablespoons butter or salad oil*
> 2 *pounds beef chuck or other beef in one piece*
> 1 *pound beef soup bones*
> 2 *pounds chicken wings*
> 3 *quarts beef bouillon or water*
> 2 *bay leaves*
> 4 *whole cloves*
> 4 *sprigs parsley*
> ½ *teaspoon dried thyme*
> 6 *peppercorns, bruised*
> 1 *tablespoon salt*

3 *medium-sized leeks, white parts only, cleaned and*
   thickly sliced
4 *medium-sized carrots, scraped and thickly sliced*
4 *medium-sized white turnips, peeled and quartered*
1 *loaf French bread, sliced thick and toasted*
Grated Parmesan cheese, preferably freshly grated

Sauté onions in heated butter or oil in a large kettle until
tender. Add beef, beef bones, chicken wings, bouillon or water,
bay leaves, cloves, parsley, thyme, peppercorns, and salt. Bring
slowly to a full simmer. Skim off any scum. Cook slowly,
covered, 2½ hours. Add leeks, carrots, and turnips. Continue to
cook slowly another 30 minutes, or until meat and vegetables are
tender. Remove from stove. Take out and discard bay leaves,
cloves, parsley, and peppercorns. Remove beef, beef bones, and
chicken wings. Keep broth and vegetables warm over low heat.
Cut beef into slices. Remove any meat from beef bones and
chicken wings. To serve, put some of beef, chicken, and vegetables in individual large soup plates. Cover with hot broth. Serve
with toasted French bread and grated cheese. Serves 8 to 10.

Iranian Beef-Rice Soup

In Iran, rich soups laced with yogurt and well-flavored with
seasonings, are called *ashes*. This is one popular variation.

   ¾ *pound lean ground beef*
   ¼ *cup minced onion*
   1 *teaspoon salt*
   ⅛ *teaspoon pepper*
   4 *cups plain yogurt*
   4 *cups water*
   2 *tablespoons all-purpose flour*

 2 *medium-sized eggs, beaten*
 ¼ *cup uncooked long-grain rice*
 ¼ *cup sliced scallions, with some tops*
 1/3 *cup chopped fresh parsley*
 2 *teaspoons dried mint (optional)*

Combine beef, onion, salt, and pepper in a medium-sized bowl. Mix well. Shape mixture into tiny meatballs. Heat yogurt in a large saucepan. Combine ½ cup water, flour, and eggs in a small bowl; mix well. Add, with rice, to heated yogurt; mix well with a whisk or fork. Stir in remaining water. Cook over a low fire, stirring constantly, until mixture thickens. Add meatballs and continue to cook slowly, covered, 25 minutes, or until rice and meatballs are cooked. Stir in scallions, parsley, and mint. Remove from heat. Serve at once. Serves 6 to 8.

German Sausage-Lentil Pot

This hearty soup can be made with German sausages or frankfurters.

 6 *thin slices bacon, chopped*
 2 *large onions, peeled and chopped*
 2 *large carrots, scraped and diced*
 2 *cups (1 pound) dried lentils, washed and picked over*
 5 *cups water*
 1 *medium-sized celery stalk, with leaves, diced*
 ½ *teaspoon dried thyme*
 Salt, pepper to taste
 1 *can (1 pound) tomatoes, undrained and chopped*
 4 *cups tomato juice*
 10 *frankfurters, thickly sliced*

2 *cups broken pasta (spaghetti, macaroni, or noodles),*
   cooked and drained
3 *tablespoons cider vinegar*
1/3 *cup chopped fresh parsley*

Fry bacon in a large kettle. Add onions and carrots. Sauté 5 minutes. Add lentils, water, celery, thyme, salt, and pepper. Bring to a boil. Lower heat and cook slowly, covered, about 30 minutes, or until most of liquid is absorbed and lentils are soft. Add tomatoes, tomato juice, frankfurters, and pasta. Cook another 10 minutes. Stir in vinegar and parsley. Serves 8 to 10. Note: For a thinner soup, add more tomato juice.

West African Beef Soup

This well-seasoned soup includes yams.

   2½ *pounds boneless stew beef, cut into 1½-inch cubes*
   1 *large onion, peeled and chopped*
   2 *cloves garlic, crushed*
   2 *tablespoons peanut or salad oil*
   1 *tablespoon curry powder*
   1 *teaspoon cayenne powder*
   Salt, pepper to taste
   1 *can (1 pound) tomatoes, undrained and chopped*
   1 *can (6 ounces) tomato paste*
   4 *cups water*
   2 *cups cut-up cooked or canned yams*
   ¼ *cup chopped fresh parsley*

Wipe beef cubes dry. Sauté onion and garlic in heated oil in a large kettle until tender. Add curry powder and cayenne pepper and cook several seconds. Push aside and add beef cubes, several at a time, and brown on all sides. Add salt, pepper, tomatoes, tomato paste, and water. Mix well. Cook slowly, covered, about 2 hours, until meat is tender. Add yams and parsley 10 minutes before cooking is finished. Serves 6 to 8.

Mexican Meat-Vegetable Pot

This colorful soup is made with a medley of favorite Mexican foods. It is a good weekend luncheon or supper dish.

> 1 pound boneless stew beef or pork, cut in small cubes
> 1 large onion, peeled and chopped
> 2 cloves garlic, crushed
> 2 tablespoons salad oil
> 2 large tomatoes, peeled and chopped
> 1 teaspoon dried oregano
> 1½ teaspoons salt
> ¼ teaspoon pepper
> 8 cups beef bouillon or water
> 3 medium-sized potatoes, peeled and cubed
> 2 cups whole kernel canned or frozen corn
> 2 cups frozen cut-up green beans
> 1 can (1 pound, 4 ounces) chick-peas, drained
> 2 tablespoons chopped fresh parsley

Wipe meat cubes dry. Sauté onion and garlic in heated oil in a large kettle until tender. Push aside and add meat. Brown on all sides. Add tomatoes, oregano, salt, and pepper and cook briskly 5 minutes. Add bouillon or water. Lower heat and cook slowly, covered, 1 hour. Add potatoes and continue cooking 30 minutes, or until ingredients are tender. Mix in remaining ingredients during last 10 minutes of cooking. Serves 8.

Michigan Venison Soup

2½ pounds boneless venison, cut into 1½-inch cubes
2 medium-sized onions, peeled and chopped
3 tablespoons salad oil
6 cups cold water
1 can (1 pound) tomatoes, undrained and chopped
1 teaspoon dried thyme
2 teaspoons salt
¼ teaspoon pepper
2 cups diced pared turnips
2 cups diced scraped carrots
2 cups diced peeled potatoes
¼ cup chopped fresh parsley

Wipe venison cubes dry. Sauté onions in heated oil in a large kettle. Push aside and add venison. Brown on all sides. Add water, tomatoes, thyme, salt, and pepper. Bring to a boil. Lower heat and cook slowly, covered, 2 hours. Skim to remove any scum. Add vegetables and continue cooking about 30 minutes longer, until ingredients are cooked. Stir in parsley just before serving. Serves 8 to 10.

Yugoslav Lamb Corba

This traditional Balkan soup includes spinach and rice.

2 pounds breast of lamb, cut into large pieces
3 tablespoons butter or margarine
1 large onion, peeled and chopped
1 tablespoon paprika

2 teaspoons salt
¼ teaspoon pepper
2½ quarts water
½ cup uncooked long-grain rice
2 packages (10 ounces each) frozen chopped spinach
2 tablespoons chopped fresh parsley
1 cup plain yogurt at room temperature
2 tablespoons chopped fresh dill

Wipe lamb pieces dry. Brown in heated butter or margarine on all sides in a large kettle. Push meat aside; add onion; sauté until tender. Stir in paprika, salt, and pepper; cook several seconds. Add water; bring to a boil; skim. Lower heat and cook slowly, covered, 2 hours. Add rice, spinach, and parsley; cook another 30 minutes, or until ingredients are cooked. Take out lamb; cut off lean meat, discarding bones and fat. Return lamb to soup. Combine yogurt and dill; mix into soup and leave over low heat long enough to heat through. Serves 8 to 10.

Australian Oxtail Soup

Oxtails, a flavorful meat, are well worth looking for to make this interesting soup.

2 oxtails (about 3 pounds)
About ½ cup all-purpose flour
1½ teaspoons salt
¼ teaspoon pepper
3 tablespoons shortening or salad oil
1 bay leaf
3 whole cloves
2 quarts water
1 large onion, peeled and sliced

2 *large carrots, scraped and chopped*
2 *stalks celery with leaves, chopped*
3 *tablespoons dry sherry (optional)*

Have oxtails cut into short lengths. Dredge in flour seasoned with salt and pepper. Brown in heated shortening or oil in a large kettle. Add bay leaf, cloves, and water. Bring slowly to a boil; skim. Cook slowly, covered, 3 hours, until meat is tender. Remove from heat; strain broth; cool; remove fat. Remove meat from bones and add with onion, carrots, and celery to broth. Bring to a boil; reduce heat; simmer, covered, 30 minutes. Correct seasoning. Remove from heat and stir in sherry. Serves 6.

Swedish Tuesday Soup

This pork-vegetable soup is called *Tisdagssoppa,* Tuesday soup, because it is traditionally prepared on that day.

1 *pound cured pork shoulder or butt in one piece*
3 *tablespoons pearl barley*
6 *cups water*
2 *medium-sized carrots, scraped and sliced*
1 *parsnip, scraped and sliced*
½ *celery root, peeled and cubed*
3 *medium-sized potatoes, peeled and cubed*
2 *teaspoons salt*
¼ *teaspoon pepper*
2 *cups milk*
3 *tablespoons chopped fresh parsley*

Put pork, barley, and water into a large kettle. Bring to a boil; skim. Reduce heat and cook slowly, covered, 1 hour. Add vegetables, salt, and pepper. Continue to cook slowly another 30 minutes, or until ingredients are tender. Remove from heat. Take out pork and cut into small pieces, removing and discarding any fat or gristle. Return with milk to soup. Leave over low heat long enough to heat through. Serve sprinkled with parsley. Serves 6.

Catalan Ouillade

A traditional soup in the French area of Catalan and the nearby Spanish region of Catalonia is called *ouillade*. It takes its name from the earthenware dishes, *ouilles*, in which it is cooked. Although the ingredients vary, beans and cabbage, cooked separately, are essential. This version also includes bacon and salt pork.

> *1 cup dried white beans, washed and picked over*
> *3 thick slices bacon, chopped*
> *2 tablespoons olive or vegetable oil*
> *1 large onion, peeled and chopped*
> *1 large carrot, scraped and diced*
> *3 cloves garlic, crushed*
> *3½ cups shredded green cabbage*
> *½ teaspoon dried thyme*
> *2 tablespoons chopped fresh parsley*
> *Salt to taste*
> *¼ teaspoon pepper*
> *3 medium-sized potatoes, pared and quartered*
> *¼ pound salt pork*
> *1 tablespoon chopped fresh herbs (rosemary, tarragon, oregano or ½ teaspoon dried herbs*

Put beans into an earthenware pot or a kettle and cover with water. Bring to a boil. Boil 2 minutes. Remove from heat and let stand, covered, 1 hour. Meanwhile, prepare ingredients for cabbage mixture to put on the stove at the same time as the bean mixture. For cabbage mixture, combine bacon, oil, onion, carrot, and 2 cloves garlic in an earthenware pot or kettle. Sauté 5 minutes. Add 4 cups water, shredded cabbage, thyme, parsley, salt, and pepper. Bring to a boil. Turn heat as low as possible and cook, tightly covered, 1½ hours. Add potatoes after mixture has cooked 1 hour.

Drain beans after soaking 1 hour; cover with 2 cups water. Add remaining garlic clove, salt pork, and herbs. Season with salt and pepper, if desired. Bring to a boil. Lower heat and cook very slowly about 1½ hours, or until just tender. Add more water while cooking, if needed. Combine with cabbage mixture just before serving. Serves 6.

German Beef Soup With Noodles

In Germany's region of Swabia this soup is served with a local specialty called *Spaetzle,* "noodles."

Spaetzle *(recipe below)*
8 cups beef bouillon
1 cup diced cooked lean beef
3 medium-sized potatoes, peeled and diced
Salt, pepper to taste
1 medium-sized onion, peeled and chopped
2 tablespoons butter or margarine
3 tablespoons chopped fresh parsley

Prepare *Spaetzle;* drain. Bring bouillon to a boil in a large saucepan. Add beef, potatoes, salt, and pepper. Lower heat and cook slowly, covered, until potatoes are just tender, about 25 minutes. Meanwhile, sauté onion in butter or margarine until tender. Add, with parsley and *Spaetzle,* to soup. Serves 8.

Spaetzle

2½ cups all-purpose flour
½ teaspoon salt
2 eggs, lightly beaten
Water

Sift flour and salt into a large bowl. Make a well in center and add eggs and ½ cup water. Beat, adding more water as necessary, to make a stiff dough. Beat with a wooden spoon until smooth and light. Let stand 30 minutes. Dampen a wooden cutting board or pastry board and turn out dough on it. Roll out to a thickness of about ⅛ inch. Cut off small strips or slivers with a sharp knife, and drop several of them at a time into boiling salted water. While cutting, dampen board and dip knife in boiling water as necessary. Cook until noodles rise to surface, 3 to 5 minutes. Remove from water with a slotted spoon and drain.

Russian Borsch

This famous soup, prepared in numerous variations throughout the western republics of Russia, as well as in Poland, is an ancient dish that probably originated in the Ukraine, where it is still a favorite. The name *borsch*, or derivations of it, comes from an old Slavic word for beet. This one ingredient appears in all versions and provides the soup's characteristic red color. While *borsch* can be made simply with beets and broth, it may also include additional vegetables, meats, poultry, or game. It can be served hot or cold, and is often garnished with sour cream. While there are extravagant versions that feature game and wine, *borsch* is generally a family dish built around inexpensive meat and vegetables. This hearty Ukrainian version includes garlic, tomatoes, and pork, as well as beef and several vegetables. It is an excellent one-dish meal that can be prepared beforehand and reheated. Serve with pumpernickel or rye bread.

8 medium-sized beets
Salt
½ cup vinegar
2 pounds soup beef
3 cracked soup bones
½ pound lean fresh pork
1 bay leaf
8 peppercorns
2 sprigs parsley
1 clove garlic, halved
3 medium-sized carrots, scraped and sliced
2 medium-sized onions, peeled and chopped
2 medium-sized leeks, white parts only, washed and sliced
½ small head green cabbage, coarsely chopped
3 medium-sized tomatoes, peeled and chopped
1 or 2 teaspoons sugar
1 cup sour cream at room temperature

Wash beets and cook 7 of them whole and unpeeled, in salted water to cover, with ¼ cup vinegar. Cook 30 to 40 minutes, until tender. Drain; peel beets and julienne. Put beef, bones, pork, and 2½ quarts cold water into a large kettle. Bring to a boil. Skim. Add bay leaf, peppercorns, parsley, garlic, carrots, onions, and leeks. Cook slowly, covered, 1½ hours, or until meat is tender. Add cabbage, tomatoes, and cooked beets; continue to cook slowly another 30 minutes, or until ingredients are tender. Remove meat and cut up, discarding any bones and gristle. Take out and discard bones, bay leaf, peppercorns, parsley, and garlic. Return cut-up meat to kettle. Season with salt. Peel and grate remaining beet. Place in a saucepan with 1 cup hot soup, the remaining ¼ cup vinegar, and sugar. Bring to a boil. Stir into soup and warm up, if necessary. Ladle soup into bowls and garnish with a spoonful of sour cream. Serves 8 to 10.

Note: Four peeled and cubed medium-sized potatoes may be added to the soup about 20 minutes before it is finished, if desired. Borsch is excellent cold with sliced or coarsely-chopped cucumbers and hard-boiled eggs in addition to the cubed (or tiny whole) boiled potatoes (and sour cream, of course).

Poultry Soups

The world loves poultry soup, and there are infinite varieties, made with chicken, turkey, duck, and other domesticated birds. Chicken soup, of course, is a universal favorite in all its interesting variations.

The best of birds, chicken, is a descendant of a wild jungle fowl once found in Southeast Asia. It was domesticated as early as 2500 B.C. and has since made its home all around the world. Long ago it was revered and even worshipped as a divine gift.

Nobody knows who first put a chicken into a pot to make soup, but the early Greeks and Romans are believed to have dined on soups or stews made with chicken. In the Roman cookbook of Apicius we find a recipe for vegetables cooked with chicken legs and wings and several seasonings. In ancient China the chicken was a staple food used for making soups as well as other dishes.

During the Middle Ages chickens were cooked to make broths and potages that also included grains and vegetables. Chicken's

167

popularity was enhanced when King Henry IV of France declared: "I want there to be no peasant in my kingdom so poor that he is unable to have a chicken in his pot every Sunday." The French developed many fine preparations for *poulet au pot*, and every region had its own favorite version.

In other European countries the chicken was raised at home and treasured for clear and cream soups, for one-dish meals, and as a companion for noodles, pastas, dumplings, or pastries.

Early settlers carried chickens to Britain's American colonies in the early 1600s, and American cooks utilized the birds not only to make traditional Old World soups but in new culinary creations. The Pennsylvania Dutch were among the most imaginative. Their famous chicken-corn soup is still prepared in the home and by the gallon for annual picnics, family reunions, and fund-raising events. Garnished with popcorn, noodles, or herbs, it is as delicious as it is attractive.

Chicken soup has long owned a certain mystique; it has been heralded as a cure for half of the illnesses known to man. Governor Edward Winslow of the Plymouth Colony prescribed it for an ailing Indian chief and that Sachem immediately recovered. Early American cookbook writers recommended the soup with such advice as ". . . very strengthening to invalids, as especially benefiting to those suffering with colds or pulmonary afflictions." Often called "Jewish penicillin," it has been the subject of many jokes. Doctors claim that there is nothing special in chicken soup that relieves colds or other ailments, but the medicos' verdict hasn't shaken the faith of those who learned to believe in the efficacy of this "wonder-drug" at their grandmother's knee.

Today chicken is the cheapest of all meats and is marketed under several different names according to age and weight. While purists point out that our commercially-grown young chicken fryers have little taste and that only birds at least one year old are really suitable for soups, whole stewing chickens or cut-up parts can be used to make excellent soups.

Soups made with other poultry, such as the turkey, are served primarily in Europe and America. A wild bird from the New World, turkey arrived in Mediterranean countries in the sixteenth century and later reached northern Europe. The origin of its curious name is not certain. Some authorities claim that it was used because a similar bird had been brought to England from the country of Turkey. In any event, left-over carcass, wings, and cut-up turkey meat make appealing soups. Duck was domesticated in China over 2,000 years ago and was brought to America in the late 1800s. Duck soup is not common, however, except in some European countries.

Try these recipes for some of the world's best poultry soups.

Mexican Sopa de Tortilla

Tortilla soup is a popular Mexican specialty that is made in several variations. Each includes fried tortillas, vegetables, seasonings, and sometimes other ingredients cooked in rich chicken broth. This is one simple but delicious version.

> *6 corn tortillas, cut in thin strips*
> *About 4 tablespoons salad oil*
> *3 scallions, with some tops, cleaned and sliced*
> *1 large tomato, peeled and chopped*
> *¼ cup minced green pepper*
> *1 green chile (fresh or canned), washed, seeded, and minced*
> *4 cups rich chicken broth*
> *½ cup shredded Jack or Cheddar cheese*

Fry tortilla strips in heated oil in a medium-sized skillet until golden and crisp. Drain on paper toweling. Remove all but 2 tablespoons oil from pan. Add scallions, tomato, and green pepper. Sauté until scallions are tender. Add chile and chicken broth. Mix well. Bring to a boil. Divide tortilla strips among 4 large soup plates; sprinkle with cheese. Ladle soup over them. Serve at once. Serves 4.

Japanese Chicken-Noodle Soup

In Japan this flavorful soup is eaten as a between-meal snack.

½ pound Japanese udon *noodles or spaghetti*
6 cups chicken broth
1 tablespoon sake or sherry
2 tablespoons soy sauce
2 teaspoons sugar
4 scallions with some tops, cleaned and sliced
6 cubes tofu (bean curd) (optional)

Cook noodles in boiling water until just tender, about 5 minutes; drain. Heat chicken broth in a large saucepan. Add remaining ingredients and noodles and leave on medium heat long enough to heat through. Serves 6.

Italian Chicken-Vegetable Soup

This is an attractive first-course soup.

½ cup minced onion
1 clove garlic, crushed
2 tablespoons salad oil or butter
2 quarts chicken broth
Salt, pepper to taste
1 packatge (10 ounces) frozen green peas
½ cup tiny pasta or cut-up spaghetti
About ½ cup grated Parmesan cheese

Sauté onion and garlic in heated oil or butter in a large sauce-pan. Add chicken broth. Season with salt and pepper. Bring to a boil. Add peas and cook, uncovered, until just tender, about 10 minutes. Meanwhile, cook pasta in boiling water until just tender; drain. Add to soup and leave on medium heat 1 or 2 minutes. Serve garnished with grated cheese. Serves 8.

Yucatán Sopa de Lima

This chicken-based soup, spiked with the tart flavor of a native bitter lime (*lima*) and garnished with fried tortilla strips, is a specialty of Mexico's region of Yucatán. The bitter lime, how-ever, is not available elsewhere. As a substitute, use a combina-tion of equal parts of fresh lime and bitter orange juice, or fresh lemon, lime, and sweet orange juice. The soup is a refreshing hot weather specialty. This version is a popular favorite.

> 2 *pounds chicken backs and wings*
> 4 *chicken gizzards*
> 2 *quarts water*
> 1 *onion stuck with 2 cloves*
> 1 *tablespoon salt*
> 1 *broiler-fryer chicken, about 3 pounds, cut up*
> 1 *medium-sized onion, peeled and minced*
> 1 *large green pepper, cleaned and minced*
> 2 *tablespoons salad oil or shortening*
> 1 *large tomato, peeled, seeded, and minced*
> 1 *teaspoon dried oregano*
> 2 *or 3 drops Tabasco*
> *Pepper to taste*
> *Juice of 1 lime or combination of lime and bitter orange juice*
> 6 *tortillas, cut in strips, fried in oil until golden and crisp and drained*

Put chicken backs, wings, gizzards, water, onion stuck with cloves, and salt into a large kettle. Bring to a boil. Skim. Reduce heat and cook slowly, covered, 1½ hours. Remove and discard chicken pieces. Strain broth. Wash kettle and return broth to it. Add broiler-fryer pieces and cook slowly, covered, about 35 minutes, until just tender. Remove chicken pieces with tongs. Take meat from bones, discarding skin and bones. Cut meat into shreds. Strain broth and skim off all excess fat. Reheat broth. Meanwhile, sauté onion and green pepper in heated oil in a small skillet until tender. Add tomato, oregano, Tabasco, and pepper. Sauté 1 minute. Add mixture to hot broth. Cook 5 minutes. Add shredded chicken and heat through. Add lime juice or lime and orange juice. Ladle soup into a tureen or large soup bowls. Top with fried tortilla strips. Serves 6.

Caucasian Lemony Chicken Soup

A characteristic soup of the Caucasus region of Russia is made with chicken or lamb and has a tart flavor achieved with lemon juice or vinegar. Egg yolks and fresh coriander add more flavor.

    6 cups chicken broth
    1 cup slivered cooked chicken
    1 large onion, peeled and chopped
    1 tablespoon butter or margarine
    1 tablespoon all-purpose flour
    2 egg yolks
    1/3 cup fresh lemon juice
    3 tablespoons chopped fresh coriander or parsley

Put chicken broth and chicken into a large saucepan and heat. Meanwhile, sauté onion in heated butter or margarine in a small skillet. Stir in flour; cook 1 minute. Spoon into hot soup and cook, stirring with a whisk, until smooth and slightly thickened. Beat egg yolks with lemon juice in a small bowl and pour in 1 cup of hot soup. Beat well and slowly pour into saucepan, stirring constantly. Simmer another 1 or 2 minutes, until soup thickens. Season with salt and pepper, if desired. Serve sprinkled with coriander or parsley. Serves 6.

Belgian Chicken Waterzooi

A characteristic dish of northern Belgium, or Flanders, is a flavorful creation called *waterzooi*, a soup-stew made with either fish or chicken. It is an excellent company luncheon or supper dish.

2 medium-sized onions, peeled and chopped
2 medium-sized leeks, white parts only, cleaned and thinly sliced
3 medium-sized stalks celery, chopped
2 medium-sized carrots, scraped and chopped
About 11 tablespoons butter or margarine
4½ to 5 pounds broiler-fryer chickens, cut in pieces, washed, and dried
6 cups chicken broth
1 bay leaf
4 whole cloves
½ teaspoon dried thyme
3 parsley sprigs
6 peppercorns
1 tablespoon salt
¼ cup all-purpose flour
2 egg yolks
Juice of 1 large lemon
1 large lemon, sliced
¼ cup chopped fresh parsley

Sauté onions, leeks, celery, and carrots in ¼ cup heated butter or margarine in a large kettle 5 minutes. Remove with a slotted spoon to a plate. Add ¼ cup butter or margarine to kettle and melt. Fry chicken pieces on both sides in it. Add more butter, if needed. When frying is finished, return sautéed vegetables and all chicken pieces to kettle. Add also chicken broth, bay leaf, cloves, thyme, parsley, peppercorns, and salt. Bring to a boil. Lower heat and cook slowly, covered, about 30 minutes, or until chicken is tender. Remove from stove and, with tongs, take out chicken pieces. Keep warm. Strain broth into another kettle and leave over low heat.

Melt 3 tablespoons butter or margarine in a medium-sized saucepan. Stir in flour; cook 1 or 2 minutes. Gradually add 2 cups hot broth and cook slowly, stirring, until thickened and smooth. Mix into broth in kettle, stirring constantly. Beat egg yolks slightly with lemon juice and add a little hot broth. Return to kettle. Mix well and remove at once from heat. Correct seasoning. To serve, pour broth over warm chicken pieces. Garnish with lemon slices and chopped parsley. Serves 8.

Note: If you wish to prepare soup beforehand, do not add egg yolks and lemon slices until just before serving.

Mexican Rice-Chicken Soup

This is a good one-dish meal for a weekend supper.

2 *medium-sized onions, peeled and chopped*
2 *cloves garlic, crushed*
3 *tablespoons peanut or salad oil*
2 *canned green chilies, rinsed, seeded, and minced*
3 *large tomatoes, peeled and chopped*
1 to 2 *teaspoons chili powder*
1 *can (1 pound) tomatoes, undrained*

About 2½ pounds cut-up chicken pieces, washed and dried
3 quarts chicken broth or water
½ teaspoon dried oregano
2 teaspoons salt
¼ teaspoon pepper
1 cup uncooked long-grain rice
2 cans (12 ounces each) whole kernel corn
2 medium-sized ripe avocados, peeled, pitted, and cubed
1/3 cup chopped fresh coriander or parsley

Sauté onions and garlic in heated oil in a large kettle until tender. Add chilies, chopped fresh tomatoes, and chili powder and sauté 3 minutes. Then add canned tomatoes, chicken pieces, broth, oregano, salt, and pepper and bring to a boil. Reduce heat and cook slowly, covered, 30 minutes. Add rice and continue to cook slowly another 30 minutes, until chicken and rice are cooked. Add corn and avocados 10 minutes before cooking is finished. Remove from heat and take out chicken pieces. Cut chicken from bones and return to soup. Discard skin and bones. Stir in coriander or parsley. Reheat, if necessary. Serves 8.

Yugoslavian Chicken-Noodle Pot

This hearty soup includes green peas and mushrooms.

1 stewing chicken, about 4 pounds, washed and cut up
4 quarts water
1 bouquet garni (parsley sprigs, thyme, bay leaf)
1 tablespoon salt
¼ teaspoon pepper
1 cup uncooked green peas
1 large green pepper, cleaned and chopped
1 cup chopped fresh mushrooms

> 1 *package (½ pound) fine egg noodles*
> 2 *tablespoons butter or margarine*
> 2 *tablespoons chopped fresh chives*

Put cut-up chicken, water, *bouquet garni,* salt, and pepper into a large kettle. Bring to a boil. Skim. Reduce heat and cook slowly, covered, about 1½ hours, until tender. Take chicken pieces with tongs from broth. When cool enough to handle, take meat from bones, discarding skin and bones. Return chicken to broth. Add peas, green pepper, and mushrooms. Cook slowly, covered, about 25 minutes, until vegetables are tender. Add noodles during last 10 minutes of cooking. Stir in butter and chives just before removing from heat. Serves 8 to 10.

Mulligatawny

This flavorful chicken soup originated in India but was popularized and changed by the British. The name is derived from an Indian word meaning "pepper water," and the soup was sometimes called "curry soup," as it is well-seasoned with exotic spices from the East. This version always wins applause.

> 1 *frying chicken, about 3 pounds, cut up*
> 1 *medium-sized onion stuck with 4 cloves*
> 2 *medium-sized carrots, scraped and thickly sliced*
> 1 *stalk celery, thickly sliced*
> 6 *cups chicken broth*
> 1½ *teaspoons salt*
> ¼ *teaspoon pepper*
> ¼ *cup butter or margarine*
> 1 *large onion, peeled and thinly sliced*
> 2 *tablespoons turmeric powder*
> 1 *teaspoon ground coriander*

1 teaspoon cayenne pepper
1 clove garlic, crushed
1/3 cup all-purpose flour
1½ cups grated coconut, preferably unsweetened
About 2 cups hot cooked rice
1 large lemon, sliced

Put chicken into a large kettle. Add onion with cloves, carrots, celery, chicken broth, salt, and pepper and bring to a boil. Lower heat and cook slowly, covered, about 30 minutes, until chicken is tender. Take out chicken pieces with tongs and when cool enough to handle remove meat from bones. Cut meat into bite-size pieces; discard skin and bones. Strain and reserve broth. Melt butter or margarine in a large kettle. Add onion and sauté until tender. Add turmeric powder, coriander, cayenne, and garlic and cook slowly 1 minute. Stir in flour; cook 1 or 2 minutes. Gradually add strained broth and then the coconut. Cook slowly, stirring, 10 minutes. Add cooked chicken pieces and leave on stove long enough to heat through. Serve in wide soup bowls. Put hot cooked rice in a bowl and lemon slices on a plate. Pass them to each person to be added to soup as garnishes. Serves 6.

Nigerian Chicken-Vegetable Soup

This well-seasoned soup is good for a company supper.

Juice of 2 lemons
1 broiler-fryer chicken, about 3 pounds, cut up
6 cups chicken broth or water
1 large onion, peeled and chopped
3 tomatoes, peeled and chopped
1 can (6 ounces) tomato paste

2 *cups or 1 can (15½ ounces) sliced okra, drained*
1/3 *cup uncooked long-grain rice*
2 *teaspoons salt*
¼ *teaspoon pepper*
½ *teaspoon ground red pepper*
1 *teaspoon ground turmeric*

Rub lemon juice over chicken pieces. Put into a large kettle with chicken broth or water. Bring to a boil. Lower heat and cook slowly, covered, 12 minutes. Add remaining ingredients and continue to cook slowly about 30 minutes, until chicken and rice are tender. Remove chicken pieces with tongs. When cool enough to handle take meat from bones. Remove and discard skin and bones. Cut meat into small pieces and return to kettle. Reheat, if necessary. Serves 4 to 6.

Cambodian Minted Chicken Soup

This well-seasoned soup has an appealing tart flavor.

1 *broiler-fryer chicken, about 3 pounds, cut up*
2 *quarts water*
3 *tablespoons uncooked long-grain rice*
1 *or 2 cloves garlic, crushed*
3 *scallions, with some tops, sliced*
1½ *teaspoons salt*
¼ *teaspoon pepper*
3 *tablespoons fresh lime or lemon juice*
1 *teaspoon sugar*
2 *tablespoons chopped fresh mint*

Put chicken pieces, water, rice, garlic, scallions, salt, and pepper into a large kettle. Bring to a boil; skim. Lower heat and cook slowly, covered, 35 to 40 minutes. Remove chicken pieces with tongs. When cool enough to handle take meat from bones. Discard skin and bones. Cut meat into bite-size pieces and return to kettle. Add lime or lemon juice, sugar, and mint. Leave on low heat long enough to heat through. Serves 6 to 8.

West African Chicken-Peanut Butter Soup

This unusual soup is well-flavored with curry powder, red pepper, tomatoes, and peanut butter.

1 broiler-fryer chicken, about 3 pounds, cut up
1 large onion, peeled and chopped
2 cloves garlic, crushed
3 to 4 tablespoons peanut or salad oil
1 tablespoon curry powder
1 teaspoon ground red pepper
2 quarts water
1 cup smooth peanut butter
2 tablespoons tomato paste
2 medium-sized tomatoes, peeled and chopped
Salt, pepper to taste

Wash chicken pieces and dry. Sauté onion and garlic in heated oil in a large kettle until tender. Add curry powder and red pepper. Cook several seconds. Push aside and add chicken pieces, a few at a time, and sauté in drippings until golden. Add water and bring to a boil. Reduce heat and cook slowly, covered, 25 minutes. Combine peanut butter, tomato paste, and tomatoes. Stir into soup. Season with salt and pepper. Continue cooking another 20 minutes, or until chicken is tender. Serves 6 to 8.

Puerto Rican Chicken-Vegetable Soup

This hearty soup can be made with a variety of vegetables. It is a good one-dish meal for luncheon or supper.

> 1 stewing chicken, about 4 pounds, cut up
> 2½ quarts water
> 1 large onion, peeled and sliced
> 2 cloves garlic, crushed
> ½ cup diced cooked ham
> 1 tablespoon salt
> ¼ teaspoon pepper
> 3 medium-sized potatoes, peeled and cubed
> 2 cups shredded green cabbage
> 2 large tomatoes, peeled and chopped

Put chicken pieces, water, onion, garlic, ham, salt, and pepper into a large kettle. Bring to a boil. Skim. Reduce heat and cook slowly, covered, 30 minutes. Add potatoes, cabbage, and tomatoes. Continue cooking another 30 minutes, or until chicken is tender. Remove chicken pieces with tongs. When cool enough to handle take meat from bones. Discard skin and bones. Cut meat into bite-size pieces and return to kettle. Reheat if necessary. Serves 8.

Brazilian Chicken-Rice Soup

This traditional Brazilian soup, called *canja*, is made in many variations. This is one of the best.

> 1 broiler-fryer chicken, about 3 pounds, cut up
> 1 large onion, peeled and chopped
> 1 or 2 cloves garlic, crushed

½ *cup diced cooked ham*
3 *to 4 tablespoons salad oil*
2½ *quarts water*
¾ *cup uncooked long-grain rice*
3 *tomatoes, peeled and chopped*
1 *cup scraped, diced carrots*
Salt, pepper to taste
3 *tablespoons chopped fresh parsley*

Wash chicken pieces and dry. Sauté onion, garlic, and ham in heated oil in a large kettle, until onion is tender. Add chicken pieces, a few at a time, and fry until golden. Add water and bring to a boil. Lower heat and cook slowly, covered, 25 minutes. Add rice, tomatoes, carrots, salt, and pepper. Continue cooking about 20 minutes longer, until chicken and rice are tender. Remove chicken pieces with tongs. When cool enough to handle take meat from bones. Discard skin and bones. Cut meat into bite-size pieces and return to kettle. Add parsley. Reheat if necessary. Serves 8 to 10.

Scotch Feather Fowlie

This creamy chicken soup is believed to have been introduced to Scotland by French cooks. The name "fowlie" is perhaps a corruption of *volaille*, chicken.

1 *stewing chicken, about 4 pounds, cut up*
6 *cups water*
1 *medium-sized onion, peeled and sliced*
¼ *cup diced cooked ham*
1 *stalk celery, with leaves, chopped*
½ *teaspoon dried thyme*
⅛ *teaspoon ground mace or nutmeg*

2 teaspoons salt
¼ teaspoon pepper
½ cup light cream
2 egg yolks
3 tablespoons chopped fresh parsley

Put chicken, water, onion, ham, celery, thyme, mace or nutmeg, salt, and pepper into a large kettle. Bring to a boil. Reduce heat and cook slowly, covered, 1 hour, or until chicken is cooked. Remove chicken. When cool enough to handle take meat from bones. Discard skin and bones. Cut white meat into bite-size pieces. Use dark meat for another dish. Strain broth. Reheat broth and chicken pieces. Mix some of hot broth with cream and egg yolks in a small bowl. Return to soup and cook over low heat, stirring, until slightly thickened and smooth. Serve garnished with parsley. Serves 8.

Supper Turkey Soup

This hearty soup is made with a left-over turkey carcass.

1 roast turkey carcass
2 quarts water
1 medium-sized onion, peeled and chopped
1 cup diced celery
½ cup chopped celery leaves
1 bay leaf
2 sprigs parsley
1 tablespoon salt
¼ teaspoon pepper
2 cups elbow macaroni
1 can (1 pound) tomatoes, undrained and chopped
1 can (12 ounces) whole kernel corn

½ *teaspoon dried thyme*
3 *cups tomato juice*
1 *green pepper, cleaned and chopped*

Remove any stuffing from carcass and break up carcass so it will fit into a large kettle. Add water, onion, celery, celery leaves, bay leaf, parsley, salt, and pepper. Bring to a boil. Lower heat and cook slowly, covered, 2 hours. Remove from heat. Take out carcass. Remove any meat from bones. Discard skin and bones. Cut meat into bite-size pieces and return to kettle. Remove and discard bay leaf and parsley. Cook macaroni in salted boiling water until just tender. Drain; add to soup. Add tomatoes, corn, and thyme. Pour in tomato juice. Cook slowly 10 minutes. Add green pepper and cook 5 minutes longer. Serves 8.

Provençal Duck Soup

This is a good soup to make with a frozen duckling or wild duck, if available.

1 *duckling, 4 to 5 pounds, cut up*
1 *large onion, peeled and sliced*
2 *cloves garlic, crushed*
1 *large carrot, scraped and chopped*
3 *tablespoons olive or salad oil*
2 *thin slices bacon, chopped*
2 *quarts water*
4 *medium-sized tomatoes, peeled and chopped*
½ *teaspoon dried thyme*
1 *bay leaf*
Salt, pepper to taste
1 *cup thickly sliced fresh mushrooms*
3 *tablespoons chopped fresh parsley*

Wash duckling pieces and wipe dry. Sauté onion, garlic, and carrot in heated oil and bacon 5 minutes in a large kettle. Push aside. Add duckling pieces and fry on all sides. Cook over a medium flame, covered, about 20 minutes, or until most of fat from duckling has been released. Spoon off fat and discard. Add water, tomatoes, thyme, bay leaf, salt, and pepper. Bring to a boil. Cook slowly, covered, 1 hour, or until duckling is tender. Remove duckling; cool. Remove meat from bones; cube. Discard bones and skin. Remove and discard bay leaf. Add meat and mushrooms to soup; cook 5 minutes. Add parsley. Serves 8.

Pennsylvania Dutch Chicken-Corn Soup

This traditional soup may also include thin, homemade noodles, if you wish.

> 1 *stewing chicken, about 4 pounds, cut up*
> 3 *quarts water*
> 1 *medium-sized onion, peeled and chopped*
> 1 *cup chopped celery and celery leaves*
> 3 *cups whole-kernel corn*
> 1½ *teaspoons salt*
> ¼ *teaspoon pepper*
> 2 *hard-cooked eggs, crumbled*
> 3 *tablespoons chopped fresh parsley*

Put chicken pieces, water, and onion into a large kettle. Bring to a boil. Skim. Reduce heat and cook slowly, covered, 1 hour, or until tender. Remove chicken; cool. Remove meat from bones; cube. Discard bones and skin. Strain broth; return to kettle; bring to boiling. Add celery, corn, salt, and pepper. Cook 10 minutes. Add eggs and parsley and remove from heat. Serves 10 to 12.

Scotch Cock-a-Leekie

This famous Scotch soup, featuring chicken and leeks, probably obtained its name because it was once made with a cockerel or young rooster. Possibly this was in the days when cock fighting was a popular sport and the defeated bird ended up in the soup pot. Some recipes call for the addition of prunes. This one includes barley, a favorite Scotch food.

> *1 stewing chicken, about 5 pounds*
> *5 quarts water*
> *12 leeks, white parts and 2 inches green stems, washed and cut into ¼-inch lengths*
> *4 parsley sprigs*
> *1 bay leaf*
> *½ teaspoon dried thyme*
> *1 tablespoon salt*
> *½ teaspoon pepper*
> *½ cup pearl barley*
> *¼ cup chopped fresh parsley*

Put chicken and water into a large kettle. Bring to a boil. Skim. Add remaining ingredients, except parsley, and lower heat. Cook slowly, partially covered, about 2½ hours, until chicken is tender. Remove chicken to a platter. When cool enough to handle, remove chicken, discarding skin and bones, and cut into bite-size pieces. Remove and discard parsley and bay leaf from liquid. Skim liquid. Return chicken to kettle. Put soup back on stove long enough to heat through. Serve garnished with parsley. Serves 10.

Jewish Chicken Soup with Matzo Balls

This treasured golden chicken soup, *goldene yoich*, is a staple dish in Jewish homes and is traditional for the Sabbath eve meal. Either noodles or matzo balls are added to or served with the soup.

> 1 *stewing chicken, about 4 pounds, cut up*
> 3 *quarts water*
> 1 *tablespoon salt*
> 1 *large onion, peeled and sliced*
> 2 *medium-sized carrots, scraped and sliced*
> 2 *stalks celery, with leaves, chopped*
> 3 *sprigs parsley*
> *Pepper*
> *Matzo balls (recipe below)*

Put chicken, water, salt, onion, carrots, celery, and parsley into a large kettle. Bring to a boil. Skim. Reduce heat and cook slowly, covered, about 1 hour, or until chicken is tender. Remove chicken; cool. Remove meat from bones; cube. Discard bones and skin. Strain broth; return to kettle; bring to boiling. Add more salt, if desired, and pepper to taste. Put chicken in a tureen or soup plates. Pour hot broth over it. Serve with matzo balls in the soup or with it. Serves 10 to 12.

Matzo Balls

> 2 *eggs*
> 3 *tablespoons chicken fat or shortening*
> 1 *cup matzo meal*
> 1 *teaspoon salt*
> 1/3 to ½ *cup water*

Combine eggs, fat or shortening, matzo meal, and salt in a medium-sized bowl. Mix well. Add enough of the water to make a stiff dough. Mix again. Chill 2 hours. With wet hands shape into small balls. Drop carefully into 2 quarts salted boiling water. Lower heat and cook at a steady boil, covered, about 30 minutes, or until done. Test one ball to see if it is cooked. Remove with a slotted spoon and serve in or with the chicken soup.

Colombian Ajiaco

This innovative soup from Colombia is prepared there in many forms ranging from simple to elaborate. Traditionally it includes chicken, two or more kinds of potatoes, ears of corn, cream, and such garnishes as capers, parsley, avocado slices, or chopped hard-cooked eggs. It is an excellent dish for a company luncheon.

1 stewing or broiler-fryer chicken, 3½ to 4 pounds, cut up
2 quarts water
1 large onion, peeled and chopped
1 bay leaf
3 sprigs parsley
⅛ teaspoon cumin seeds
1 tablespoon salt
¼ teaspoon pepper
4 medium-sized potatoes, peeled and thickly sliced
3 ears corn, husked and broken in thirds
1 cup heavy cream
2 tablespoons capers, drained
1 ripe avocado, peeled, pitted, and sliced

Put chicken pieces, water, onion, bay leaf, parsley, cumin seeds, salt, pepper, and 2 potatoes into a large kettle. Bring to a boil. Skim. Reduce heat and cook slowly, covered, 45 minutes to 1 hour, until chicken is cooked. Remove chicken pieces with tongs; cool. Remove meat from bones, discarding skin and bones; cut into large pieces. Remove potatoes from broth; mash. Remove fat from top of broth; strain broth. Put mashed potatoes and remaining 2 potatoes in broth. Cook slowly, covered, 15 minutes. Add chicken and corn and cook about 10 minutes longer, until corn and potatoes are tender. To serve, put 3 tablespoons cream and 1 teaspoon capers into each of 6 wide soup plates. Ladle soup with corn and potatoes into each plate. Top with avocado slices. Serves 6.

Note: Ears of corn are removed and eaten by holding in the hands.

Chinese Hot And Sour Soup

This popular Chinese soup is a colorful dish that includes shredded pork, mushrooms, bamboo shoots, and bean curd.

> *4 dried Chinese black mushrooms*
> *½ cup warm water*
> *1 quart chicken broth*
> *¼ pound boneless pork, trimmed of fat and finely shredded*
> *½ cup shredded canned bamboo shoots*
> *1 to 2 tablespoons soy sauce*
> *¼ teaspoon pepper*
> *2 ounces bean curd, washed and shredded*
> *2 to 3 tablespoons rice or white vinegar*
> *2 tablespoons cornstarch mixed with 3 tablespoons cold water*
> *1 egg, lightly beaten*
> *2 scallions, with some tops, cleaned and sliced*
> *2 to 3 teaspoons sesame oil (optional)*

Put mushrooms into a small bowl. Add water and leave to soak 20 minutes. Drain. Cut off and discard stems. Cut mushrooms into thin strips. Put chicken broth into a large saucepan and bring to a boil. Add mushrooms, pork, bamboo shoots, soy sauce, and pepper. Reduce heat to medium and cook covered, 5 minutes. Add bean curd and vinegar. Stir cornstarch-water mixture and pour into soup, stirring. When slightly thickened, remove from heat. Pour in egg and stir until cooked. Add sesame oil. Serve at once garnished with scallions. Serves 4 to 6.

Seafood Soups

Among the world's great culinary creations, none is more satisfying to prepare and savor than soups starring seafood. A varied and bountiful supply of fish and shellfish from both fresh and salt waters has provided cooks with ingredients for a magnificent collection of seafood soups. Many are actually soup-stews and make excellent one-dish meals.

Men have always gone fishing and it has been both an engrossing pastime and a profitable occupation. Without this source of nutritious and inexpensive food, humankind probably would not have survived. Denizens of the deep abound in the waters of the world in incredible diversity, yet some are found only in limited geographical regions. This book tells you how to cook only the best-known varieties that are readily available.

Early Greeks esteemed the products of the sea, and writers of the time extolled the virtues of these foods. Without benefit of recipes or modern culinary know-how, their cooks created some

191

of the first great soup-stews, dishes which are still prepared with native seasonings.

The ancient Romans had a definite affinity for seafood, and their soups made with such local specialties as eel, *langouste,* and octopus, among others, were liberally seasoned with sweet-sour flavorings and spices.

During the Middle Ages seafood gained importance in the rest of Europe; it was an essential supplement to the meager everyday diet. The Church contributed greatly to the increasing consumption of "fysshe," as Christians were enjoined to eat fish on Fridays, during Lent, and on the numerous fast days. Little wonder that hundreds of soups were prepared with a number of fish, often with other foods put into the pot.

In southern Europe, where fresh fish was in plentiful supply, soups were well-seasoned with garlic, onions, lemon juice, wine, and herbs. Dried salt cod also became the basis of many staple soups.

Eels were particularly popular fare in Europe and were used in a number of national soups such as French bouillabaisse and Portuguese *caldeirada.* Such a diversity of fish is used in Europe that it's impossible to mention every type, but carp and members of the mollusk family, such as mussels and squid, were essential ingredients of many notable dishes.

The best-known European soup-stew is certainly bouillabaisse, which has inspired cooks, delighted diners, and evoked the praise of poets and writers for centuries. The noted epicure Curnonsky, extolled ". . . this incomparable golden soup which embodies and concentrates all the aromas of our shores and which permeates, like an ecstasy the stomachs of astonished gastronomes."

And Thackeray was equally ecstatic:

This Bouillabaisse a noble dish is—
A sort of soup, or broth, or brew,

A hotch-potch of all sorts of fishes,
That Greenwich never could outdo.

According to legend this soup was the creation of Venus, the goddess of love. Some cognoscenti contend that the recipe was brought to France in ancient times by Greek fishermen who settled in Marseille. No matter, the true bouillabaisse, for which there are many variations even in southern France, is generally conceded to be that made in the colorful port of Marseille and nearby locales. The name is a combination of "boil," *bouille*, and "let down," *baisse*, and the cooking of the soup is exactly that. It should never be lengthy. The necessary ingredients are olive oil, garlic, tomatoes, saffron, seasonings of fennel, thyme, bay leaf, and orange peel, and, of course, seafood. There's much controversy, however, about the latter. In Marseille the soup must include a great variety of crustaceans and fish, some of which are found only in the Mediterranean off the French coast. The most important or "soul" ingredient is an ugly spiny creature, rascasse, not good when cooked by itself but widely sought after in rocky crevices to impart a special characteristic flavor to bouillabaisse. Other seafood often included are the conger eel, *rouget*, *Saint-Pierre*, and *loup*. Some persons insist that *langouste* (the Mediterranean lobster) is essential; others say never. Most purists agree that mussels, freshwater fish, and white wine are taboo, and that the soup should never be thickened with other ingredients.

Although the seafood of the Mediterranean is not available all over the world, you can use excellent substitutes that are readily available.

Early American cooks utilized the New World's bounty of fish and shellfish to create excellent soups, which were primarily chowders, gumbos, bisques, and cream soups. These recipes have appeared in previous chapters. Recipes for a few other seafood specialties are included here.

Every Caribbean and Latin American country has created notable seafood soups, and there are also good ones in Africa. Those prepared in the Orient are made with some familiar white-fleshed fish but also utilize exotic varieties native to the area. All these soups are well-seasoned with local flavorings.

Whenever possible, seafood soups should be prepared with fresh fish or shellfish, but frozen items may be used. All seafood should be cooked only briefly and seasoned to enhance its natural flavor.

The recipes below comprise only a few of the world's great seafood soups but constitute a representative selection.

Bouillabaisse

This version of bouillabaisse can be prepared in American kitchens with local seafood.

> *4 pounds mixed fish and shellfish (lobsters, crabs; firm-fleshed fish such as cod, haddock, sea bass, rockfish, mackerel; soft-fleshed fish such as sole, sea perch, flounder, red snapper, whiting)*
> *1/3 cup olive oil*
> *2 medium-sized onions, peeled and chopped*
> *2 or 3 cloves garlic, crushed*
> *3 large tomatoes, peeled, seeded, and chopped*
> *1 bay leaf*
> *1 large piece of fennel, chopped, or ½ teaspoon fennel seeds*
> *1 large piece of orange peel, diced*
> *1 tablespoon chopped fresh parsley*
> *¼ teaspoon dried thyme*
> *Salt, pepper to taste*
> *⅛ teaspoon saffron*
> *Slices of plain or toasted French bread*
> Rouille *sauce (recipe below)*

Have fish and shellfish cleaned and ready beforehand. Small ones can be left whole. Larger ones should be cut into uniform-sized pieces. If lobster or large crabs are to be used, cut them up. Separate firmer-fleshed varieties from the more delicate; the former should be added before the latter.

Heat oil in a large kettle. Add onions and sauté until tender. Add garlic, tomatoes, bay leaf, fennel, orange peel, parsley, and thyme. Cook slowly, stirring, 5 minutes. Lay any crustaceans and firm-fleshed fish atop the mixture and cook over fairly high heat 5 minutes. Add the more delicate fish and boiling water to cover. Season with salt and pepper. Add saffron. Bring to a boil. Lower heat and cook slowly, covered, about 10 minutes, until seafood is tender. To serve, ladle broth over one or more pieces of crusty bread in a large soup plate. Serve seafood on a separate platter. Pass *rouille* sauce, previously prepared, separately. Serves 6 to 8.

Rouille Sauce

2 or 3 garlic cloves
2 small hot red peppers, seeded and rinsed
¼ cup soft dry bread crumbs
¼ cup olive oil
¾ to 1 cup hot broth from soup

Pound together garlic and red peppers with a pestle or wooden spoon in a mortar or small bowl. Add bread crumbs and pound again. Slowly add oil to make a thick paste and thin with hot broth. Mix well. Serve with soup. Makes about 1¼ cups.

Russian Fish Soup

This traditional soup is called *solianka* and is generally made with sturgeon, but any firm white-fleshed fish will do. It is tart and colorful.

> 2½ *pounds whole white-fleshed fish (halibut, haddock)*
> 3 *medium-sized onions, peeled and chopped*
> 1 *bay leaf*
> 3 *sprigs parsley*
> 2 *whole cloves*
> 6 *peppercorns*
> *Salt*
> 2 *tablespoons butter or margarine*
> 2 *large tomatoes, peeled and chopped*
> 1 *medium-sized salted cucumber, peeled and chopped*
> 3 *tablespoons capers, drained*
> 12 *pitted black olives*
> 2 *tablespoons chopped fresh dill or parsley*
> 1 *lemon, thinly sliced*

Have fish dealer dress and fillet fish. Take home trimmings, heads, and bones, as well as fillets. Cut fillets into bite-size pieces. To cook, put trimmings, heads, and bones into a kettle with 1 chopped onion, bay leaf, parsley, cloves, peppercorns, salt, and 2½ quarts water. Cook, covered, over medium heat 30 minutes. Strain broth and discard solid ingredients. Sauté remaining 2 onions in heated butter or margarine until tender. Add tomatoes and cook 2 minutes, stirring. Put this mixture, with cucumber, capers, olives, fish pieces, and strained broth, in a large kettle. Cook slowly, covered, until fish is tender, about 8 minutes. Remove and discard bay leaf, cloves, and peppercorns. Correct seasoning to taste. Serve in soup bowls garnished with lemon slices and dill. Serves 6.

Italian Seafood Soup

This thick and flavorful soup is called *cacciucco alla livornese*. It takes its name from the colorful Tuscan port of Livorno or Leghorn. The dish traditionally is made with a mixture of local seafood including octopus and strange and spiny shellfish. Here is an adaptation.

> *3 pounds mixed seafood (lobster, shrimp, cod, haddock, mackerel, snapper, sea bass, or rockfish)*
> *1 large onion, peeled and chopped*
> *2 or 3 cloves garlic, minced*
> *1/3 to ½ cup olive oil*
> *½ teaspoon crumbled dried sage*
> *2 bay leaves*
> *Salt, black and red pepper to taste*
> *¼ cup tomato paste*
> *½ cup dry white wine*
> *6 thick slices of garlic toast*

Cut fish into good-sized serving pieces. If lobster is used, clean and separate body from claws. Cut into similar-sized pieces. Sauté onion and garlic in heated oil, the amount according to taste, in a large kettle until tender. Add sage, bay leaves, salt, and peppers; mix well. Cook 1 minute. Stir in tomato paste; add wine. Bring to a boil. Add seafood and lower heat. Cook very slowly, covered, about 15 minutes, until seafood is tender. (If seafood varies considerably in texture, add firmer pieces first and then softer pieces.) Meanwhile, prepare garlic toast by spreading crusty Italian bread slices with a mixture of crushed garlic and olive oil. Bake in preheated 350° oven about 12 minutes, until crisp. To serve, put toast in large soup bowls. Put pieces of seafood over bread and spoon broth over it. Or serve broth separately. Serves 6.

Norwegian Fish-Vegetable Soup

This hearty soup is flavored with sour cream.

2 pounds raw fish trimmings (bones, heads, skin, tails)
1 medium-sized onion stuck with 3 cloves
1 bay leaf
6 peppercorns, bruised
Salt to taste
4 quarts water
3 tablespoons butter or margarine
1 cup sliced leeks
1 small celery root, pared and cubed
1 cup sliced carrots
4 medium-sized potatoes, peeled and diced
1½ pounds boneless white-fleshed fish, cleaned
2 egg yolks
1/3 to ½ cup sour cream, at room temperature
1/3 cup chopped fresh parsley

Put fish trimmings, onion with cloves, bay leaf, peppercorns, salt, and water into a large kettle. Bring to a boil. Lower heat and simmer, covered, 30 minutes. Strain broth. Melt butter or margarine in a large kettle. Add leeks, celery root, carrots, and potatoes. Sauté 5 minutes. Add fish and cook about 10 minutes longer, until fish is tender. Remove fish to a platter and keep warm. In a small bowl, beat egg yolks; add a little hot broth. Pour back into soup. Add sour cream to soup and leave on low heat a few minutes, stirring. Break up fish into bite-size pieces and add to soup. Remove from heat. Serve garnished with parsley. Serves 6 to 8.

Spanish Quarter-of-an-Hour Soup

This seafood soup is a well-known Spanish restaurant specialty. It's tasty and relatively quick to prepare.

1/3 cup diced bacon or ham
1 or 2 tablespoons olive oil
1 medium-sized onion, peeled and chopped
2 cloves garlic, crushed
1 large tomato, peeled and chopped
1 teaspoon paprika
6 cups chicken broth
2 cans (7½ to 8 ounces each) minced clams, cleaned
½ cup raw long-grain rice
Salt, pepper to taste
1 cup fresh or frozen green peas
1 cup small or medium-sized cooked fresh or canned shrimp, cleaned
2 hard-cooked eggs, chopped
About 12 thin strips canned pimiento

Combine bacon or ham, oil (use 2 tablespoons if ham rather than bacon is used), onion, and garlic in a large kettle. Heat and sauté 5 minutes. Add tomato and paprika. Sauté 3 minutes. Pour in broth; add clams, with liquid; bring to a boil. Stir in rice. Season with salt and pepper. Lower heat and cook over medium heat, uncovered, about 15 minutes. Add peas and shrimp and cook 10 minutes longer if fresh peas are used, 5 minutes for frozen peas. Serve garnished with eggs and pimiento. Serves 6 to 8.

California Cioppino

This excellent soup-stew is believed to have been created in

San Francisco, but nobody knows how it got the name *cioppino*. Restaurants along Fishermen's Wharf started serving it about 1900, and it has been a treasured specialty in California ever since. This is one of many marvelous variations.

1 large onion, peeled and chopped
2 or 3 cloves garlic, crushed
1 medium-sized green pepper, seeded and diced
1/3 cup olive oil
2 cans (1 pound each) tomatoes, undrained and chopped
1 can (8 ounces) tomato sauce
1 bay leaf
¼ teaspoon dried oregano or thyme
Salt, pepper to taste
2 pounds firm white-fleshed fish (bass, halibut, cod, haddock)
1 large Dungeness crab or lobster
1 dozen fresh clams in shells
1 pound large shrimp in shells
About 2 cups dry white or red wine

Sauté onion, garlic, and green pepper in heated oil in a large kettle until onion is tender. Add tomatoes, tomato sauce, bay leaf, and oregano or thyme. Season with salt and pepper. Bring to a boil. Lower heat and cook slowly, covered, 30 minutes. While sauce is cooking, cut fish into serving pieces. Clean and crack crab or lobster and put in a large kettle. Scrub clams to remove all dirt. Cut shrimp shells down the backs and remove any black veins. Put clams and shrimp over crabs. Add fish. Pour sauce over seafood. Add wine. Cook slowly, covered, 20 to 30 minutes, until clams open and seafood is cooked. Add more wine while cooking, if needed. Remove and discard bay leaf. Serves 6.

Portuguese Seafood Soup

This traditional soup-stew is prepared in villages along the Portuguese coast. It is called *caldeirade* and is made with a mixture of seafood from the daily catch.

3 pounds mixed fish and shellfish, cleaned
3 large onions, peeled and sliced
1 or 2 cloves garlic, crushed
1/3 cup olive or vegetable oil
3 large tomatoes, peeled and chopped
6 medium-sized potatoes, peeled and thinly sliced
½ cup chopped fresh coriander or parsley
Salt, pepper to taste
1 cup dry white wine

If fish is small, leave it whole; otherwise, cut it into serving pieces. Clean clams and crabs or other shellfish, and crack any shellfish. Sauté onions and garlic in heated oil in a large kettle until tender. Add tomatoes and cook slowly, 5 minutes. Arrange fish, shellfish, and potatoes in layers in the kettle. Add coriander or parsley, salt, pepper, and wine. Cook slowly, covered, about 25 minutes, until ingredients are tender. Serves 8.

Breton Fish Soup

An inviting fish soup called *cotriade* is made with a variety of fish taken from the day's catch in the coastal towns of the French province of Brittany. The soup has a pungent flavor derived from onions and herbs.

3 pounds mixed fish (halibut, haddock, sea bass, flounder,
cod, mullet, mackerel)

2 large onions, peeled and thinly sliced
1 garlic clove, crushed
3 tablespoons butter or margarine
6 medium-sized potatoes, pared and quartered
2½ quarts water
2 bay leaves
½ teaspoon dried thyme
3 parsley sprigs
½ teaspoon dried marjoram
Salt, pepper to taste
6 or 8 slices crusty French bread

Cut fish into chunks or slices of equal size. Sauté onions and garlic in heated butter or margarine in a large kettle. Add potatoes, water, bay leaves, thyme, parsley, marjoram, salt, and pepper; bring to a boil. Add prepared fish and lower heat to moderate. Cook, covered, about 20 minutes, or until fish are just tender and potatoes are cooked. Ladle broth over slices of bread in wide soup plates and serve potatoes and fish separately on a platter. Serves 6 to 8.

Burmese Fish Soup

This soup, called *hsan byoke*, includes rice and vegetables.

1 whole white-fleshed fish (bass, haddock, flounder), about 2 pounds
2 quarts water
1 small onion, peeled and chopped
2 teaspoons salt
2 to 3 tablespoons soy sauce
2 tablespoons vinegar

Black and red pepper to taste
¼ cup raw long-grain rice
1 cup shredded Chinese or green cabbage
½ cup slivered celery

Have head, tail, skin, and bones cut from fish. Put these trimmings into a kettle. Add water, onion, and salt. Bring to a boil. Lower heat and cook slowly, covered, 30 minutes. Strain broth. Meanwhile, cut fish into cubes. Put with soy sauce, vinegar, and peppers in a small bowl. Leave to marinate while broth is cooking. Reheat broth to boiling. Add rice and reduce heat. Cook slowly, covered, 20 minutes. Add fish cubes with seasonings, cabbage, and celery and continue cooking about 10 minutes longer, or until rice and fish are tender. Serves 4 to 6.

American Oyster Stew

This traditional American soup is best simply flavored but can be made as rich as you wish, using milk, half milk and cream, or heavy cream, and seasoned with Worcestershire sauce, red pepper sauce, or paprika.

1 pink shucked oysters with liquor
3 cups light cream or half cream and milk
Salt, pepper, cayenne to taste
4 teaspoons butter

Cook oysters in their liquor in a medium-sized saucepan until edges curl, about 5 minutes. Add cream and seasonings. Leave over low heat until hot. Do not boil. Put a teaspoon of butter into each of four warm soup bowls. Ladle soup into bowls and serve at once, with oyster crackers if desired. Serves 4.

Corsican Soupe de Poisson

A characteristic fish soup of the Mediterranean island of Corsica and southern France is a flavorful rich broth made with several kinds of local seafood. The recipe is not easy to make elsewhere because the traditional shellfish aren't available. This is an adaptation.

> *1 large onion, peeled and finely chopped*
> *2 cloves garlic, crushed*
> *3 tablespoons olive oil*
> *3 medium-sized tomatoes, peeled, seeded, and chopped*
> *1 bay leaf*
> *1 small piece orange rind*
> *1 tablespoon chopped fresh parsley*
> *6 cups water*
> *2 cups dry white wine*
> *2 pounds mixed cleaned fish and shellfish (small lobster, crab, red snapper, haddock, sea bass, rockfish), cut into large pieces of equal size or cracked*
> *Salt, pepper to taste*
> *Pinch saffron (optional)*
> *Toasted slices of crusty French bread*

Sauté onion and garlic in heated oil in a large kettle until tender. Add tomatoes, bay leaf, orange rind, parsley, water, and wine. Bring to a boil. Add fish and shellfish and salt and pepper. Reduce heat and cook, uncovered, about 30 minutes. Carefully remove seafood to a platter and keep warm. Add saffron to hot broth, if used. Strain broth. To serve, put portions of seafood over bread in wide soup plates. Ladle broth over it. Serves 4 to 6.

Thailand Shrimp Soup

This flavorful soup is an adaptation of a traditional dish that includes native seasonings.

> 2 *whole chicken breasts, halved*
> 6 *cups water*
> 1 *small onion, peeled and chopped*
> 1 *small bay leaf*
> 2 *sprigs parsley*
> ½ *teaspoon dried thyme*
> 1 *teaspoon salt*
> ⅛ *teaspoon pepper*
> 1 *clove garlic, crushed*
> 2 *teaspoons ground coriander*
> 1½ *teaspoons chili powder*
> 1 *tablespoon soy sauce*
> ½ *pound small raw shelled shrimp, deveined*
> 2 *cups sliced mushrooms*
> 6 *scallions, with tops, sliced*
> 1/3 *cup chopped fresh coriander or parsley*
> 3 *cups hot cooked rice*

Remove skin from chicken breasts. Carefully cut meat from bones and pull out pieces of cartilage. Cut meat into strips and set aside. Put bones in a large saucepan. Add water, onion, bay leaf, parsley, thyme, salt, and pepper. Bring to a boil. Lower heat and cook slowly, covered, 1 hour. Strain broth into a large saucepan. Combine garlic, coriander, chili powder, and soy sauce. Stir into broth. Bring to a boil. Add chicken, shrimp, and mushrooms. Cook slowly, covered, about 5 minutes, until shrimp turn pink and chicken is tender. Stir in scallions and coriander or parsley. Remove and discard bay leaf. Serve in soup bowls over or with rice. Serves 6.

Spanish Fish Soup

This soup from Spain's Costa Brava is thickened with bread
and includes almonds.

> 1 *pound white-fleshed fish fillets (cod, bass, halibut, hake)*
> *All-purpose flour*
> *Salt, pepper to taste*
> ¼ *cup olive oil*
> 1 *medium-sized onion, peeled and chopped*
> 2 *cloves garlic, crushed*
> 2 *medium-sized tomatoes, peeled and chopped*
> ½ *teaspoon crushed red peppers or paprika*
> 2 *quarts water*
> 1½ *cups soft bread cubes, crusts removed*
> 1/3 *cup chopped blanched almonds*
> 1/3 *cup chopped canned pimiento*
> 3 *tablespoons chopped fresh parsley*

Cut fish into large cubes. Dust lightly with flour, seasoned
with salt and pepper. Heat oil in a large kettle. Add fish and sauté
lightly on all sides. Remove with a slotted spoon to a plate. Add
onion and garlic to drippings and sauté until tender. Add tomatoes and peppers or paprika. Sauté 1 or 2 minutes. Pour in water
and bring to a boil. Return fish to kettle. Reduce heat and cook
slowly, uncovered, 10 minutes. Add bread, almonds, and
pimiento and cook about 3 minutes longer, until fish is tender.
Stir in parsley. Serves 4 to 6.

Hungarian Fish Soup

A treasured Hungarian soup-stew, called *halaszle*, is made
with several local freshwater fish and flavored with paprika.

Traditionally, it is cooked in a large kettle over an open fire.

4 large onions, peeled and sliced
3 tablespoons lard or fat
2 to 3 tablespoons paprika, preferably Hungarian
4 pounds mixed fresh fish (catfish, carp, pike, perch),
*   cleaned and cut into large cubes*
Salt, pepper to taste

Sauté onions in heated lard or fat in a large kettle until tender. Stir in paprika; cook 1 minute. Carefully place fish over onions; season with salt and pepper. Add water to cover. Cook very slowly, covered, until fish is tender, about 25 minutes. Serves 6 to 8.

Greek Fish Soup

Greek cooks prepare a great many tantalizing fish soups from local catches. This one also includes pasta.

2 large onions, peeled and chopped
2 or 3 garlic cloves, crushed
6 tablespoons olive or salad oil
¾ cup tomato paste
2 quarts water
1½ teaspoons dried oregano
2 bay leaves
Salt, pepper to taste
2 pounds white-fleshed fish fillets (flounder, cod, halibut),
*   cut into bite-size pieces*
1 cup cut-up macaroni or pasta sea shells, cooked and
*   drained*
1/3 cup chopped fresh parsley

Sauté onions and garlic in heated oil in a large kettle until tender. Add tomato paste; mix well. Pour in water. Add oregano, bay leaves, salt, and pepper. Bring to a boil. Reduce heat and add fish. Cook slowly, covered, about 12 minutes, until fish is tender. Add macaroni or sea shells and parsley and continue cooking about 5 minutes longer. Remove and discard bay leaves. Serves 6 to 8.

Caribbean Callaloo

A favorite soup in South America and the Caribbean is a mixed seafood dish that usually includes greens, vegetables, and spicy seasonings. This is one renowned version.

> 1 *large onion, peeled and chopped*
> 2 *stalks celery, chopped*
> 3 *tablespoons butter or margarine*
> 6 *cups water*
> ½ *pound smoked ham, diced*
> 2 *cups washed spinach leaves, trimmed of stems*
> 1 *cup sliced okra*
> 1 *pound medium-sized shrimp, shelled and deveined*
> ½ *teaspoon dried thyme*
> 1½ *teaspoons salt*
> ¼ *teaspoon pepper*
> *Dash hot sauce*

Sauté onion and celery in heated butter or margarine in a large kettle until tender. Add water and ham. Bring to a boil. Cook briskly, covered, 10 minutes. Add remaining ingredients and cook slowly, covered, about 12 minutes, until shrimp turn pink. Serves 4.

Provençal Bourride

One of the best French fish soups is a thick, creamy specialty called *bourride;* it is made only with white fish—two or three different firm-fleshed varieties such as sea bass, sole, mullet, flounder, or bream. The fish should be purchased with the trimmings, which are necessary for the stock. A pungent garlic mayonnaise, *aioli*, is stirred into the soup to make a lovely, smooth, yellow sauce. Serve with hot boiled potatoes, if you like.

> *3½ pounds mixed firm-fleshed white fish (sea bass, rock*
>   *cod, haddock, flounder)*
> *6 cups water*
> *½ cup dry white wine*
> *2 tablespoons wine vinegar, preferably white*
> *2 medium-sized onions, peeled and thinly sliced*
> *2 bay leaves*
> *1 teaspoon fennel seeds*
> *1 teaspoon dried thyme*
> *2 small strips orange peel, white zest removed*
> *2 teaspoons salt*
> *3 egg yolks*
> *Aioli* (recipe below)
> 1 tablespoon fresh lemon juice (optional)
> 12 pieces toasted French bread

When purchasing fish, if you have them filleted, ask that heads, bones, and trimmings be wrapped as well.

Put heads, bones, and trimmings into a large kettle. Add water, wine, vinegar, onions, bay leaves, fennel, thyme, orange peel, and salt. Bring to a boil. Lower heat and cook slowly, partially covered, 30 minutes. Skim off scum occasionally. When cooked, strain broth into a bowl, pressing ingredients with a wooden spoon to extract all juices Wash kettle and return

strained liquid to it. About 15 minutes before serving, bring broth to a boil and add fish, cut into serving pieces. Lower heat and simmer, covered, 5 to 8 minutes, until firm to the touch. Do not overcook. Carefully remove fish with a slotted spoon to a warm platter and cover to keep the fish warm. Then quickly beat egg yolks, one at a time, with a wire whisk into 1 cup of *aioli* sauce in a saucepan. Slowly stir in 1 cup hot fish broth and cook over low heat, stirring constantly, until broth is thick enough to coat the whisk lightly. Season with salt and pepper and add lemon juice. To serve, pour broth into a tureen or large bowl and bring to the table with warm toast, platter of warm fish, and reserved *aioli*. Each diner puts two slices of toast in the bottom of his own wide soup plate and tops the bread with one or two pieces of fish and some hot broth. Pass *aioli* separately.
Serves 6-8.

Aioli (Garlic Mayonnaise)

> 6 *medium-sized garlic cloves, peeled and crushed*
> 3 *egg yolks at room temperature*
> ¼ *to ½ teaspoon salt*
> *White pepper to taste*
> 1½ *cups olive oil at room temperature*
> 2 *to 3 tablespoons fresh lemon juice*

Pound garlic in a mortar or bowl with a pestle or wooden spoon. Add egg yolks, one at a time, and pound together until well blended and thick. Season with salt and pepper. Then begin adding oil, drop by drop, beating constantly with a wire whisk until mixture begins to thicken. Add half remaining oil in a steady stream, beating constantly. Then add lemon juice and remaining oil, still beating steadily, until thickened and smooth. Put 1 cup sauce in a small bowl to be added to the soup and put remaining sauce in another small bowl or saucepan to be passed with soup at the table. Makes about 1¾ cups.

Note: The *Aioli* may be prepared beforehand or may be made while the soup stock is cooking. It can also be prepared in an electric blender if the oil is added very slowly.

Finnish Dilled Fish-Potato Soup

This soup, called *kalakeitto,* is a favorite supper dish in Finland. Serve with rye bread and cheese.

4 medium-sized potatoes, peeled and diced
4 cups water
1 medium-sized onion, peeled and chopped
2 teaspoons salt
1-1½ pounds white-fleshed fish fillets (cod, haddock, flounder), cubed
2 cups hot milk
Pepper to taste
2 tablespoons butter or margarine
¼ cup chopped fresh dill

Put potatoes, water, onion, and salt into a large saucepan and bring to a boil. Reduce heat and cook slowly, covered, 10 minutes. Add fish and continue cooking about 12 minutes, until fish is tender. Add hot milk, pepper, butter or margarine, and dill. Serves 4 to 6.

West African Fish Soup

This well-seasoned soup is a good lunch specialty.

1 large onion, peeled and chopped
2 tablespoons salad oil
2 teaspoons curry powder

½ teaspoon cayenne
1 can (6 ounces) tomato paste
6 cups water
1½ pounds white-fleshed fish fillets (cod, haddock, rock bass), cubed
Juice of 1 lime or lemon
Salt, pepper to taste
1 green pepper, cleaned and cubed

Sauté onion in heated oil in a large saucepan until tender. Add curry powder and cayenne. Cook several seconds. Mix in tomato paste and water. Bring to a boil. Add fish cubes and reduce heat. Cook slowly, covered, about 12 minutes, until tender. Add lime or lemon juice, salt, pepper, and green pepper. Cook 5 minutes longer. Serves 4 to 6.

Chinese Garnished Fish-Rice Soup

1/3 cup uncooked long-grain rice
2 teaspoons minced ginger root
6 cups fish broth or water
1 pound white-fleshed fish fillets (cod, flounder, haddock), cubed
2 canned bamboo shoots, sliced
2 tablespoons soy sauce
1 tablespoon vinegar
Pepper to taste
4 scallions, with some tops, sliced

Put rice, ginger root, and broth or water into a large saucepan and bring to a boil. Reduce heat and cook slowly, covered, 15 minutes. Add fish, bamboo shoots, soy sauce, vinegar, and pepper. Continue cooking about 12 minutes longer, until fish is tender. Add scallions 1 or 2 minutes before serving. Serves 4 to 6.

Peruvian Shrimp-Vegetable Soup

This attractive soup includes tomatoes, potatoes, corn, and shrimp. Serve with warm cornbread.

1 large onion, peeled and chopped
1 or 2 cloves garlic, crushed
2 tablespoons salad oil
2 large tomatoes, peeled and chopped
2 medium-sized potatoes, peeled and chopped
6 cups fish broth or water
2 red chile peppers, seeded and chopped
Salt, pepper to taste
2 cups canned or frozen whole-kernel corn
16 medium-sized shrimp, shelled and deveined
3 tablespoons chopped fresh coriander or parsley

Sauté onion and garlic in heated oil in a large saucepan until tender. Add tomatoes and cook 1 or 2 minutes. Add potatoes, fish broth or water, chile peppers, salt, and pepper. Bring to a boil. Reduce heat and cook slowly, covered, 12 minutes. Add corn and shrimp and cook about 3 minutes, until shrimp are pink. Serve garnished with coriander or parsley. Serves 4 to 6.

Tunisian Fish-Vegetable Soup

This is a tempting luncheon or supper soup.

1 large onion, peeled and sliced
2 cloves garlic, crushed
2 tablespoons olive oil
2 medium-sized carrots, scraped and thinly sliced
2 medium-sized zucchini, stemmed and sliced
1 can (6 ounces) tomato paste

6 cups water
1½ pounds white-fleshed fish fillets, cubed
½ teaspoon dried oregano
½ teaspoon ground red pepper
Salt, pepper to taste
3 tablespoons chopped fresh coriander or parsley

Sauté onion and garlic in heated oil in a large saucepan. Add carrots and sauté 1 minute. Add zucchini, tomato paste, and water. Bring to a boil. Cook slowly, covered, 20 minutes. Add fish, oregano, red pepper, salt, and pepper. Continue cooking about 15 minutes, until fish is tender. Mix in coriander or parsley. Serves 4 to 6.

Flemish Seafood Soup

In Belgium's northern province of Flanders an everyday soup is made with saltwater fish, shrimp, and flavorings. This is one of many versions.

1 medium-sized onion, peeled and chopped
1 leek, white part only, cleaned and sliced
1 medium-sized carrot, scraped and chopped
3 tablespoons butter or margarine
6 cups fish broth or water
1½ pounds white-fleshed fish fillets, cubed
1½ cups shelled and cleaned small shrimp, cooked
1 cup light cream
1 tablespoon fresh lemon juice
Salt, pepper to taste

Sauté onion, leek, and carrot in heated butter or margarine in a large kettle for 5 minutes. Add broth or water and bring to a boil.

Add fish. Lower heat and cook slowly, covered, 12 minutes. Add shrimp, cream, lemon juice, salt, and pepper and continue cooking about 5 minutes longer to blend flavors. Serves 4 to 6.

Mexican Spicy Fish Soup

This *caldo de pescado* is a good luncheon or supper dish.

2 *large onions, peeled and sliced*
2 *cloves garlic, crushed*
2 *tablespoons olive or salad oil*
1 *tablespoon chili powder*
2 *large tomatoes, peeled and chopped*
1 *large green pepper, cleaned and cubed*
1 *green chile pepper, seeded and minced*
6 *cups water*
1½ *pounds white-fleshed fish, cut into large pieces*
½ *teaspoon dried oregano*
Salt, pepper to taste
3 *tablespoons chopped fresh parsley*
6 *thick slices crusty white bread, toasted*

Sauté onions and garlic in heated oil in a large saucepan until tender. Add chili powder and cook a few seconds. Add tomatoes and cook 1 or 2 minutes. Add green pepper, chile pepper, and water. Bring to a boil. Reduce heat and add fish, oregano, salt, and pepper. Cook slowly, covered, about 20 minutes, until fish is tender. Mix in parsley. Put a slice of toasted bread in each of six wide soup plates. Top with fish pieces. Ladle soup over fish. Serves 6

Basque Fish-Onion Soup

A flavorful soup-stew, called *ttoro* or *tioro,* is prepared in the Basque region of southern France and northern Spain with local fish, onions, and seasonings.

3 large onions, peeled and sliced
2 or 3 cloves garlic
½ cup olive oil
2 large tomatoes, peeled and chopped
2 quarts water
½ cup dry white wine
½ teaspoon dried thyme
1 bay leaf
2 tablespoons chopped fresh parsley
Salt, pepper to taste
4 large and thick pieces boneless white-fleshed fish (hake, cod, haddock)
4 thick slices crusty white bread

Sauté onions and garlic in ¼ cup heated olive oil in a large saucepan until tender. Add tomatoes and cook 1 minute. Add water, wine, thyme, bay leaf, parsley, salt, and pepper. Bring to a boil. Reduce heat. Cook slowly, uncovered, 10 minutes. Add fish and continue cooking, covered, about 25 minutes, until fish is tender. Meanwhile, fry bread in remaining heated oil until golden on each side. Rub with a cut clove of garlic, if you like. To serve, put a slice of fried toast in each of six soup plates. Top with fish. Ladle broth over fish. Serves 4.

Vegetable Soups

Of all the world's superb soups, those made with vegetables are particularly notable for their rich and interesting variety. The fascination of these soups is in part due to the many intriguing ways that both familiar and unfamiliar vegetables can be used.

The practice of placing one or more vegetables and the necessary liquid, with or without other foods, into some sort of pot dates back to prehistoric times.

As more than three hundred kinds of edible vegetables are known, man has long had plenty of plants, roots, and herbs from which to choose for making soup. We have leaves, stems, tubers, flower seeds, pods, and even fruits that are classified as vegetables. All of them have been used at some place or time to make delectable soups.

In the Middle East, where many of our familiar plants originated, early soups were made with greens and herbs. Legumes have been inventively used in that area ever since Jacob supplied his brother Esau with the Biblical "pottage of lentils." Beans,

217

peas, and chick-peas, as well as lentils, are still important ingredients in soups that are carefully flavored to enhance the appeal of bland foods. Garlic, onions, herbs, spices, yogurt, olive oil, lemon juice, and peppers appear in many of them.

From the Mediterranean countries have come some of the world's best fresh and dried vegetable soups, notably Italy's famous minestrone and the *pistou* of France. Very often pasta and grains supplement the roster of ingredients. Rice is a popular addition in the western Mediterranean, as is cracked wheat or *bulgur* in the Middle East.

While vegetables were most often used as flavorings or as supplements in meat soups, European cooks also created individual dishes starring these foods. In Russia, for example, the most common soup has long been made with cabbage and is called *shchi,* or *s'chee.* During the summer it is made with fresh cabbage and called "lazy s'chee." In the winter sauerkraut is used, and the name is changed to "sour s'chee." Other basic Russian soups are made with beets, mushrooms, and cucumbers.

Eastern Europeans make full-flavored soups with root vegetables, fresh and dried mushrooms, and greens. Balkan cooks are fond of preparing dried-bean soups. Northern European specialties feature green and yellow split peas. The Welsh favor leek soups, and Germans enjoy those made with celery root, turnips, kohlrabi, and white asparagus.

Early American settlers found that homemade vegetable soups were indispensable. Healthful and economical, these steaming dishes also tasted good. The hardy colonists were brought up with so-called family soups that were thick, stuck to the ribs, and often served as a complete meal. The best of them all is still old-fashioned vegetable soup, made with a number of fresh and dried vegetables, often using whatever varieties the cook happened to have on hand.

Particularly desirable soup vegetables are any of the onion family, especially leeks and yellow onions, as well as carrots, white turnips, green cabbage, potatoes, and dried beans. But in some areas of the world, for example Latin America, pumpkin, squash, black beans, and corn are soup staples. East Asians make marvelous soups with their varieties of cabbage, bean sprouts, soy beans, and various root vegetables.

These soups should be made with fresh vegetables that are ripe but not overly so, well-colored, crisp or firm, and free of blemishes and bruises. Frozen and canned vegetables are also good for making soups.

There are so many fine vegetables in the world that it's not possible to do justice to the soup potential of each of them here. This collection of traditional recipes, however, will draw kudos from your family and guests.

Oriental Celery Cabbage-Mushroom Soup

This soup is made with celery cabbage, also called Chinese cabbage, long cabbage, and *pe-tsai*. It has wide delicate crisp, long leaves that are whitish and firm in the stemlike center part and light green and fringed at the sides and top.

> *6 scallions, cleaned and sliced, with some tops*
> *2 cloves garlic, crushed*
> *3 tablespoons peanut or salad oil*
> *½ pound fresh mushrooms, cleaned and sliced*
> *6 cups beef bouillon*
> *1 teaspoon minced fresh ginger*
> *2 to 3 tablespoons soy sauce*
> *¼ teaspoon pepper*
> *4 cups shredded celery cabbage leaves*

Sauté scallions and garlic in heated oil in a large saucepan until tender. Add mushrooms and sauté 3 minutes. Add bouillon, ginger, soy sauce, and pepper. Bring to a boil; lower heat and cook slowly, covered, 10 minutes. Stir in cabbage leaves and cook, still covered, 5 minutes longer. Serves 6.

Polish Vegetable-Barley Soup

This traditional soup, called *krupnik,* is made with various ingredients but always includes barley and, usually, dried mushrooms, potatoes, and other vegetables. It is very nutritious and flavorful.

> *4 dried mushrooms, preferably Polish*
> *1 soup bone with meat, about 1 pound*
> *1 large carrot, scraped and chopped*
> *1 large onion, peeled and chopped*
> *6 peppercorns, bruised*
> *Salt to taste*
> *¼ cup pearl barley*
> *3 tablespoons butter or margarine*
> *3 medium-sized potatoes, peeled and diced*
> *1 cup sour cream, at room temperature*
> *3 tablespoons chopped fresh dill*

Soak mushrooms in lukewarm water to cover in a small bowl for 20 minutes. Drain and slice, reserving liquid. Put soup bone and 8 cups water into a large kettle. Bring to a boil; skim. Add carrot, onion, peppercorns, and salt; lower heat. Cook slowly, covered, for 1½ hours. Meanwhile, put barley and water to cover in a saucepan and cook slowly, covered, until barley is cooked, 1 hour or longer. Stir in butter or margarine. When soup has cooked the designated time, remove from heat and take out soup bone and meat. Cut meat from bone. Discard any gristle and dice meat. Return to kettle. Add sliced mushrooms, reserved liquid, and potatoes and put kettle back on stove. Continue to cook slowly, covered, until tender, about 25 minutes. Stir in cooked barley. Add sour cream and dill; mix well. Serves 6 to 8.

Note: Use fresh mushrooms as a substitute for dried mushrooms, if desired. Slice and clean ½ pound fresh mushrooms. Add to soup 15 minutes before the soup is finished. Fresh mushrooms do not have as much flavor as dried ones.

Majorcan Cauliflower Soup

This rich soup, called *sopa Mallorquinas,* is from the lovely island of Majorca, the largest of the Balearic Isles in the western Mediterranean.

> 1 *cauliflower, about 1½ pounds*
> 1 *large Bermuda onion, peeled and thinly sliced*
> 3 *medium-sized leeks, white parts only, cleaned and thinly sliced*
> 2 *garlic cloves, crushed*
> 3 *tablespoons olive or salad oil*
> 4 *large tomatoes, peeled and chopped*
> 6 *cups water*
> 1 *bay leaf*
> ½ *teaspoon dried thyme*
> *Salt, pepper to taste*
> 2 *medium-sized potatoes, peeled and diced*
> 6 *thick slices crusty white bread*

Cut stem and tough outer leaves from cauliflower. Wash in cold running water and drain. Set aside. Sauté onion, leeks, and garlic in heated oil in a large kettle until tender. Add tomatoes and sauté 2 minutes. Place whole cauliflower over sautéed vegetables. Add remaining ingredients, except potatoes and bread. Bring to a boil. Lower heat and cook slowly, covered, 20 minutes. Add potatoes and cook about 20 minutes longer, until cauliflower is tender. Break into flowerets before serving. Ladle over slices of bread in wide soup bowls. Serves 6.

African Lentil-Spinach Soup

This is a nutritious basic soup that can be flavored with various seasonings.

1 cup dried lentils
2 quarts water
1 medium-sized onion, peeled and chopped
1 clove garlic, crushed
1/3 cup olive oil
Juice of 1 lemon
½ teaspoon ground red pepper
Salt, pepper to taste
1 pound fresh spinach, washed, cleaned, and chopped
1/3 cup chopped fresh coriander or parsley

Wash and pick over lentils. Combine with water in a large kettle. Bring to a boil. Lower heat and cook slowly, uncovered, about 1¼ hours. Meanwhile, sauté onion and garlic in heated oil in a small skillet until tender. When lentils are cooked, add onion mixture and remaining ingredients. Mix well. Cook several minutes longer, until spinach is tender. Serves 6.

Peruvian Mixed Vegetable Soup

This colorful soup is made with an assortment of vegetables and includes chick-peas and rice.

1 *large onion, peeled and chopped*
2 *cloves garlic, crushed*
2 *tablespoons butter or margarine*
1 *can (1 pound) tomatoes, undrained and chopped*
½ *cup uncooked long-grain rice*
¼ *teaspoon dried oregano or thyme*
Salt, pepper to taste
4 *cups water*
1 *cup fresh or frozen green peas*
1 *cup canned chick-peas, drained*
3 *tablespoons chopped fresh coriander or parsley*

Sauté onion and garlic in heated butter or margarine in a large saucepan until tender. Add tomatoes, rice, oregano or thyme, salt, and pepper. Pour in water. Bring to a boil. Reduce heat and cook slowly, covered, 25 minutes. Add green peas and chick-peas. Continue cooking about 10 minutes longer, until ingredients are tender. Mix in coriander or parsley. Serves 6.

Hungarian Bean Soup with Noodles

This traditional family soup is called *Bableves Csipetkével*. It is flavored with sour cream and dill.

2 *cups (1 pound) dried white beans*
6 *cups water*
1 *large carrot, scraped and diced*
2 *tablespoons chopped fresh parsley*
1 *large onion, peeled and chopped*
3 *tablespoons butter or margarine*
2 *tablespoons all-purpose flour*
1 *cup sour cream, at room temperature*
Pinched noodles (recipe below)
2 *tablespoons chopped fresh dill*

Combine beans and water in a kettle. Bring to a boil; boil 2 minutes. Remove from heat. Let stand, covered, 1 hour. Add carrot and parsley; mix well. Bring to a boil. Reduce heat and cook slowly, covered, 2 hours, until beans are tender. Sauté onion in heated butter or margarine in a small skillet. Stir in flour; cook 1 or 2 minutes. Pour in 1 cup hot bean broth; mix well. Return to soup. Cook 1 or 2 minutes, stirring. Stir in sour cream; add pinched noodles. Cook until they rise to the surface. Add dill. Serves 8.

Pinched noodles

> 1 cup all-purpose flour
> ½ teaspoon salt
> 1 egg

Sift flour and salt into a small bowl. Make a well in center and break egg into it. Add a little water, enough to make a soft dough. Mix well. Knead to make smooth. Roll out to ⅛-inch thickness. Pinch off little pieces of dough with fingers and add to soup. Cook until noodles rise to surface.

Midwestern Corn Soup

This soup can be made with freshly-cut corn, or frozen or canned whole-kernel corn.

> 1 small onion, peeled and minced
> 2 tablespoons butter or margarine
> 2 tablespoons all-purpose flour
> 1½ cups hot water
> 2 cups fresh, canned, or frozen whole-kernel corn

1½ cups light cream or milk
Salt, pepper to taste
3 tablespoons chopped fresh parsley

Sauté onion in heated butter or margarine in a large saucepan until tender. Stir in flour; cook 1 or 2 minutes. Gradually add hot water, stirring constantly. Cook slowly until thickened and smooth. Add corn and cream or milk; mix well. Cook over moderate heat about 12 minutes, allowing a few minutes longer for fresh than frozen or canned corn. Season with salt and pepper. Add parsley. Serves 4.

Caribbean Black Bean Soup

A universal Caribbean black bean specialty is a thick and dark substantial soup called *sopa de frijol negro* that is made in considerable variety but is always hot in taste as well as in temperature. The soup is served with or over hot cooked rice and garnished with chopped onions.

1 pound (2 cups) dried black beans
8 cups cold water
¼ cup diced salt pork
¼ cup olive or salad oil
1 large onion, peeled and diced
2 cloves garlic, crushed
1 medium-sized green pepper, cleaned and chopped
1 cup diced cooked ham (optional)
3 medium-sized fresh or canned whole tomatoes, chopped
1 bay leaf
1 teaspoon dried oregano or thyme
Salt, pepper to taste
2 tablespoons wine vinegar
About 1 cup chopped onions

Pick over and wash beans. Put beans and water into a kettle. Bring to a boil; boil 2 minutes. Remove from heat and let stand, covered, 1 hour. Meanwhile, fry salt pork in a small skillet to render all fat. Add oil and heat. Add onion, garlic, and green pepper; sauté until onion is tender. Add ham, if used, tomatoes, bay leaf, oregano or thyme, salt, and pepper. Cook slowly, uncovered, stirring occasionally, 15 minutes. After beans have rested 1 hour, add sautéed mixture; mix well. Return to heat. Bring to a boil. Lower heat and simmer, covered, about 1½ hours, until beans are tender. Remove from heat. Mix in vinegar. Remove and discard bay leaf. Serve with beans whole, or whirl soup in a blender, or purée. Serve garnished with chopped onions, and over, or with, hot cooked rice, if desired. Serves 8 to 10.

Finnish Potato Soup

This is a nourishing soup for supper. Serve with dark bread and butter.

> 1 *medium-sized onion, peeled and chopped*
> 2 *tablespoons butter or margarine*
> 5 *cups vegetable broth or water*
> 3 *cups diced, peeled potatoes*
> 1 *cup grated raw carrots*
> 1½ *teaspoons salt, and ¼ teaspoon pepper, or to taste*
> 2 *tablespoons all-purpose flour*
> 1 *cup sour cream, at room temperature*
> ¼ *cup chopped fresh dill or parsley*

Sauté onion in heated butter or margarine in a large saucepan until tender. Add broth or water; bring to a boil; add potatoes. Reduce heat and cook over medium heat, covered, 15 minutes. Stir in carrots. Add salt and pepper. Cook a little longer if potatoes are not tender. Mix some of hot liquid with flour in a small bowl. Add to soup and cook, stirring, until thickened. Mix in sour cream and dill or parsley and leave over low heat 5 minutes. Serves 6 to 8.

Russian Cabbage Soup

This basic soup, called *schi* or *s'chee*, is hearty and nutritious; it is often served with buckwheat groats and sour cream. This variation has a large following.

> 1 large onion, peeled and sliced
> 1 leek, white part only, cleaned and sliced
> 2 medium-sized carrots, scraped and sliced ¼-inch thick
> 1 stalk celery, cleaned and sliced
> ½ white turnip, peeled and cubed (optional)
> 3 tablespoons bacon fat or shortening
> 8 cups beef bouillon or water
> 1 head green cabbage, about 1½ pounds, cored, cleaned, and shredded
> 1 can (6 ounces) tomato paste
> 3 tablespoons chopped fresh dill or parsley

Sauté onion, leek, carrots, celery, and turnip in heated bacon fat or shortening in a kettle 5 minutes. Add bouillon or water; bring to a boil. Stir in cabbage and tomato paste. Reduce heat and cook slowly, covered, about 1 hour, or until vegetables are cooked. Sprinkle with dill or parsley. Serves 6 to 8.

French Onion Soup

A rich soup topped with toasted French bread and grated cheese, this is marvelous any time of the day or night but is especially esteemed in France as a restorative after a night of celebrating.

> 1½ *pounds (about 5 cups sliced) onions, peeled and thinly*
> *sliced*
> 3 *tablespoons butter*
> 3 *tablespoons salad oil*
> 1 *teaspoon sugar*
> *Salt, pepper to taste*
> 6 *cups beef bouillon*
> ½ *cup dry white wine*
> 6 *or more slices toasted French bread*
> *About 1½ cups grated Gruyére or Swiss cheese*
> *Melted butter*

Sauté onions in heated butter and oil in a large, heavy saucepan over moderate heat until limp. Add sugar and mix well. Season with salt and pepper. Pour in bouillon and bring to a boil. Reduce heat and simmer, covered, 20 minutes. Add wine and continue to cook slowly 10 minutes. Ladle into earthenware or other ovenproof bowls. Top with one or more slices toasted French bread. Sprinkle generously with cheese. Sprinkle top with melted butter. Put into a preheated 375° oven 20 minutes, or until cheese is melted. Then put under broiler a few minutes, until golden and crusty on top. Serve in the same dishes. Serves 6.

Soupe au Pistou

This characteristic soup of France's Provence is very similar to minestrone, but it includes a spicy sauce, or *pistou*, made of crushed garlic, olive oil, grated cheese, and fresh basil, which is added at the end of the cooking. It is made in early spring with small, fresh white beans. Dried, white navy beans are a good substitute.

> 1 *large onion, peeled and diced*
> 2 *leeks, white parts only, cleaned, washed, and sliced*
> 3 *tablespoons butter or olive oil*
> 2 *large tomatoes, peeled and chopped*
> 3 *quarts water*
> *Salt, pepper to taste*
> 2 *cups diced raw potatoes*
> 2 *cups cut-up green beans*
> 2 *unpeeled medium-sized zucchini, washed and diced*
> 1 *can (1 pound) cannellini or navy beans, drained; or 1½*
>   *cups cooked dried white beans, pea beans, or navy beans*
> ½ *cup broken spaghettini or vermicelli*
> 3 *cloves garlic, crushed*
> ½ *cup chopped fresh basil, or 1½ tablespoons dried basil*
> ½ *cup freshly grated Parmesan cheese*
> ¼ *cup olive oil*

Sauté onion and leeks in heated butter or oil in a kettle until tender. Add tomatoes and cook 2 minutes. Add water and bring to a boil. Season with salt and pepper. Mix in potatoes and green beans. Reduce heat and simmer, uncovered, 15 minutes. Add zucchini, cannellini or beans, and spaghettini or vermicelli, and cook another 15 minutes, until vegetables are tender. While soup is cooking, prepare *pistou* sauce. Pound garlic and basil to form a paste in a mortar with a pestle, or mash in a bowl with a wooden spoon. Stir in cheese. Add oil, 1 tablespoon at a time, and beat to make a thick paste. Just before serving, add 2 cups hot soup to paste. Slowly stir into hot soup and serve at once. Pass grated cheese with soup, if you like. Serves 12.

Tunisian Chick-Pea Soup

Made in several variations in northern African countries, this nutritious soup is flavored with red peppers.

> 1¾ *cups chick-peas, washed and drained*
> 1 *or 2 cloves garlic, crushed*
> 1 *tablespoon red pepper sauce (*harissa*) or crushed red peppers*
> ½ *teaspoon ground cumin seed*
> *Juice of 1 lemon*
> *Salt to taste*
> 1 *to 2 tablespoons olive oil*

Soak chick-peas overnight in 4 cups water. Do not drain. Cook slowly, covered, about 1½ hours, until tender. Add more water while cooking, if needed to make a thinner soup. When cooked, add remaining ingredients, except oil, and cook slowly another 5 minutes to blend flavors. Serve sprinkled with the oil. Serves 4.

Portuguese Kale-Potato Soup

This traditional soup of Portugal's northwestern region of Minho is called *caldo verde,* green soup. It is made with a deep-green kale unlike that grown elsewhere. Serve with warm cornbread.

> 1 *pound fresh kale*
> 4 *medium-sized potatoes, peeled*
> 8 *cups water*
> ¼ *cup olive oil*
> *Salt, pepper to taste*
> ¼ *pound smoked garlic sausage, cooked and sliced into ¼-inch rounds*

Wash kale and cut off stems. Slice into shreds as thin as possible. Put potatoes, water, oil, salt, and pepper into a large saucepan and bring to a boil. Reduce heat and cook slowly, covered, about 25 minutes, or until potatoes are tender. Remove from stove and put mixture through a sieve or purée it. Return to saucepan; add kale strips. Continue cooking about 15 minutes longer, until kale is tender. Serve with sausage placed on top of soup. Serves 6.

Welsh Leek-Potato Soup

In Wales the leek is not only a favorite food but also the national emblem. It is used to make many delectable dishes including this soup.

> 4 leeks, white parts only, trimmed, washed, and sliced
> 2 tablespoons butter or margarine
> 4 medium-sized potatoes, peeled and sliced
> 2 cups water
> 1 bay leaf
> ¼ teaspoon dried thyme
> 2 sprigs parsley
> Salt, pepper to taste
> 3 cups milk or light cream
> 1 tablespoon chopped chives or fresh parsley

Sauté leeks in heated butter or margarine in a large saucepan until tender. Add potatoes, water, bay leaf, thyme, parsley, salt, and pepper. Bring to a boil. Reduce heat and cook slowly, covered, until potatoes are tender, about 25 minutes. Remove from heat and remove and discard bay leaf and parsley. Purée. Return to heat and gradually add milk or cream. Gently reheat. Serve garnished with chives or parsley. Serves 4 to 6.

Basque Vegetable Soup

If you want a hearty soup to serve for a winter supper, you'll want to prepare this. It's made with favorite foods of the Basque region in northern Spain.

1 *cup dried navy beans, washed*
8 *cups water*
1 *large onion, peeled and chopped*
2 *cloves garlic, crushed*
2 *tablespoons olive or salad oil*
1 *can (6 ounces) tomato paste*
2 *bay leaves*
½ *teaspoon dried thyme*
Salt, pepper to taste
3 *medium-sized potatoes, peeled and cubed*
3 *small zucchini, stemmed and sliced*
3 *cups shredded green cabbage*

Put beans and water into a large kettle. Bring to a boil. Boil 2 minutes. Remove from heat and let stand, covered, 1 hour. Bring again to a boil. Reduce heat and cook slowly, covered, 1 hour. Meanwhile, sauté onion and garlic in heated oil in a small skillet until tender. Add with remaining ingredients to beans. Continue cooking about 50 minutes longer, until ingredients are tender. Remove and discard bay leaves. Serves 8 to 10.

Shaker Green Soup

This soup, made with greens and herbs, was a favorite dish of the Shakers who formed communities in America during the 1800s.

6 *scallions, with some tops, cleaned and sliced*
2 *tablespoons butter or margarine*
½ *cup shredded lettuce*
½ *cup shredded spinach*
3 *tablespoons minced sorrel*
½ *cup minced watercress*
1 *tablespoon minced chervil*
2 *teaspoons sugar*
6 *cups chicken broth*
Salt, pepper to taste
1 *cup light cream or milk*

Sauté scallions in heated butter or margarine in a large saucepan until tender. Add lettuce, spinach, sorrel, watercress, and chervil. Simmer, covered, 10 minutes. Mix in sugar, chicken broth, salt, and pepper. Continue cooking slowly 30 minutes longer. Add cream or milk and leave on stove long enough to heat. Serves 6.

Tuscan Bean Soup with Cheese

This is a favorite soup in the northern Italian province of Tuscany. Tuscans consume beans in such large quantities that they are goodnaturedly called *mangiafagioli* (bean eaters) by other Italians.

2 *cups (1 pound) dried white beans*
1 *large onion, peeled and chopped*
2 *cloves garlic, crushed*
1 *large carrot, scraped and diced*
2 *stalks celery, with leaves, cleaned and chopped*
1 *cup diced cooked ham*

¼ cup olive oil
⅛ teaspoon ground red pepper
1 teaspoon crumbled dried rosemary
Salt, pepper to taste
½ cup chopped fresh parsley
8 to 10 slices toasted crusty white bread
½ cup grated Parmesan cheese, preferably freshly grated

Wash and pick over beans. Put into a large kettle. Cover with water; bring to a boil; boil 2 minutes. Remove from heat and let stand, covered, 1 hour. Drain beans, reserving water. Add enough fresh cold water to make 3 quarts. Sauté onion, garlic, carrot, celery, and ham in heated oil in a large kettle for 5 minutes. Add beans with water, red pepper, rosemary, salt, and pepper. Bring to a boil. Reduce heat and cook slowly, partially covered, about 1½ hours, until beans are tender. Remove about half the beans from the soup and purée; return to soup. Add parsley. Simmer over low heat, stirring, 1 or 2 minutes. Put toast in bottom of soup plates. Ladle soup over toast. Pass cheese to sprinkle over soup. Serves 8 to 10.

Turkish Vegetable Soup with Yogurt

For a luncheon or supper entrée, this is great.

1 beef soup bone with meat, about 1¼ pounds
6 cups water
1 bay leaf
1½ teaspoons salt
¼ teaspoon pepper
1 large onion, peeled and chopped
1/3 cup uncooked long-grain rice

1 cup diced scraped carrots
1 cup cut-up green beans
1 cup green peas
2 cups tomato juice
½ teaspoon dried oregano or thyme
Dash cayenne
1 cup plain yogurt

Put soup bone, water, bay leaf, salt, and pepper into a large kettle. Bring to a boil; skim. Reduce heat and cook slowly, covered, 1½ hours. Skim again. Add onion, rice, carrots, beans, peas, tomato juice, oregano or thyme, and cayenne. Continue to cook slowly, covered, about 30 minutes, until meat, rice, and vegetables are tender. Remove and discard bay leaf. Take out soup bone, and cut any meat into small pieces. Discard bone and return meat to soup. Stir in yogurt and leave on stove long enough to heat through. Serves 10 to 12.

Italian Minestrone

The best known of the great repertoire of Italian soups is the thick vegetable soup called minestrone. The ingredients vary greatly, but there are usually a number of dried and fresh vegetables. The name derives from the Latin for "hand-out." Long ago monks kept pots of the soup on their monastery stoves to hand out to hungry wayfarers, and here is one version of the friars' soup.

3 thin slices bacon, chopped
1 tablespoon olive or salad oil
1 large onion, peeled and chopped
3 leeks, white parts only, cleaned and thinly sliced

    1 or 2 cloves garlic, crushed
    1 large carrot, scraped and diced
    2 cups chopped green cabbage
    2 small zucchini, stemmed and sliced
    1 can (1 pound) tomatoes, undrained and chopped
    1½ cups diced raw peeled potatoes
    8 cups beef bouillon or water
    Salt, pepper to taste
    1 can (1 pound) white or kidney beans, drained
    1 cup small pasta or broken-up spaghetti
    Grated Parmesan cheese, preferably freshly grated

Combine bacon, oil, onion, leeks, and garlic in a kettle. Sauté 5 minutes. Add carrot and cabbage and sauté another 5 minutes. Add zucchini, tomatoes, potatoes, and bouillon or water. Bring to a boil. Season with salt and pepper. Reduce heat and cook slowly, covered, about 30 minutes, until ingredients are tender. Add beans and pasta and cook over moderate heat about 12 minutes longer, until pasta is tender. Serve with grated cheese. Serves 10.

Romanian Vegetable Soup

This characteristic soup has an appealing tart flavor.

    5 large onions, peeled and chopped
    About 1/3 cup butter or margarine
    5 cups beef bouillon
    3 tablespoons cleaned and chopped leeks, white parts only
    1 large potato, peeled and diced
    Salt, pepper to taste
    3 tablespoons wine vinegar
    2 teaspoons sugar

2 tablespoons chopped fresh parsley
1 cup sour cream, at room temperature

Sauté onions in butter or margarine in a large saucepan until tender. Add bouillon, leeks, and potato. Season with salt and pepper. Cook slowly, covered, until onions and potato are tender, about 30 minutes. Purée. Return to kettle; add vinegar and sugar, bring to a boil. Stir in parsley and sour cream. Leave over low heat long enough to heat through. Serves 6.

French-Canadian Pea Soup

This staple winter soup, also called habitant pea soup, is made with dried yellow peas. Serve with hot cornbread.

2 cups dried yellow peas, washed and picked over
2 quarts water
1/3 to ½ pound salt pork, blanched and diced
1 medium-sized onion, peeled and diced
1 medium-sized carrot, scraped and diced
1 tablespoon minced fresh parsley or ½ teaspoon dried sage
Salt, pepper to taste

Soak peas in water in a large kettle overnight or for 9 hours. Add remaining ingredients and bring to a boil. Reduce heat and simmer, covered, about 1½ hours, until tender. Serves 6 to 8.

Finnish Vegetable Soup

In Finland an excellent summer soup, called *kesäkeitto*, is made with a combination of fresh vegetables. It can be made, however, with fresh and/or frozen vegetables.

2 *cups thinly sliced peeled onions*
1 *cup thinly sliced scraped carrots*
2 *cups cut-up cauliflower*
2 *cups cut-up green beans*
1 *cup green peas*
5 *cups boiling water*
1 *tablespoon sugar*
Salt, pepper to taste
6 *tablespoons all-purpose flour*
6 *cups hot milk*
2 *tablespoons butter or margarine*
1/3 *cup chopped fresh parsley*

Put vegetables and boiling water into a kettle. Add sugar, salt, and pepper. Bring to a boil. Reduce heat and cook slowly, covered, until vegetables are just tender, about 25 minutes. Combine flour and milk; mix until smooth. Gradually stir into soup; mix well. Continue to cook several minutes longer, until liquid has thickened and vegetables are tender. Remove from heat. Add butter and parsley. Serves 8 to 10.

Mexican Corn Soup

Serve with hot cornbread or muffins for supper or luncheon.

1 *large onion, peeled and chopped*
1 *or 2 cloves garlic, crushed*
2 *tablespoons vegetable oil*
1 *to 2 tablespoons chili powder*
2 *medium-sized tomatoes, peeled and chopped*
½ *teaspoon dried oregano*
Salt, pepper to taste
1½ *cups fresh or frozen corn niblets*
½ *cup fresh or frozen cut-up green beans*

3 cups milk
3 tablespoons chopped fresh coriander or parsley

Sauté onion and garlic in heated oil in a large saucepan until tender. Add chili powder and cook 1 minute. Stir in tomatoes, oregano, salt, and pepper. Cook 1 or 2 minutes. Add corn, green beans, and milk and cook over low heat, covered, about 15 minutes, until ingredients are tender. Serve garnished with coriander or parsley. Serves 4 to 6.

French Garbure

In France a thick soup-stew called *garbure* is a traditional dish in several regions and is made in many variations. The dish is basically a hearty vegetable soup that often includes bacon, salt pork, sausages, or preserved goose. This is one kind. In some locales, as each diner gets close to the bottom of the soup bowl, he adds a glass of wine to the remaining soup.

2 cups (1 pound) dried navy or pea beans
2 quarts water
½ pound bacon or salt pork in one piece
4 cloves garlic, minced
4 large onions, peeled and sliced
4 large carrots, scraped and sliced
4 white turnips, peeled and sliced
6 medium-sized potatoes, peeled and sliced
1 medium-sized head green cabbage, cored and shredded
½ teaspoon dried thyme
1 bay leaf
Salt, pepper to taste

Cover beans with water in a kettle. Bring to a boil; boil 2

minutes. Let stand, covered, 1 hour. Put bacon or pork in center of beans. Cook 1 hour. Add remaining ingredients and continue cooking until ingredients are tender, about 45 minutes. Remove bacon or pork and slice. Serve on the side or in the bowls. Serve soup in wide bowls over pieces of crusty white bread previously fried until golden in butter, if desired. Serves 8 to 10.

Quick
and Easy Soups

Although the purpose of this book is to demonstrate the fascination and satisfaction of making soups from scratch, this chapter is for those who, by either preference or force of circumstance, use shortcuts.

It is possible to prepare palatable soups quickly and easily with canned, dehydrated, or frozen soups, with or without the addition of other foods, and by using electric blenders and/or food processors. All sorts of recipes lend themselves to these methods of cookery.

In the late 1890s an important milestone in the commercial preparation of canned soups was the introduction of Campbell's condensed products. The famous red-and-white can became one of the most familiar sights on any grocery store shelf. Other products soon followed, and condensed soups in cans became household staples.

Ready-made soups are good when heated individually, but they can be combined with other canned soups to produce interesting variations, or enhanced with additional seasonings or solid foods. Combining canned soups has been popular in America for many decades. Many favorite "soup mates" have been recommended by the manufacturers or created by cooks at home.

Smooth and flavorful soups, either hot or cold, can be made quickly in electric blenders and food processors. This type of soup-making is particularly desirable either for impromptu snacks or to serve at meals. You can save time, energy, and sometimes money with these soups, but don't expect the flavor to be as good as that of soups made from scratch.

For blender and food-processor soups, read the instructions that come with the appliance. If you don't, you may damage the machine and ruin the soup. You must understand how and when to operate the machine, the proper way to add the ingredients, and how to remove the container from the motor stand.

The recipes in this chapter include some well-known and innovative shortcut soups that are good for every day as well as entertaining.

Mock Lobster Soup

1 *can (10½ ounces) condensed pea soup*
1 *can (10¾ ounces) condensed tomato soup*
2 *soup cans light cream or milk*
3 *tablespoons dry sherry*
1 *teaspoon Worcestershire sauce*
Dash Tabasco
Salt, pepper to taste

Combine ingredients in a blender and whirl, covered, smooth or mix with a whisk to blend. Serve chilled or hot. Serves 6.

Senegalese Potage

1 can (10½ ounces) condensed cream of chicken soup
1 soup can light cream
1 teaspoon curry pwder
1 teaspoon paprika
⅛ teaspoon ground cinnamon
1 cup crushed ice

Put soup, cream, curry powder, paprika, and cinnamon into a blender. Blend, covered, 15 seconds. Add ice and blend 15 seconds. Serve cold garnished with grated coconut or chopped nuts, if desired. Serves 4.

Frosty Tomato Soup

1 can (10¾ ounces) condensed tomato soup
1 soup can water
1 cup dairy sour cream or yogurt
2 teaspoons horseradish
1 teaspoon paprika
1 large tomato, peeled, seeded, and chopped
2 tablespoons chopped fresh dill or parsley

Put soup, water, sour cream or yogurt, horseradish, and paprika into a blender. Blend, covered, smooth. Pour into a container. Chill 2 hours or longer. Add chopped tomato; mix well. Serve in chilled soup cups garnished with dill or parsley. Serves 4.

Purée Mongole

1 can (10½ ounces) condensed tomato soup
1 can (11¼ ounces) condensed green pea soup
1 soup can milk
1 soup can water
1 teaspoon curry powder

Combine soups, milk, and water in a medium-sized saucepan. Mix to blend well. Heat to boiling. Stir in curry powder. Remove from heat. Serves 4.

Blender Vichyssoise

1 medium-sized onion, peeled and quartered
1½ cups chicken broth
1½ cups diced cooked potatoes
½ teaspoon salt
¼ teaspoon white pepper
1 cup crushed ice
¾ cup light cream or milk
¼ cup finely chopped chives

Put onion and ½ cup chicken broth into blender. Blend on high speed, covered, 10 seconds. Add remaining cup of chicken broth, potatoes, salt, and pepper. Blend 20 seconds. Add ice and cream or milk and blend 15 seconds. Serve in chilled soup bowls or cups garnished with chives. Serves 6.

Oriental Spinach Soup

2 cans (10½ ounces each) condensed beef bouillon
2 soup cans water

2 tablespoons soy sauce
2 tablespoons sliced scallions
½ cup sliced canned bamboo shoots
1 cup shredded fresh spinach

Combine bouillon, water, and soy sauce in a medium-sized saucepan. Heat. Add remaining ingredients and heat over moderate heat 5 minutes. Serves 6 to 8.

Elegant Asparagus-Mushroom Soup

1 can (10 ounces) condensed cream of asparagus soup
1 can (10 ounces) condensed cream of mushroom soup
2 soup cans milk
Salt, pepper, freshly grated nutmeg to taste
1/3 cup dry sherry
2 tablespoons finely chopped chives

Combine soups, milk, salt, pepper, and nutmeg in a large saucepan. Mix well and heat. Cook slowly, covered, 5 minutes to blend flavors. Remove from heat and add sherry. Serve garnished with chives. Serves 4 to 6.

Cold Beet Soup

½ small onion
1 cup cooked or canned sliced beets
1 cup beef bouillon
2 tablespoons wine vinegar
1 teaspoon salt
¼ teaspoon pepper
1 cup dairy sour cream

Put ingredients into blender. Blend, covered, smooth. Pour into a container. Chill several hours. Serve in chilled soup bowls garnished with sour cream, if desired. Serves 6.

Potage Saint Germain

1 can (11¼ ounces) condensed green pea soup
1 can (10½ ounces) condensed cream of chicken soup
2 cups milk
½ cup heavy cream
½ cup cooked or canned green peas

Combine soups, milk, and cream in a medium-sized saucepan. Mix until smooth. Heat, stirring occasionally. Add peas and remove from heat. Serves 4 to 6.

Southern Black Bean Soup

2 cans (10½ ounces each) condensed black bean soup
2 soup cans hot water
2 tablespoons bourbon whiskey
1 teaspoon salt
¼ teaspoon pepper
8 thin lemon slices
¼ cup minced onion

Combine soup, water, and whiskey in a large saucepan. Mix well. Bring to a boil. Add salt and pepper. Put 1 slice lemon in each of 8 soup cups or bowls. Pour in soup. Garnish each serving with a little minced onion. Serves 8.

Easy Gazpacho

1 *can (10¾ ounces) condensed tomato soup*
1 *can (10½ ounces) condensed beef bouillon*
1 *soup can water*
2 *tablespoons wine vinegar*
1 *tablespoon olive oil*
1 *or 2 cloves garlic, crushed*
1 *cup finely chopped cucumber*
½ *cup finely chopped green pepper*
¼ *cup finely chopped scallions, with some tops*

Combine ingredients in a large bowl. Chill at least four hours. Serve in chilled soup bowls or cups garnished with croutons, if desired. Serves 4.

Southern Gumbo

½ *cup diced cooked ham*
¼ *cup chopped onion*
¼ *cup chopped green pepper*
2 *tablespoons butter or margarine*
2 *cans (10½ ounces each) condensed chicken gumbo soup*
1 *soup can tomato juice*
1 *soup can water*
1 *cup cooked or canned small shrimp, cleaned and shelled*
½ *teaspoon dried thyme*

Cook ham, onion, and green pepper in heated butter or margarine in a large saucepan until onion is tender. Add remaining ingredients. Cook over low heat, stirring, 5 minutes. Serves 6.

The Complete International Soup Cookbook

Swiss Cheese-Onion Soup

2 medium-sized onions, peeled and sliced
¼ cup butter or margarine
2 cans (10¾ ounces each) condensed Cheddar cheese soup
1 soup can milk
1 soup can water
1 teaspoon dried basil

Sauté onions in heated butter or margarine in a medium-sized saucepan until tender. Add remaining ingredients. Mix well. Heat, stirring occasionally. Serve garnished with croutons, if desired. Serves 4.

Chicken-Watercress Potage

½ bunch watercress
2 cans (10½ ounces each) condensed cream of chicken soup
2 cups milk
⅛ teaspoon pepper

Pick over and wash watercress; chop fine. Whirl soup, milk, pepper, and watercress in a blender, covered, until smooth. Heat in a large saucepan and serve hot or chill and serve cold. Serves 4 to 6.

Seafood Bisque

1 can (6½ ounces) crab meat, drained and cleaned
3 tablespoons butter or margarine
2 tablespoons fresh lemon juice
¼ teaspoon paprika

¼ *teaspoon salt*
Dash pepper
1 *can (10 ounces) frozen cream of shrimp soup*
1 *can (about 7 ounces) tuna, drained and flaked*
3 *cups light cream or milk*
3 *tablespoons chopped fresh dill or parsley*

Sauté crab meat in heated butter or margarine, lemon juice, and seasonings in a large saucepan 2 or 3 minutes. Add remaining ingredients, except dill or parsley, and heat to boiling. Pour into soup bowls or cups and serve garnished with dill or parsley. Serves 6.

Potage Saint Cloud

2 *cans (10½ ounces each) condensed pea soup*
1½ *soup cans light cream or milk*
½ *soup can heavy cream*
½ *cup shredded lettuce*
½ *cup cooked green peas*
1/3 *cup chopped fresh parsley*

Combine soup and creams in a blender. Blend, covered, smooth. Turn into a medium-sized saucepan and heat to boiling. Serve in soup bowls garnished with lettuce, peas, and parsley. Serves 4 to 6.

Boula Boula

2 *cans (10½ ounces each) condensed pea soup*
1 *can (10 ounces) green turtle soup*
¼ *cup dry sherry*
½ *cup whipped cream*

Combine soups in a saucepan and heat to boiling. Remove from heat and stir in sherry. Pour into ovenproof cups or bowls. Top each with 2 large spoonfuls of whipped cream. Put under heated broiler until light golden. Serves 4.

Tomato-Tuna Bisque

1 can (10¾ ounces) condensed tomato soup
2 cups light cream or milk
½ teaspoon dried basil
1 can (about 7 ounces) tuna, drained and flaked
2 tablespoons dry sherry

Combine soup, cream or milk, and basil in a large saucepan. Mix well. Bring to a boil. Add tuna and mix well. Remove from heat and stir in sherry. Serves 4.

Mexican Avocado Soup

1 large ripe avocado
1 clove garlic, crushed
¼ cup chopped onions
2 large tomatoes, peeled, seeded, and quartered
1 teaspoon chili powder
2 tablespoons fresh lemon juice
1 can (10½ ounces) condensed chicken broth
1 soup can water or tomato juice
Salt, pepper to taste

Cut avocado in half lengthwise with a stainless-steel knife. Remove seed. Cut off skin. Put into blender. Add garlic, onions, tomatoes, chili powder, and lemon juice. Blend, covered, until smooth. Add chicken broth, water or tomato juice, salt, and pepper; blend a few seconds. Turn into a container. Chill two hours or longer. Serve in chilled soup bowls garnished with a sprinkling of paprika, if desired. Serves 4.

Summer Vegetable Soup

1 *envelope onion soup mix*
4 *cups water*
1 *medium-sized cucumber, peeled, seeded, and chopped*
2 *large tomatoes, peeled and chopped*
1 *cup chopped celery*
½ *teaspoon dried thyme or basil*
3 *tablespoons chopped fresh parsley*

Prepare soup mix with water and basil, following label directions. Pour into a container. Chill. Divide vegetables between 6 chilled soup cups. Pour soup over vegtetables. Garnish tops with parsley. Serves 6.

Mushroom-Salmon Bisque

1 *envelope mushroom soup mix*
1 *tablespoon grated onion*
1 *tablespoon fresh lemon juice*
2 *cups water*
2 *cups light cream*
1 *can (about 4 ounces) salmon, drained and flaked*
½ *teaspoon crumbled dried rosemary*

Prepare soup mix with onion, lemon juice, and water, following label directions. Put into a large saucepan. Add cream, salmon, and rosemary. Bring to a boil. Heat over low heat 5 minutes. Serves 4 to 6.

Food Processor Soups

Italian Tomato-Zucchini Zuppa

1 medium-sized onion, peeled and quartered
2 cloves garlic, peeled
2 medium-sized zucchini, stemmed and quartered
1 can (1 pound, 12 ounces) peeled tomatoes, undrained
½ teaspoon dried basil
1 tablespoon parsley flakes
1½ teaspoons salt
½ teaspoon pepper
2 tablespoons olive or salad oil
2 cups beef bouillon

   With metal blade in place, put onion and garlic through feed tube into work bowl. Process, turning on and off, until finely chopped. Turn into a small bowl. Replace metal blade with slicing disk. Add zucchini pieces to feed tube and slice, using moderate pressure on plunger. Remove to a plate. Replace slicing disk with metal blade. Add tomatoes and liquid, basil, parsley, salt, and pepper. Process, turning on and off, until puréed. Remove from base and set aside. To cook soup, sauté chopped onion and garlic in heated oil in a large saucepan until tender. Add zucchini and sauté 2 minutes. Then add puréed tomato mixture and bouillon. Mix well. Bring to a boil. Reduce heat and cook slowly, covered, 30 minutes. Serves 6.

German Sauerkraut Soup

1 large onion, peeled and quartered
1 large carrot, scraped and quartered
1 large green pepper, cleaned and quartered

1 can (1 pound, 11 ounces) sauerkraut, drained
3 cups beef bouillon
4 cups tomato juice
½ teaspoon dried thyme
2 teaspoons parsley flakes
½ teaspoon salt
¼ teaspoon pepper

With metal blade in place, put onion and carrot through feed tube into work bowl. Process, turning on and off, until finely chopped. Combine chopped vegetables with sauerkraut in a large saucepan or kettle. Mix well. Add remaining ingredients and mix. Bring to a boil. Reduce heat and cook slowly, covered, 45 minutes. Serves 6 to 8.

Belgian Dilled Carrot-Potato Soup

1 medium-sized onion, peeled and quartered
2 medium-sized potatoes, peeled and halved
4 medium-sized carrots, scraped and cut into thirds
3 cups water
1 tablespoon butter or margarine
1 tablespoon all-purpose flour
1 cup light cream
1 teaspoon dillweed
1½ teaspoons salt
½ teaspoon pepper

With metal blade in place, put onion, potatoes, and carrots through feed tube into work bowl. Process, turning on and off, until finely chopped. Turn into a large saucepan. Add water and mix well. Bring to a boil. Reduce heat and cook slowly, covered, 30 minutes. Reinsert metal blade in work bowl. Spoon vegetable mixture through feed tube into work bowl. Process until smooth. Melt butter or margarine in a large saucepan. Mix in flour and cook 2 minutes. Gradually add cream, stirring constantly, and cook until smooth and slightly thickened. Add dillweed, salt, and pepper and cook slowly, stirring occasionally, 5 minutes. Add puréed vegetable mixture and leave on stove long enough to heat through. Serves 4 to 6.

Provençal Fish Soup

1 *large onion, peeled and quartered*
2 *cloves garlic, peeled*
2 *large tomatoes, peeled, seeded, and quartered*
2 *tablespoons olive or salad oil*
6 *cups water*
1 *pound white-fleshed fish fillets (flounder, cod, halibut),*
  cut into thirds
1 *bay leaf*
½ *teaspoon dried thyme*
1 *teaspoon salt*
¼ *teaspoon pepper*
3 *tablespoons chopped fresh parsley*

With metal blade in place, put onion and garlic through feed tube into work bowl. Process, turning on and off, until finely chopped. Turn into a small bowl. Add tomatoes and process, turning on and off twice, or until evenly chopped. Remove from base and set aside. To cook soup, sauté chopped onion and garlic in heated oil in a large saucepan until tender. Add tomatoes and cook 1 minute. Add water, fish, bay leaf, thyme, salt, and pepper. Bring to a boil. Reduce heat and cook slowly, covered, about 25 minutes, until fish is tender. Mix in parsley. Serve over toasted, crusty white bread in large soup bowls, if desired. Serves 4 to 6.

French-Canadian Onion Soup

2 *large onions, peeled and quartered*
2 *tablespoons butter or margarine*
2 *tablespoons all-purpose flour*
8 *cups beef bouillon*
Salt, pepper to taste
3 *to 4 ounces Cheddar cheese*
6 *slices toasted crusty white bread*

With slicing blade in place, put onion through feed tube into work bowl and slice, using moderate pressure on plunger. Sauté onion in heated butter or margarine in a large saucepan until tender. Add flour and stir well; cook 2 minutes. Gradually add bouillon, stirring constantly. Bring to a boil. Reduce heat and cook slowly, covered, 20 minutes. Meanwhile, with shredding disk in place, shred cheese, using moderate pressure on pusher. To serve, ladle soup into individual oven-proof soup bowls. Top each with a slice of toast and sprinkle with cheese. Put under broiler 3 or 4 minutes, until cheese is melted and bubbly. Serves 6.

Exotic Soups

Unusual, curious, or exotic soups, prepared with foods or methods that are not commonplace everywhere are not only worthy of note, but may well add piquant interest to your menu.

Fashions in soups have changed over the years. While we still make some kinds that have been popular for centuries, many favorites of our forefathers have been largely forgotten today. Others are prepared with rare ingredients that aren't always readily available, or must be gathered wild or purchased at specialty food markets.

The content of these exotic soups is fascinating. For example, there are recipes using every kind of cereal grain, breads, milk, and nuts, and even soups featuring a single spice such as saffron or turmeric. Cooks in some countries prepare soups with armadillos, bison, wild boar, grasshoppers, kangaroos, larks, lions, pigeons, pronghorns, woodcocks, and zebras. Eskimo soups are made with reindeer, ptarmigan, caribou, oogruk intestines, and fish duck.

257

Mollusks and crustaceans have long been used to make soups, and many of these dishes feature cockles, frogs' legs, limpets, mussels, terrapins, turtles, whelks, and winkles.

Hundreds of unusual wild and edible greens and plants may be used in soups. East Asians and northern Europeans are fond of a variety of seaweed soups. Soups made with dandelions, lotus roots, white radishes, and bitter, pickling, and winter melons are also popular in East Asia. There are Caribbean plantain, cassava, breadfruit, chayote, and pigeon pea soups. In Hawaii there is a basella soup and in West Africa an interesting melon seed soup.

Marvelous soups have been made for hundreds if not thousands of years with mushrooms and other edible fungi such as the great European favorites: *cèpe, chanterelle, morel,* and field mushroom. In the Orient, rich brownish and black mushrooms such as the textured cloud ear, fragrant *matsutake, shiitake* (oak mushroom), and padi straw mushrooms are used to make flavorful soups.

The rarest fungi, however, are truffles; these usually aren't associated with soups. In northern Italy where white truffles are a specialty they sometimes add perfume and color to soups, usually as a garnish. Black truffles found in Perigord, elsewhere in France, and in some other areas of Europe are so treasured that they are called "black diamonds." They have been brilliantly featured in one of the world's most luxurious and expensive soups, called *Soupe aux Truffles Elysée,* created by the famous chef Paul Bocuse, for a celebrity dinner given by French President and Mrs. Valéry Giscard d'Estaing on February 25, 1975 when Bocuse was awarded the coveted Legion of Honor.

The soup, still prepared by Bocuse, is a marvelous combination made with a mushroom-vegetable *brunois,* topped with sliced fresh truffles and cubes of truffled *foie gras,* containing dry vermouth, truffle liquid, and rich chicken broth, put into small individual bowls, and crowned with a glazed pastry that is baked until puffed and golden. This elegant soup is a sight to behold and a delight to savor.

For centuries, flowers have added distinction, flavor, color, and décor to soups. Once grown for medicinal purposes and to please gourmets' palates, medieval cooks believed that flowers "maketh a man merrie and joyfull, putteth away all melancholie and madness." Soup recipes in 18th-century cookbooks featured daylilies, marigolds, nasturtiums, roses, and violets. Some soups used three or four kinds of flowers, greens, and fruits, which were simmered in broth or water. Others were made with flower petals, leaves, and roots.

Some Mexican soups feature squash and pumpkin blossoms. In the American Southwest soups are made with cactus flowers and yucca (Indian banana) blossoms. The chrysanthemum, which has an aromatic, crisp, and exciting flavor, is a favorite in the Orient. The Chinese believe the flower imparts longevity, and their cooks prepare a celebrated ceremonial dish called Chrysanthemum Bowl, a flavorful soup made at the table and finished with the addition of several colorful petals from "mums."

In *The Food of France,* Waverly Root describes several unusual French soups. *Cousinette* is a sort of salad-soup made with several kinds of greens and herbs, and *soupe au farci* features a whole seasoned-sausage-stuffed cabbage. *Soupe des vendanges,* grape-pickers' soup, is made in great quantity to serve crews who harvest grapes. Large vats contain clean rocks or stones; sizable chunks of beef stuffed with fresh grape seeds, garlic, and spices; veal; several vegetables, aromatics, herbs, spices, fresh grapes, and water, all of which are slowly simmered.

Very old north European soups, called black soups, seem bizarre to the uninitiated but are treasured native specialties. In Sweden, *Svartsoppa,* black soup, is still prepared for a traditional November holiday with a recipe that dates back to the

Vikings. It is made with a mixture of pig and goose blood, giblet stock, red and white wine, fortified wines, gin, fruit juice, several herbs and spices, and is garnished with cooked goose liver and giblets, apples, and prunes. In France's Perigord region a black pudding water soup, *soupe à l'eau de boudin,* features fried vegetables, bread, and flour cooked in the liquid from a blood pudding.

The earliest American soups, prepared by the Indians, were made with acorn meal, arrowhead, beans, cattails, greens, wild onions, potatoes, sunflower seeds, hominy, sago, seafood, turtles, squirrels, and wild turnips, among other foods.

American Indian recipes include a Pine Nut Soup made by cooking pine nuts with hot charcoal and then rolling and grinding them to a meal, which was mixed with water to make a broth called "milk of life." A Meat Skin Soup was a simple preparation of boiled meat skins, roasted until brown, and cooked in water thickened with cornmeal. Yellow Jacket Soup was made with browned yellow jackets cooked in water and seasoned with grease and salt.

American colonists created soups with everyday staples such as bread or cornmeal and milk, wild greens, green kern (corn) and other grains, and a variety of nuts and game. Many of the soups had innovative titles. Cake Soup, for example, was actually a type of portable soup like the pocket soup mentioned in the first chapter. Squatter's Soup included venison, boiled corn on the cob, and cornmeal. You could easily make Poor Boy Oyster Soup with a can of sardines and hot milk, or Mock Oyster Soup with shredded cabbage, milk, and butter.

In *The Carolina Housewife,* published in 1847, there are recipes for Lamb's Head Soup, Omelette Soup, Seminole Soup (squirrel, hickory nuts, and sassafras leaves), Nut Soups, and one named Soup With (So-Called) Green Frogs. The "frogs" were made with butter, egg, bread, and green peas, wrapped in spinach leaves, shaped like frogs, cooked in butter, and served in bouillon.

Of all the exotic and unusual soup recipes I uncovered while doing research for this book, the following is the most outstanding. It is a "recipe" from *Fez, Traditional Moroccan Cooking*, translated from the French by J. E. Harris.

> *Fortifying Broth For Pregnant Women "Tadeff"*
> "During the final birth pangs it is the custom to prepare a strong broth which the pregnant woman, as soon as she is delivered and has returned to bed, will take after having first swallowed a few raw eggs.
>
> "It is composed of chopped garlic, powdered saffron flowers, much pepper, thyme, and wild mint, called peppermint."

Here are recipes for cosmopolitan exotic soups; you can be sure no one at your table is "tired of" these already.

Chinese Soups

The Chinese prepare some of the world's most exotic soups, featuring a fascinating selection of ingredients. For millennia the Chinese have had a taste for many foods that most Westerners would find weird or peculiar.

Virtually every variety of fauna and flora have been found in Chinese soups. You'll find confirmation when looking over Chinese menus and cookbooks, and dining in Chinese restaurants in the Orient. There are soups made with lotus seeds and roots, walnut dates, pigeons, dried fish tripe, melon seed plant, deer heads and kidneys, pigs' feet, birds' tongues, bear meat, sea slugs, crabs' eggs, seaweeds, flower petals and roots, all sorts of nuts, black "tree ear" mushrooms and other fungi, baby bite-size sparrows, fish cheeks and lips, chicken feet, greens, dried oysters, tangerine peel, whelks, preserved parsnips, cuttlefish, duck eggs, and many other imaginative ingredients.

The Chinese esteem many soups as cures. Those prepared with fish or seaweed and spices are for colds. Women drink a restorative made with pigs' feet and fresh ginger after childbirth. Broths laced with ginseng, a popular Oriental aphrodisiac, are taken to enhance virility or to keep singers' voices in shape.

One popular Chinese soup is made with winter melon and called Winter Melon Pond. This melon, a member of the squash family, is green and may be very large. It has a distinctive and attractive appearance and an appealing white flesh noted for its flavor and texture. In the Orient it's prepared in many interesting ways.

Winter melon soup is a restaurant specialty that can be a simple preparation or an elaborate combination of diverse ingredients such as winter melon pieces, mushrooms, lotus seeds, diced chicken and ham, bamboo shoots, shrimp, greens, seaweed, and other foods, cooked in a tasty broth and served from a decorated whole melon that has been parboiled and hollowed out. Winter melon is sold by the slice or whole in Chinese groceries in America.

Soups made with birds' nests are an ancient, famous, and luxurious delicacy enjoyed in China, throughout the rest of Southeast Asia, and wherever people of Chinese extraction have settled.

The nests are made by swifts or swallows, which subsist on certain types of seaweed and construct the cuplike forms with driblets of their gelatinous saliva dropped in lengths one on top of the other. Finding and collecting the nests is extremely diffi-cult and dangerous because the birds build them high upon rugged cliffs and in caves off the China coast and some other South Sea areas that can be reached only at some hazard. For this reason the nests have been served only at special feasts and are still extremely expensive.

The nests vary somewhat in shape and content, are graded black, white, or yellow, and are used for different dishes. Those made almost entirely of saliva and that are free of debris are the best. All are rich in protein and are commercially available ready for use in many Asian countries and some American Oriental markets.

Before using, the nests must be cleaned of feathers and leaves, soaked in water to swell and become transparent, and reshaped after cooking to resemble the original nest. Birds' nests have no color or flavor but when they are cooked in well-seasoned broths with other foods, such as shredded chicken and a garnish of smoked ham, they make attractive rich soups.

So-called "birds' nests" are sold in Europe, but they are man-made with agar-agar, a gelatinous substance derived from sea-weed, and the finished product cannot compare with the flavor of the original.

Another cherished and expensive Chinese soup is made with sharks' fins; they are widely used in Far Eastern cooking. The soupfin shark has a gelatinous fin rich in protein and vitamins. It must be sun-dried or cured to develop its richness and then has to be soaked in water before cooking. It is sold unprocessed (with skin and bone) or in prepared form in dry strips or "needles" and is expensive. The best quality is pale ivory in color. The fins have an unusual, appealing, and chewy consistency and are served in flavorful soups with mushrooms and chicken or other ingredients.

You'll find a recipe for a Chinese exotic soup below as well as some other intriguing international recipes.

Chinese Winter Melon Soup

8 cups chicken broth
1 whole chicken breast, skinned, boned, and diced
½ cup diced Chinese or celery cabbage
1 pound winter melon, peeled and diced

½ cup chopped canned water chestnuts
1 teaspoon monosodium glutamate
1 tablespoon cornstarch
3 tablespoons cold water
Garnishes: ½ cup diced smoked ham, ½ cup chopped scal-
lions, 1 cup fried noodles

Put chicken broth into a large saucepan. Bring to a boil. Add chicken, cabbage, winter melon, water chestnuts, and monosodium glutamate. Reduce heat and cook slowly, covered, 30 minutes. Add cornstarch, dissolved in cold water, and mix well. Cook several seconds, stirring, until thickened. Serve sprinkled with garnishes. Serves 4 to 6.

A Novelist's Beef Soup
The following "recipe" is from *Famous Recipes by Famous People,* compiled and edited by Herbert Cerwin.

How To Write A Novel
Louis Bromfield, Novelist

"Boil three pounds of good beef as well as four or five pieces of shin bone for at least twelve hours in an iron pot. Add one dozen young carrots, one-half pound of beans, two bunches of celery chopped moderately fine, parsley, sage, pepper, salt, one dozen medium sized potatoes, one dozen yellow onions, one clove of garlic, three tomatoes (in fact the more vegetables the merrier). Serve the meat cold with mustard and the soup hot.
Then let it rain."

Swedish Rose Hip Soup

In Sweden a soup called *nyponsoppa*, rose hip soup, is a cherished national dish and is made in the home or sold in cans and packages. Rose hips are the fleshy swollen red seed capsules of any of the various kinds of roses, but especially those of wild roses, which are very rich in vitamin C and eaten as a health food. Rose hips may vary in size from tiny to large; the larger ones are more tasty. They can be gathered in the autumn as soon as they turn bright red and are sold dried whole, cut, or powdered. Scandinavians make flavorful rose hip soups that are served hot or cold, often garnished with shredded almonds and whipped cream. Some are flavored with wine or a liqueur. This is one favorite recipe for the soup.

> *2 cups fresh rose hips, cleaned*
> *Water*
> *½ cup sugar*
> *1 tablespoon cornstarch*

Put rose hips and 4 cups of cold water into a large saucepan. Bring to a boil. Reduce heat and cook slowly, covered, 30 minutes, or until rose hips are tender. Strain to remove seeds and skins. Add enough water to make 4 cups. Add sugar and cornstarch, mixed with a little cold water. Return to heat and bring slowly to a boil, stirring constantly. Cook, stirring, until thickened and smooth. Serve garnished with almonds and whipped cream, if desired. Serves 4.

New Zealand Toheroa Soup

In New Zealand a traditional soup is made with a rare shellfish called a *toheroa*, which must be dug by hand with considerable skill from the sands of the country's North Island and South Island beaches. The toheroa season is short and the catch is limited. Canned toheroas are sold in many American specialty food stores. If they are not available, clams may be substituted.

> 2 *tablespoons all-purpose flour*
> 2 *tablespoons butter or margarine, melted*
> 4 *cups fish broth*
> 2 *cups hot milk*
> 2 *cups minced toheroas or clams*
> *Few grains grated nutmeg*
> *Salt, pepper to taste*
> *Juice of ½ lemon*
> *Whipped cream (optional)*

Combine flour and melted butter or margarine in a large saucepan and cook slowly 2 minutes. Gradually add fish broth and cook slowly, stirring, until thickened and smooth. Add hot milk, toheroas or clams, and nutmeg. Season with salt and pepper. Cook about 5 minutes. Add lemon juice. Serve garnished with a little whipped cream, if desired. Serves 4 to 6.

Japanese Steamed Egg Soup

A steamed egg dish, similar to a custard, called *chawanmushi*, is served as a soup or as one of the main courses of a Japanese dinner. This is a traditional recipe for the soup.

> 3 *eggs*
> 2 *cups* dashi*
> 5 *teaspoons soy sauce*
> ½ *teaspoon monosodium glutamate*
> 8 *bite-size pieces of cooked white chicken*

4 small shrimp, cooked, deveined, and shelled
4 small mushroom caps
4 small strips canned bamboo shoots

Beat eggs in a medium-sized bowl. Add *dashi* and 4 teaspoons soy sauce. Put through a strainer into another bowl. Add monosodium glutamate. Combine chicken, shrimp, mushroom caps, and bamboo shoots with remaining 1 teaspoon soy sauce in a bowl and mix well. Put into 4 Japanese-style soup bowls or custard cups, dividing evenly. Pour strained egg mixture into bowls. Set bowls in a fireproof dish of simmering water and cover custard cups with foil if Japanese soup bowls are not used. Steam over simmering water on medium heat 10 to 15 minutes, until custard is set. Serve warm in bowls. Serves 4.
*See recipe on page 60.

Italian Squid Soup

Delicious thick soups are made with squid, octopus, or cuttlefish, saltwater mollusks that are similar but differ slightly, in several Mediterranean countries, especially Greece, Italy, Spain, and southern France. Squid has a tender sweet flesh that is highly prized for many dishes, including a variety of soups. It must be tenderized, skinned, and cleaned, and the tentacles cut into rings before cooking. For some soups the "ink" taken from the thin sac or bag of the mollusk imparts a characteristic dark appearance. This Italian creation includes red wine and herbs.

1 large onion, peeled and chopped
2 cloves garlic, crushed
1/3 cup olive oil
1 medium-sized squid, about 2 pounds, cleaned and cut
  into small rings

2 large tomatoes, peeled and chopped
1 teaspoon dried oregano or basil
2 tablespoons chopped fresh parsley
Salt, pepper to taste
2 cups dry red wine
4 cups water

Sauté onion and garlic in heated oil in a kettle until tender. Add squid rings and fry 5 minutes. Add tomatoes, oregano or basil, and parsley. Season with salt and pepper. Cook 5 minutes. Add wine and water and bring to a boil. Reduce heat and simmer, covered, about 25 minutes, until the squid is tender. Serve over slices of crusty white bread previously fried in hot olive oil, if desired. Serves 6.

Irish Nettle Soup

Nettles, a number of related weeds with stinging hairs that have to be picked and prepared with gloves on, are highly prized in Ireland and Scotland, where they are eaten as a green, either plain or topped with poached eggs, or used to flavor potato and oatmeal dishes and beer, and to make soups. Nettles, which have a spinachlike flavor, are rich in iron and vitamins. In the spring, when nettles are young and tender, the Irish and Scots traditionally drink quantities of nettle broth to insure good health the rest of the year. Nettles grow wild in America and must be washed thoroughly before using. This recipe is for a typical Irish nettle soup.

1 medium-sized onion, peeled and chopped
2 tablespoons butter or margarine
2 tablespoons oatmeal
6 cups vegetable or chicken broth
2 cups chopped clean nettles

Salt, pepper to taste
½ cup cream

Sauté onion in heated butter or margarine in a large saucepan until tender. Add oatmeal and fry until crisp and brown. Add broth and bring to a boil. Reduce heat and add nettles. Season with salt and pepper. Cook slowly, covered, about 30 minutes. Add cream. Serves 4 to 6.

Turtle Soup

Prized by gourmets, turtle soup has long been served at special dinners and on royal tables. It is universally regarded as the unrivaled King of Soups, and it is generally believed that Lewis Carroll's "Beautiful Soup, so rich and green, Waiting in a hot tureen" is the finest and richest soup that has ever been created.

Turtles are the descendants of prehistoric sea reptiles. Tortoises are turtles that live on land or in fresh water, and terrapins exist in brackish or fresh water. Of the sea turtles, the most famous is the edible green turtle, noted for its fine flavor and gelatinous meat.

Culinary creations, including soups, made with turtles have been more popular in America than in Europe. The exception is England, where turtle soup has long been regarded as a delicacy and is still served as the first course at traditional banquets.

Because of its intricate preparation and expense, turtle soup is not made in English homes. An ancient recipe begins "Take a turtle weighing about 50 pounds." But the soups made in London today require three 140-pound turtles, imported from the West Indies, to make some fifty gallons of soup such as are required for a large gathering like the Lord Mayor's traditional banquet for a thousand or more guests. Also needed are vast amounts of rich stock and a considerable quantity of sherry and sweet white wine.

In early America the tedious task of making turtle soup apparently did not phase housewives. All cookbooks of the 1800s gave lengthy instructions for this "king of soups." A typical recipe began, "Kill it at night in winter, and in the morning in summer. Hang it by the hind fins." Then directions were given for dressing, cutting, and shelling turtles. Soups were made with the meat, innards, and shell boiled in water with bacon, onions, and salt, and the flesh was combined with wine, catsup, lemon pickle, mace, nutmegs, cloves, thyme, parsley, marjoram, and savory, and thickened with flour and butter.

Green turtle meat is very lean and has a flavor something like veal, which is why popular soups of the 1800s, called mock turtle, were usually made with calf's heads.

In Philadelphia a favorite specialty has long been snapper soup made with the snapping turtle, a large freshwater species native to North America. Another turtle prized for its flesh for soups was the diamondback terrapin, which is now rare and generally is raised only at commercial breeding stations.

Green sea turtles are threatened with extinction and are on the endangered species list. Their sale in the United States has been banned for some time. Our turtle meat now comes from the Grand Cayman Islands.

Canned green turtle soup is an excellent substitute for the fresh variety, and while expensive it is top quality. Depending on the brand, clear turtle soup may either be condensed and require diluting, or be ready to serve. Allow at least one cup per serving and prepare according to label directions, adding a scant tablespoon of Madeira wine or dry sherry and a slice of lemon, if desired, to each serving. Canned thick turtle soup including the meat is also available. In New Orleans a rich Creole turtle soup that is dark brown and very thick and flavored with sherry is a restaurant specialty. It may be garnished with lemon slices and chopped hard-cooked egg or with small yellow turtle eggs.

Scottish Cullen Skink

This interesting soup is made with smoked haddock, a Scottish favorite that is popularly called by a corruption of the name, finnan haddie. *Skink* is an old Gaelic word that originally meant "essence" but is now used for a soup-stew. The soup is nutritious and hearty, enriched with milk, butter, and mashed potatoes.

1 finnan haddie, whole or fillets, about 2 pounds
Boiling water
1 medium-sized onion, peeled and chopped
3 to 4 cups hot milk
About 1 cup mashed potatoes
2 tablespoons butter or margarine
Salt, pepper to taste

Cover finnan haddie with boiling water in a large saucepan. Simmer 5 minutes. Take from kettle and remove skin. Return to pan. Bring liquid to a boil. Add onion. Reduce heat and cook slowly, covered, about 10 minutes, until the fish flakes. Take from kettle again and remove all bones. Flake the fish and set aside. Return bones to saucepan and simmer 20 minutes. Strain liquid. Put liquid in saucepan and bring just to a boil. Reduce heat and add fish and milk. Add potatoes, enough to make a creamy mixture. Add butter and season with salt and pepper. Serve at once. Serves 4.

Beer Soups

Soups made with light or dark beer or ale have long been popular in northern Europe, where they are prepared in several variations. They may be clear or creamy, hot or cold, and may be flavored with eggs, cream, lemon juice, sugar, sour cream, raisins, butter, or spices. Some of the soups include slices or cubes of pumpernickel or rye bread. The Danes are devotees of a beer-bread soup, called *øllebrød*, to which milk is added to produce lumpy curds. The English drink a spiced ale soup that includes vegetables. Beer soups are not to everyone's taste, but there are many who like them. The two beer soup recipes below are excellent.

German Beer Soup

> 2 cans (12 ounces each) beer
> 1 tablespoon fresh lemon juice
> 2 teaspoons sugar
> 1 small stick cinnamon
> 1 or 2 whole cloves
> 1 or 2 teaspoons cornstarch

Put beer, lemon juice, sugar, cinnamon, and cloves into a large saucepan and bring to a boil. Moisten cornstarch with a little cold water and add to soup. Cook slowly, stirring, 3 or 4 minutes. Remove and discard cinnamon and cloves. Serves 4.

Belgian Beer Soup

> 1 tablespoon all-purpose flour
> 1 quart beer
> 1 tablespoon sugar
> Pinch each of ground cinnamon and ginger
> Salt, pepper to taste
> 3 tablespoons heavy cream
> Toasted cubes of French bread

Mix flour with a little beer until smooth. Set aside. Combine remaining beer, sugar, cinnamon, ginger, salt, and pepper in a saucepan and bring to a boil. Reduce heat and add flour mixed with the beer. Cook slowly, uncovered, 5 minutes. Remove from heat and stir in cream. Serve over bread cubes. Serves 4.

Australian Kangaroo Tail Soup

In Australia a delectable rich and heavy soup made with kangaroo tail is regarded as a delicacy. The tail meat, not available except in Australia and Tasmania, is cut into joints, cooked with onions, carrots, celery, turnips, stock, spices, and herbs and then flavored with sherry or claret. In America the soup is sold in cans in specialty food stores. Given below is an amusing recipe for the soup which appeared in a spiral-bound cookbook called *Fabulous International Specialties,* compiled by the Frankfurt International School in Germany.

Kangaroo Tail Soup (A Popular Australian Family Diet)
1. Call and catch a medium-sized kangaroo.
2. Ride him home, tie him down, and shake his paw until he dies of strangulation.
3. Quickly skin him, hang his hide on the shed (and save for winter coat trimmings).
4. The tail may be cut, chopped, or broken into six pieces and thrown into a pot of boiling gum leaves.
5. Boil intensely for 12 to 24 hours, stirring continuously.
6. Just before serving add 5 to 6 handfuls of emu egg noodles. Save the remainder of the meat, either smoked or salted, for snacks and for serving on toast as a main breakfast dish. This soup serves a family for the whole winter but it can be skimmed and chilled as a summer appetizer and served with sour cream, gherkins, and chopped mint.

Japanese Soybean Paste Soup

A traditional Japanese clear soup, called *misoshiru*, is flavored with *miso*, a pungent salty paste made from fermented soy beans. The paste may be white or red; the white is sweeter than the red. *Miso* is sold in Japanese markets and may vary in strength or pungency. This soup is handsomely garnished with several foods such as dried seaweed or fish, soybean curd, small meatballs, seafood, sliced mushrooms, scallions, or white radishes.

> *6 cups* dashi*
> *1/3 to ½ cup red or white* miso
> *Garnishes: 2 scallions with some tops, sliced; 2 mushroom caps, sliced; 6 small cubes* tofu *(soybean curd); 6 paper-thin carrot slices*

Bring *dashi* to a boil. Press *miso* through a sieve into *dashi* and mix well. Divide garnishes between six individual soup bowls. Pour in soup. Serve at once. Pick out garnishes with chopsticks and drink soup from the bowl. Serves 6.
*See recipe on page 55.

Garlic Soups

Some of the world's oldest soups are made with a base of garlic, a hardy bulbous plant of the lily family, which also includes onions and leeks. Garlic has been cultivated for thousands of years in Mediterranean countries, where it has long been eaten in considerable quantity and regarded as a health food. Characteristic garlic soups of Spain, southern France, and Italy are made in great variety and relished not only to satisfy hunger but to cure any number of ailments. The soup may be a simple one based on several crushed or minced garlic cloves and bread browned in olive oil and cooked in water. Often the broth is ladled over toasted crusty bread which has been soaked in olive oil, sprinkled with grated cheese, toasted, and topped with a poached egg. Some garlic soups also include sausage or other meats, seafood, poultry, vegetables, herbs, spices, nuts, or cheese. Garlic soups have a special appeal in that the garlic loses its harsh potency during cooking and imparts a pleasing delicate flavor to the liquid. This garlic soup is from Spain, where it is served traditionally in small earthenware bowls and eaten with wooden spoons. Similar soups are prepared in several Central and South American countries.

¼ *cup olive oil*
3 *tablespoons minced garlic*
4 *slices bread, crusts removed and crumbled*
Salt, pepper to taste
¼ *teaspoon cayenne pepper*
4 *cups beef bouillon*
2 *tablespoons chopped fresh parsley*
2 *eggs, lightly beaten*

Heat oil in a heavy saucepan. Add garlic and fry gently for several minutes, being careful not to brown. Add bread and fry until golden. Stir in salt, pepper, and cayenne. Add bouillon and bring to a boil. Mix well. Reduce heat and cook slowly, covered, 15 minutes. Stir in parsley. Pour in eggs. Simmer, stirring 1 or 2 minutes, until eggs are set. Serves 4.

Vermont Cider Soups

Cider, apple juice that may be "sweet" or "hard," unfermented or fermented, has long been a treasured traditional drink in northern France and England. Early New Englanders prepared and consumed great quantities of cider and used it in their cookery. In *The American Cider Book* by Vrest Orton, who operates The Vermont Country Stores, the author writes that stock called for in soup may be replaced with the same amount of cider and suggests that this works best for pea and onion soup. Here are two recipes from his book.

Cider Apple Soup

3 cups water
½ cup brown sugar
Salt
About 6 winter apples
1 cinnamon stick
1 lemon
½ cup bread crumbs
2 cups hard cider
4 tablespoons lemon juice
3 tablespoons apple jelly
Cinnamon or nutmeg

Put water, sugar, and a pinch of salt into a pan and cook to boiling point. Add apples, which have been peeled, cored, and sliced, and cinnamon stick, sliced rind of the lemon, and bread crumbs. Let cook until apples are tender. Then remove cinnamon stick and lemon rind, and strain. Turn the strained mixture into a saucepan. Add cider, and 4 tablespoons lemon juice, and jelly. Let simmer until it is all dissolved. Serve with some grated cinnamon or nutmeg on top. Can be served hot or cold. Serves 4 to 6.

Herb Cider Soup

1 *cup water*
2 *tablespoons flour*
3 *cups sweet cider*
½ *teaspoon basil*
1 *cinnamon stick*
2 *cups scalded milk*
2 *beaten egg yolks*
1 *teaspoon sugar and salt*

Make a smooth mixture of water and flour. Pour this slowly into the cider, which has been made to boil. Stir fast, then add basil and cinnamon stick and cook 8 minutes. Remove cinnamon stick. Add hot milk, but do not boil this mixture. Pour all this into a dish which has the beaten egg yolks in it, and add sugar and a pinch of salt. Serves 4 to 6.

Milk Soups

From earliest times simple soups have been prepared with various kinds of milk; milk by-products such as sweet cream, sour cream, yogurt, and buttermilk; and milk liquids like coconut milk and so-called milks made from nuts. These soups were usually made by combining the hot or cold liquid with some form of bread, cooked pasta, grains or cereals, or fruits. Russians make a sweetened milk soup with vermicelli, rice, or noodles, and butter and sugar, to which dried fruit is sometimes added. The French prepare a milk soup flavored with onions, celery, rice, and herbs. English milk soups usually have been thickened with almonds, arrowroot, or oats. Early American cookbooks often suggested that milk soups be served to invalids and to children, and to other folks late at night before retiring. Most of the old-fashioned American favorites were sweetened with sugar and flavored with butter, spices, or nuts. One, called Five Minute Soup, was made with crumbled biscuits fried in butter, covered with hot milk, and seasoned with salt and pepper. This is a typical milk soup recipe.

Milk-Bread Soup

1 cup coarsely chopped stale bread
3 tablespoons butter or margarine
6 cups milk
1 tablespoon sugar
Few grains ground nutmeg
6 slices white bread, toasted

Fry bread in melted butter or margarine in a large saucepan until golden. Add milk, sugar, and nutmeg. Leave on the stove long enough to heat and blend flavors, about 10 minutes. Serve in soup plates over slices of toasted bread. Serves 6.

Wine Soups

In Europe and America it has long been customary to flavor some soups with fortified dry or sweet wines just before they are served. A variety of good soups are made with wines, too. Eastern Europeans prepare highly-seasoned fruit and red wine soups. The Swiss are fond of an apple, raisin, and red wine soup. Scandinavians like cold wine-flavored fruit and berry soups and hot, spicy wine soups. In Germany, stimulating sweet-wine soups are favorite party specialties. The French enjoy both red and white wine soups. In America wine soups have been prepared frequently in the Midwest and Northwest as well as in California with local wines. This is a typical recipe for a wine soup you may like.

Red Wine Soup

2 cups beef bouillon
2 tablespoons sugar
1 teaspoon ground allspice
2 cups dry red wine

Bring bouillon to a boil. Add sugar and allspice. Cook slowly, covered, 15 minutes. Add wine and cook 1 or 2 minutes. Serves 4.

Bread and Grain Soups

While soups featuring bread or grains can hardly be called exotic, they are rare today since few of them appear in modern cookbooks and menus. Yet there are many variations of these ancient basic dishes that are well worth remembering. The soups are interesting and delectable.

In France a soup of bread and broth became known as a *panade*. It was generally a homely dish of stock or water, or perhaps another liquid, thickened with stale slices or cubes of firm crusty white bread, to which butter, salt, pepper, and a beaten or whole egg might be added.

Old recipes for a *panade*, called bread *rustique*, bread and butter *rustique*, or *soupe rustique*, sometimes also included other ingredients such as onions, leeks, garlic, or carrots and flavorings like cream, wine, herbs, or spices. The *panade* could be cooked on top of the stove or baked.

Elsewhere in Europe there are traditional preparations similar to the *panade*. In Spain, for example, the soup is well-seasoned with garlic. The Austrians and Germans make the soup with pumpernickel or rye bread and broth or beer to which onions or fruit are added. In Switzerland a traditional supper dish is made with alternate layers of bread and cheese, topped with cooked onions and bouillon, and then baked.

The Italians prepare some of the best bread soups. *Zuppa di fontina* is a baked dish of layered bread and fontina cheese covered with stock. Paradise Soup or *millefanti* is a traditional bread soup made from bread crumbs, grated parmesan cheese, nutmeg, and eggs beaten into stock. Others are well-seasoned with garlic, herbs, tomatoes, and/or cheese, while an elaborate version includes bread rounds filled with ham and chicken.

Early American cooks made many innovative bread soups. One recipe for a *panade* included split whole crackers sprinkled with powdered sugar and grated nutmeg, which were covered with boiling water and more sugar. Some soups were prepared with left-over coffee-cake crumbs, fried bread cubes, and milk or water, or heated broth, into which small pieces or lumps of dough or scraps of leftover bread were dropped.

Grain soups have long been popular in the Middle East and Europe. Armenians still prepare a traditional holiday dish with cracked wheat, nuts, raisins, and sugar cooked in broth. In Turkey there are well-seasoned farina and flour soups. Scandinavians prepare several soups that are similar to porridges but served at the beginning of the meal and include rice, oats, or sago flavored with fruit juices, raisins, and perhaps nuts. Oatmeal soups are described below.

Here are some recipes for bread and grain soups.

German Pumpernickel Soup

The Germans make several variations of *Brotsuppe,* bread soup, that is made with pumpernickel or rye bread simmered in broth. This is one delectable version.

6 *slices stale pumpernickel, broken into cubes*
8 *cups hot beef bouillon*
1 *medium-sized onion, peeled and chopped*
2 *tablespoons butter or margarine*
Salt, pepper to taste
2 *tablespoons chopped fresh parsley*
½ *cup sour cream, at room temperature (optional)*
Paprika

Cover bread cubes with some of the hot bouillon in a large bowl and let stand until soft, about 10 minutes. Meanwhile, sauté onion in melted butter or margarine in a large saucepan until tender. Add bread cube-bouillon mixture and remaining bouillon. Season with salt and pepper. Simmer, covered, 25 minutes. Add parsley. Serve garnished with sour cream and paprika, if desired. Serves 6.

Italian Bread-Tomato Soup

3 *cloves garlic, crushed*
1/3 *cup olive oil*
4 *medium-sized tomatoes, peeled and chopped*
6 *cups beef stock or chicken broth*
1 *bay leaf*
⅛ *teaspoon ground red pepper*
Salt, pepper to taste
6 *thick slices crusty white bread, toasted*
About 1/3 cup grated Parmesan cheese

Sauté garlic in heated oil in a large saucepan until tender. Add tomatoes and sauté about 5 minutes. Add stock or broth, bay leaf, red pepper, salt, and pepper. Bring to a boil. Reduce heat and cook slowly, covered, 25 minutes. Remove and discard bay leaf. Serve soup over toast sprinkled with cheese in individual soup bowls. Serves 6.

French Panade

2 large onions, peeled and sliced
1/3 cup butter or margarine
8 cups rich beef bouillon
6 thick slices stale firm white bread, torn into pieces
Salt, pepper to taste
1/3 cup grated Swiss or yellow cheese

Sauté onions in melted butter or margarine in a large saucepan until tender. Add bouillon and bring to a boil. Add bread pieces. Season with salt and pepper. Reduce heat and cook slowly, covered, 20 minutes. Stir in cheese and cook about 10 minutes longer. Serves 4 to 6.

Oatmeal Soups

Various kinds of soup made with oatmeal (ground or rolled oats from which the husks have been removed, regular, rather than quick-cooking) have long been staple dishes in several European countries. The Swiss, for example, make the soup with oatmeal, water, potatoes, and grated cheese. In Belgium it is a simple preparation of oatmeal and buttermilk. The Irish are devotees of soups made with oatmeal and leeks or oatmeal and nettles. In Wales there is an oatmeal-milk soup, as well as a hearty beef-vegetable soup which includes oatmeal. In Scotland oatmeal soups are extremely popular. A basic crowdie, or soup, is made with stock and oatmeal and sometimes flavorings and served with potatoes. Oatmeal is added to a traditional kale soup and is the basis of the following creamy soup.

1 medium-sized onion, peeled and chopped
2 tablespoons butter or margarine
¼ cup oatmeal
2 cups chicken broth
Salt, pepper to taste
1½ cups milk
½ cup cream
3 tablespoons chopped fresh parsley

Sauté onion in heated butter or margarine in a large saucepan. Add oatmeal and cook 1 or 2 minutes. Add chicken broth and bring to a boil. Season with salt and pepper. Reduce heat and cook slowly, covered, 30 minutes. Strain mixture. Return liquid to pan. Add milk and cream. Heat. Serve garnished with parsley. Serves 4.

Amana Brown Flour Soup

½ cup all-purpose flour
1/3 cup butter or margarine
6 cups beef bouillon
Salt, pepper to taste
3 tablespoons chopped fresh parsley
1/3 cup grated Parmesan cheese

Mix flour with melted butter or margarine in a large saucepan and cook briskly until golden. Add bouillon, salt, and pepper. Bring to a boil. Cook slowly, covered, 30 minutes. Add parsley. Serve sprinkled with cheese over toast slices, if desired. Serves 6.

Swiss Flour Soup

A popular soup in Switzerland, and in some regions of Austria and Germany, is based on flour and butter and seasoned variously. The soup, called *Mehlsuppe*, is enjoyed by the Swiss as a carnival specialty, particularly in Basel, where crowds celebrate at an early morning parade by merrymaking and drinking the soup to sustain them.

> 5 *tablespoons butter*
> 5 *tablespoons all-purpose flour*
> 6 *cups hot beef bouillon*
> 1 *medium-sized onion stuck with 4 whole cloves*
> 1 *bay leaf*
> *Salt to taste*
> 1½ *cups stale bread croutons*
> ½ *cup grated Swiss cheese*

Melt butter in a heavy saucepan. Stir in flour and cook over medium heat, stirring, until mixture is smooth and deep brown. Be careful not to burn. Remove from stove and add hot bouillon, stirring until smooth. Add onion with cloves, bay leaf, and salt. Return to stove and cook over very low heat for 30 minutes, or until thickened and smooth. Stir occasionally. Remove and discard onion and bay leaf. Serve with croutons on top and sprinkle with cheese. Serves 6.

Soup Garnishes

Edible decorations, which provide complementary color, flavor, and texture contrast for soups, add a great deal to their attractiveness and taste. An incredible number of foods may serve as garnishes. Some may be added to the soup shortly before serving or cooked in the soup for several minutes.

When choosing a garnish you should consider both the basic taste of the soup and how the garnish will be displayed. While some garnishes, such as chopped herbs, provide zestful flavor and are decorative, others, such as dumplings, are more substantial additions. The garnish should enhance the soup and harmonize with the flavor of the ingredients and the color of the soup.

As previously mentioned, garnishes are most important additions to clear soups. Many consommés are named for their garnishes. You can decorate such soups simply with thin lemon slices, julienne strips of vegetables, elaborate pastries, or pretty egg custards.

Cream soups may be garnished with foods that match those in

285

the soup, such as whole green peas for pea soup or sliced mushrooms for mushroom soup. Other good garnishes are dollops of lightly-salted whipped cream or sour cream, toasted nuts, golden croutons, or a chiffonade of slivered greens.

Thick soups can be embellished with crisp cooked bacon, croutons, noodles, or more substantial "extenders" such as sliced frankfurters, meatballs, or dumplings. Cold soups should be garnished with chilled foods such as chopped chives or dill, fruit slices, whole berries, or spoonfuls of cream.

A number of garnishes are traditional with certain national and regional soups. Those of the Mediterranean feature balls made with meats or grains, breads, pastries, and flavored yogurt.

European garnishes include many kinds of dumplings, pancake strips, plain or cheese puffs, filled pastries, carved vegetables, and whipped cream ornaments. Especially important are three French creations: *profiteroles*, plain or cheese-filled pastry balls; *quenelles*, fine fish or meat dumplings in various shapes; and *fleurons*, thinly-rolled scraps of puff pastry, shaped into ovals or crescents and baked or fried.

Some of the most attractive and innovative soup garnishes have been devised by Oriental cooks, who make elaborate decorations with unusual foods, including flower petals and roots, seafood, and many kinds of vegetables and herbs.

While American restaurant soups may be embellished with French classical garnishes or other elaborate adornments, most homemade soups are decorated simply with breads or crackers, eggs, chopped herbs, vegetable strips, dumplings, drop biscuits, or grated cheese.

Southerners add hard-cooked eggs and a lemon slice to black bean soup, serve fish soups with hush puppies, and add dumplings to chicken soup. New Englanders are partial to crackers as garnishes, while the Pennsylvania Dutch favor popcorn, pretzels, browned bread squares, and rivels (shredded dough). In the Southwest soups are often topped with crisp fried tortillas.

Here are some useful suggestions and recipes for soup garnishes. Recipes for *Spaetzle,* matzo balls, and pinched noodles appear earlier in the book.

Bread Garnishes

Bread is one of the world's oldest and best soup garnishes; it can be served in many forms in or over soups. You'll obtain better results if you use breads that are flavorful and firm, breads such as crusty white French or Italian, rye, whole-wheat, or pumpernickel. These general directions will help you prepare some of the best bread garnishes to add substance, flavor, and color to your soups.

Cheese sticks: Remove crusts from bread slices and butter one side. Cut each slice into four strips and spread each buttered side with a thick coating of grated Parmesan or yellow cheese. Toast under heated broiler. (Cheese rounds can be made in the same way.)

Cracker crumb balls: Combine 1 egg, a few grains of salt, pepper, and 1 to 2 tablespoons cracker crumbs to make a stiff dough. Shape into ½-inch balls and roll lightly in flour. Drop into rapidly boiling broth or soup and cook about 10 minutes.

Croutons: Cut stale bread into slices, 1/3- to ½-inch thick, or use sliced firm bread. Remove crusts. Spread with butter or margarine on both sides, cut into ¼-inch cubes. Brown in preheated 350° oven about 6 minutes until golden or sauté in heated butter, margarine, or oil, stirring, until golden on all sides. The length of time needed depends on the type of bread used. Drain on absorbent paper and add to soup while hot. Variations are:

Cheese: Sprinkle cubes with grated Parmesan before browning.

Curry: Add a little curry powder to butter, margarine, or oil before sautéing.

Garlic: Add ½ crushed or minced garlic clove to heated oil before sautéing.

Herb: Sprinkle cubes with dried basil, marjoram, oregano, sage, or thyme before sautéing.

Diablotins: These French garnishes for clear or thick soups are made with toasted round slices of French bread, about ¼-inch thick, which are spread with vegetable purée and sprinkled with grated cheese or thick cheese-flavored white sauce and browned under a broiler. They are served especially in fish soups or chowders.

Garlic toast: Brush French or Italian bread slices with garlic-seasoned olive or vegetable oil. Sprinkle with grated Parmesan cheese. Toast under broiler.

Parmesan Melba toast: Cut stale white or dark bread into very thin slices. Remove crusts. Put bread into a preheated 250° oven and leave until crisp and golden and all moisture is gone from bread. Spread with butter or margarine and grated Parmesan cheese and toast under broiler.

Poppy-seed bread sticks: Remove crusts from white bread slices and brush both sides with melted butter or margarine. Cut each slice into four strips and roll in poppy seeds. Bake in a preheated 350° oven about 10 minutes, until golden.

Pulled bread: Remove crusts from a loaf of French bread; tear bread into strips; bake in a preheated 250° oven until golden and crisp.

Egg Garnishes

There are several good and easy-to-prepare egg garnishes, which are used primarily for clear soups. The eggs should be cooked briefly (except for the hard-cooked) at low temperatures so they do not become tough and rubbery. Below are directions for making several of the egg garnishes.

Egg Balls

> 2 *hard-cooked eggs, sieved or minced*
> 1 *egg yolk*
> 1 *tablespoon fine dry bread crumbs*
> *Dash salt, pepper, and cayenne*
> *All-purpose flour*
> 2 *tablespoons butter or margarine*

Combine hard-cooked eggs, egg yolk, bread crumbs, salt, pepper, and cayenne. Shape into ½-inch balls and roll lightly in flour. Cook gently in heated butter or margarine until golden on all sides. Drain on absorbent paper and garnish with chopped parsley or dill, if desired. Add several to each serving of soup.

Egg drops or flakes

1 egg
2 tablespoons all-purpose flour
Salt

Break egg into a small bowl. Add flour and salt. Beat until smooth. Turn into a strainer or colander over a pot of hot broth or soup and let mixture drop into soup and cook about 3 minutes. For 2 or 3 cups soup.

Threaded eggs

1 egg
Salt, pepper

Break egg into a small bowl. Season with salt and pepper. Beat until light and creamy. Pour slowly in a fine stream into hot broth or soup, stirring constantly, until egg forms fine shreds. For 2 or 3 cups soup.

Poached eggs

Break 1 cold egg into a saucer. Slide gently into a skillet containing 1¼ inches simmering lightly-salted water. Poach egg 1 or 2 minutes, until the white is firm. If egg "sticks" to bottom of skillet, lift carefully with a spoon. Remove with a perforated spoon and trim edges to make an oval egg, if desired. Add to a bowl of hot broth or soup, allowing 1 egg per bowl.

Royal custard

A French garnish with eggs made into a kind of unsweetened custard, which can be of various colors and cut in plain or fancy shapes, is a traditional addition to consommés or other clear soups. You can make these garnishes with a base of eggs and broth and add puréed vegetables, seafood, liver, or mushrooms, if desired. Three well-known French versions are: *Royale Crécy* (made with a purée of carrots and orange in color), *Royale Vert-Pré* (made with a purée of green vegetables and herbs and green in color), and *Royale à l'écarlate* (made with a lobster purée and red in color). This is a basic recipe for royal custard.

> 2 *egg yolks*
> 1 *egg*
> ½ *cup beef stock*
> ⅛ *teaspoon salt*
> *Dash pepper*
> *Few grains cayenne or nutmeg*

Beat egg yolks and egg in a small bowl. Add stock, salt, pepper, and cayenne or nutmeg. Pour into a shallow pan or dish so mixture is about ½-inch deep. Set pan or dish in a pan of hot water. Bake in a preheated 325° oven until custard is set, about 20 minutes. Be sure custard does not form a brown crust on top. Remove from oven and cool. Cut into small cubes or fancy shapes. Carefully add a few or several to a clear soup and leave just long enough to heat through.

Note: You can add 1/3 cup vegetable purée and an extra egg yolk to the above mixture, if desired.

Herb Garnishes

Fresh herbs are the simplest of all soup garnishes. They add color and flavor to all soups but are especially desirable in clear soups.

Herb garnishes should be selected to complement ingredients and color, but must be used with discretion, generally in small quantities.

Suggestions include: basil (bean, pea, potato, spinach, and especially tomato soups), chives (cold and cream soups), dill (bean, borsch, split-pea, and tomato soups), fennel (fish soups), mint (bean and pea soups), savory (bean, lentil, and vegetable soups), and tarragon (chicken, mushroom, tomato, and turtle soups).

Vegetable Garnishes

You can make colorful and nutritious garnishes with raw or cooked vegetables, including greens, which may be used singly or in combination.

While most vegetables for garnishes are chopped, cut into thin slices, julienne-style strips, or fancy shapes, small ones such as green peas, small mushroom caps, or asparagus tips, can be left whole. Broccoli or cauliflower can be divided into small florets.

You may prepare the vegetables in any fashion as long as they complement the soup in which they will be served and are decorative.

Here are some suggestions for good vegetable garnishes.

Raw vegetables: Grated carrots or paper-thin carrot slices, diced green peppers, sliced or chopped mushrooms, minced scallions, paper-thin radish slices, shredded or chopped spinach, peeled, seeded, and diced tomatoes, and watercress sprigs.

Cooked vegetables: Green beans cut crosswise into small sections; strips of Brussels sprouts; thin slices of celery root, carrots, and turnips; cheese-flavored celery slices; parsley covered cucumber slices; lemony sautéed sliced mushrooms; strips of leeks; and chopped or shredded zucchini.

Brunoise: Chop an assortment of vegetables such as green beans, celery, carrots, onions, leeks, turnips, or mushrooms into tiny squares and simmer in heated butter until tender. Add 2 or 3 tablespoons for each quart of soup.

Chiffonade: Cut greens or leafy vegetables such as spinach, sorrel, or lettuce into fine shreds and mix with herbs, if desired. Cook briefly in butter or stock and add to soup.

Pasta Garnishes

Pasta lends itself artistically and gastronomically to a far greater variety of international soups then you might expect. There are so many pastas available today that you can enhance the appearance, flavor, and nutritional value of virtually any soup.

Use either commercial or homemade pastas. Of the former, which vary greatly in size and shape, the most familiar are versions of macaroni, spaghetti or noodles—alphabets, pastina, elbows, spaghettini, vermicelli, egg flakes, fine egg noodles, small seashells, and ditalini.

Italian grocers usually have a representative selection of more fanciful forms with intriguing names such as cockscombs; tiny rings, seeds, stars, snails, wheels, hats; the eyes of wolves, sparrows, trout; melon, apple, rosemary seeds; butterflies; clover-leaves; tiny umbrellas; or baby chicks.

The tiny pastas are best adapted to such soups as consommés and bouillons, but they and other small or thin varieties of pasta, such as those mentioned above, may be added to thicker soups. In the Orient soup noodles are long, generally translucent or cellophane varieties, or those made of wheat, which are similar to vermicelli.

Homemade pasta for soup is generally made with egg dough. Some are flat pastas, which add nourishment to thick meat and vegetable soups, but the best known are filled doughs such as the Chinese *won-ton*, Jewish *kreplach*, Central European noodle squares, Russian *pelmeny*, and Italian *cappelletti* and *tortellini*. Customarily these delectable forms of pasta, when served in soups, are simply cooked in broth or bouillon, where they are best displayed.

Try some of these superior pasta recipes.

Basic Egg Pasta

Basic fresh egg-pasta called *pasta fresca all'uovo* in Italy and by various different names in other countries, is used to make a number of types of noodles and other dishes by cutting the sheet of dough into contrasting shapes. The simplest of the Italian repertoire is *tagliatelle*, a name derived from *tagliare*, meaning "to cut." Thus there are several noodles with names beginning with *taglia*, all of the same "family," which differ only in their width.

> 3 *cups semolina or all-purpose white flour*
> 3 *large eggs at room temperature*
> ¾ *teaspoon salt*
> 2 *teaspoons olive or salad oil (optional)*
> *Lukewarm water*

Sift flour into a large bowl or onto a wooden or marble surface to form a mound. Make a well or depression in the center, and carefully break eggs into it. Add salt and oil. Working with tips of the fingers, mix flour with other ingredients to combine well. Add water, a little at a time as needed, to make a stiff paste that forms a compact ball. Knead dough on a floured surface until smooth and elastic, 5 to 10 minutes. Leave, covered, to rest for 30 minutes. Divide into halves. Firmly roll out each portion on a lightly-floured board, turning often and dusting with flour, if needed, until very thin, between ⅛-inch and 1/16-inch thick. Roll up each sheet of dough into a jelly-roll shape and cut into strips ranging from ⅛- to ½-inch wide. Unroll each strip and place on a clean towel to dry for 1 hour. (Unroll quickly before they stick together.) Cook several at a time in a kettle of boiling salted water until just tender. Drain. Separate to keep from sticking. Add to soup. Makes about 1 pound.

Russian Pelmeny

The best known of the Russian stuffed doughs is called Siberian *pelmeny* or *pelmeni*. The triangles or half circles with meat and onion filling are traditionally made by housewives and frozen for meals at home or on trips. They can be cooked in beef bouillon and served as a soup.

Filling:

1/3 cup finely chopped onion
1 tablespoon butter or margarine
½ pound lean ground beef
1 egg, beaten
2 tablespoons chopped fresh dill
Salt, pepper to taste

Sauté onion in heated butter or margarine in a small skillet. Add beef and cook, stirring, until redness disappears. Spoon off any fat. Remove from heat and cool. Stir in egg, dill, salt, and pepper; mix well.

Dough:

1½ cups unsifted all-purpose flour
1 large egg at room temperature
½ teaspoon salt
About 4 tablespoons water

Put flour into a large bowl or onto a wooden or marble surface to form a mound. Make a well in the center and break the egg into it. Add salt and 2 tablespoons water. Working with tips of the fingers, mix flour with other ingredients to combine well. Add water, a little at a time as needed, to form a stiff and compact ball of dough. Knead on a floured surface 5 to 10 minutes or until dough is smooth and elastic. Cut dough into 2 portions. Roll out each portion as thin as possible. With a tumbler or cookie cutter cut dough into 3-inch circles. Put a small spoonful of filling in center of each circle. Dip tip of a finger into cold water and rub around edge of dough. Fold over to form a crescent and pinch edges to enclose filling. When ready to cook, drop filled *pelmeny*, several at a time, into a large kettle of boiling salted water. Keeping the water at a steady boil, cook about 10 minutes or until dough is cooked. Remove with a slotted spoon and serve in hot bouillon. Makes about 36.

Chinese Won Ton

The Chinese prepare a very popular stuffed dough called *won ton* that is familiarly served in well-flavored soups. The dough for the *pay*, or skin, as it is called, is quite difficult to prepare in the home because of its thinness. Although similar to other egg-noodle doughs, it is rolled until paper thin on a board that is lightly sprinkled with cornstarch. The skins or wrappers, generally cut into 3½-inch squares and lightly sprinkled with cornstarch, are sold at Oriental stores. Most Western cooks prefer to buy the wrappers ready-made and add their own fillings before cooking. The *won ton* are generally filled with mixtures of finely-chopped chicken, pork, or seafood, with chopped vegetables and seasonings. This is an easy and delectable filling.

1 *pound ground pork*
2 *tablespoons soy sauce*
2 *teaspoons sugar*
2 *teaspoons cornstarch*
¼ *cup minced scallions with some tops*
1 *teaspoon minced fresh ginger*
Freshly ground pepper
1 *pound ready-made* won ton *wrappers, cut into 3½-inch squares*

Combine all ingredients except *won ton* wrappers. Mix well, working together with the hands to combine the foods thoroughly. To fold the *won ton*, place a square on a flat surface with one tip pointing toward you. Place a heaping teaspoon of filling on the lower half. Wet tip of a finger and run it along the outer edges. Fold top half over the filling to form a triangle (or at a slant) and press edges together. Cross left and right points of triangle, bringing together just below the bulge formed by the filling, and press points together. Repeat for the others. Makes about 60.

For soup: Drop *won ton* into heated, well-seasoned broth and cook about 10 minutes, until tender. Add garnishes of shredded raw spinach or scallions, if desired.

Pancakes

These pancakes, when cut into thin strips, are good additions to soups.

1 cup milk
1 egg
1 cup sifted all-purpose flour
¼ teaspoon salt
Butter or margarine for frying

Combine milk and egg in a bowl; mix with a whisk or fork. Stir in flour and salt; mix again. Heat a lightly greased 7-inch or 8-inch skillet and spoon 3 tablespoons batter into it by pouring batter all at once. Tip pan quickly at once to spread batter evenly. Cook until underside is done and bubbles form on top. Turn over with a spatula and cook on other side. Cut into thin shreds.

Ball and Dumpling Garnishes

Garnishes in the form of balls made with seasoned ground meat, poultry, cracker or bread crumbs, hard-cooked eggs, marrow, and cheese, and dumplings prepared with any kind of flour or meal, potatoes, or ground meat, poultry, or seafood, are standard additions to soups. Both are small and light, are bound with eggs, and are seasoned with herbs, spices, onions, cheese, or other foods. Some kinds may be filled. While some of the garnishes are usually cooked in soups, others are poached in simmering water and then added to the soup.

Here are some tempting recipes for these garnishes.

Marrow Balls

1 egg yolk
2 tablespoons marrow
About 2 tablespoons fine dry bread crumbs
Salt, pepper to taste

Combine egg yolk and marrow; add enough bread crumbs to make a stiff mixture; season with salt and pepper. Shape into tiny balls; drop into lightly-salted boiling water and cook about 10 minutes. Remove and add 3 or 4 balls to each serving of soup.

Tiny Meatballs

½ pound lean ground beef
1 egg yolk
2 to 3 tablespoons fine dry bread crumbs
Salt, pepper, ground nutmeg to taste

Combine ingredients in a bowl and mix well. Shape into tiny meatballs. Drop into simmering water and cook 10 minutes, or until they rise to the top. Remove and add to soup, allowing 4 or 5 per serving.

Parsley Dumplings

2 cups all-purpose flour
2 teaspoons baking powder
1 teaspoon salt
2 tablespoons shortening
¾ cup milk
3 tablespoons chopped fresh parsley

Combine flour, baking powder, and salt in a bowl. Cut in shortening. Add milk and parsley; mix well. Drop from a spoon into simmering broth or soup. Cover and cook about 12 minutes.

Potato Dumplings

1 cup mashed potatoes
1½ tablespoons butter or shortening
1 egg yolk
2 tablespoons grated Parmesan cheese
Salt, pepper, grated nutmeg to taste
All-purpose flour

Combine potatoes, butter or shortening, egg yolk, cheese, salt, pepper, and nutmeg; mix well. Turn onto a floured board and roll out until very thin; cut into strips and then form into balls. Drop into hot broth about 10 minutes, or until done.

A List of Soup Garnishes

Almond slivers, toasted or shredded, plain or salted
Apples with skin, diced
Asparagus tips, cooked
Avocado balls, cubes, slices, or strips, sprinkled with lemon juice
Bacon, cooked crisp and crumbled
Banana slices, sprinkled with lemon juice
Beef, chopped dried
Beets, canned or cooked, diced or sliced
Bread crumbs, plain or buttered
Capers, drained
Caraway seeds
Carrots, grated, thinly sliced, or julienne cut strips, raw
Cauliflower, buds or diced, raw or cooked
Celery, sliced or chopped, raw or cooked

Cereals

Cheese, grated American, Cheddar, Parmesan, Swiss, or crumbled blue

Chicken, cooked, diced, or slivered

Chives, chopped

Chocolate, grated

Chutney

Coconut, grated, plain or toasted

Crackers (bacon, onion, oyster, pilot, potato, rye, saltines, sesame, soda, rye) plain or spread with butter and herbs

Cream, whipped sweet or slightly salted (plain or with minced chives or parsley)

Cucumber, unpeeled raw, diced or sliced, plain or mixed with chopped fresh dill or parsley

Eggs, hard-cooked sliced or chopped or hard-cooked egg yolks

Eggs, poached

Flower petals (marigold, nasturtium, roses, violet)

Frankfurter slices

Ham, cooked, minced or cut into julienne strips

Herbs, fresh, chopped or slivered

Lemon, sliced thin, plain or sprinkled with chopped fresh parsley

Lime, sliced thin

Macaroni, elbows or other kinds, cooked

Melon, balls or diced

Mint, raw, whole leaves or chopped

Mushrooms, raw, canned, or cooked, sliced, chopped, or whole small caps

Noodles, cooked, cut-up or in fancy shapes

Olives, black, green, or stuffed, sliced or slivered

Onions, raw or cooked, chopped, sliced, or in rings

Orange, sliced thin

Paprika

Parsley, fresh, chopped

Pasta, store-bought or homemade, cooked, whole or broken
Pickles, diced or slivered
Pimiento, canned, chopped or sliced
Popcorn, unbuttered, buttered, garlic or cheese
Poppy seeds, toasted
Pretzels
Radishes, sliced thin
Raisins, whole or chopped
Rice, cooked, white or brown
Rind, grated lemon, lime, or orange
Sausages, smoked, diced or sliced
Scallions, raw, chopped, with some tops
Sesame seeds, toasted
Shrimp, small, cooked, shelled, and deveined
Spices
Sunflower seeds
Tacos, whole or crumbled
Tomatoes, peeled, seeded, and diced
Tongue, cooked, diced or cut into strips
Watercress, sprigs or chopped
Wheat germ
Zucchini, raw or cooked, chopped or shredded

Metric Measure Conversion Table

Metric Measure Conversion Table
(Approximations)

When You Know (U.S.)	Multiply by	To Find (Metric)
	WEIGHT	
ounces	28	grams
pounds	0.45	kilograms
	VOLUME	
teaspoons	5	milliliters
tablespoons	15	milliliters
fluid ounces	30	milliliters
cups	0.24	liters
pints	0.47	liters
quarts	0.95	liters
	TEMPERATURE	
degrees Fahrenheit (°F)	subtract 32° and multiply the remainder by 5/9 or .556	degrees Celsius or Centigrade (°C)

Index